D0727286

Irish Rogues and Rascals

Irish Rogues
and Rascals

Joseph McArdle

Gill & Macmillan

Gill & Macmillan Ltd
Hume Avenue, Park West, Dublin 12
with associated companies throughout the world
www.gillmacmillan.ie

© Joseph McArdle 2007
978 07171 4118 0

Typography design by Make Communication
Print origination by Carole Lynch
Printed by ColourBooks Ltd, Dublin

This book is typeset in Linotype Minion and Neue Helvetica.

The paper used in this book comes from the wood pulp of
managed forests. For every tree felled, at least one tree is
planted, thereby renewing natural resources.

A CIP catalogue record for this book is available
from the British Library.

5 4 3 2 1

Contents

Preface

The English word 'rogue' derives from sixteenth-century cant and means 'a knave, rascal, scamp, trickster, swindler or vagrant' and can even include a 'scapegrace'. In the vegetable world it is defined as 'an inferior or intrusive plant among seedlings,' and it follows naturally that, applied to animals (which include human beings), it denotes 'a variation from the standard type.'

The classification can be pejorative. A rogue elephant is a vicious animal, often isolated from the main herd; and a shirking or vicious horse is described as a rogue. Contrariwise, the word can include a hint of approval. A rogue may be charming, delightful, cheerful and saucy. To describe someone as roguish is to imply that they are mischievous or high-spirited. To call someone 'a bit of a rogue' is often a good-humoured warning.

In ninety-nine cases out of a hundred the noun is masculine; it is rare to hear it applied to a woman, but this should not preclude the inclusion of women in a rogues' gallery.

Any list of Irish rogues should take account of their degree of roguishness and should distinguish, where possible, between the vicious rogues and the scamps, while not forgetting that, deliberate or not, rogues invariably harm others. This book does not attempt to pass judgement or to categorise and indeed stresses that a rogue is not necessarily a criminal. Rogues, on the whole, stray from the norm and are often eccentric; but to be eccentric is not *ipso facto* to be a rogue. Eccentrics see and do things differently but do not necessarily deceive, cheat or harm. It is for the reader to make his or her own judgement about the category into which a particular person falls. One thing is certain: the classification 'rogue' imposes limitations that become more severe the closer we come to the present day. Because certain behaviour is regarded as romantic or quaint at a remove of three or more centuries does not mean that it is acceptable in the twenty-first century.

The rogue's deviation implies breaches of an accepted code, rather than a departure from 'normal behaviour'. This fact permits the inclusion of a particular class of rogues who, when they broke the rules, did so with the conviction that they were supporting a just cause. Lord Haw-Haw and Erskine Childers are extreme examples who paid for their deviation with their lives. They did not play the game. What distinguishes a rogue, therefore, from a yob, thug or mobster is the fact that his behaviour often wins the approval, even envy, of a substantial number of his peers, particularly if the roguish behaviour involves derring-do, the courage to flout society's oppressive norms, and risk of life. A rogue is rarely a rotter.

Jonah Barrington (1760–1834), a rogue himself, was a great chronicler of rogues. His description of John Scott, Lord Clonmell, Chief Justice of the King's Bench, is as good a description as any of many rogues, particularly the tribunal rogues whom we shall meet later in this book.

> Mr. Scott never omitted one favourable opportunity of serving himself. His skill was unrivalled and his success proverbial. He was full of anecdotes, though not the most refined; these in private society he not only told but acted: and when he perceived that he had made a very good exhibition, he immediately withdrew, that he might leave the most lively impression of his pleasantry behind him. His boldness was his first introduction, his policy his ultimate preferment. Courageous, vulgar, humorous, artificial, he knew the world well, and he profited by that knowledge: he cultivated the powerful, he bullied the timid, he fought the brave, he flattered the vain, he duped the credulous, and he amused the convivial. Half-liked, half-reprobated, he was too high to be despised, and too low to be respected. His language was coarse, and his principles arbitrary; but his passions were his slaves, and his cunning was his instrument. In public and in private he was the same character; and though a most fortunate man and a successful courtier, he had scarcely a sincere friend or a disinterested adherent.

To sum up, the majority, if not all, of the rogues in this book could be said to have suffered from anti-social personality disorder. In other words, they were individuals who had little regard for the feelings and welfare of others. They suffered from emotional immaturity, self-centredness and lack of guilt.

Such rogues do not learn from experience. They have a weak sense of responsibility and are unable to form honest relationships or to control impulses. They lack moral compass and chronically indulge in anti-social behaviour. Punishment does not change their behaviour. They are often manipulative and are prepared to lie to gain personal pleasure or profit. Their faults include impulsiveness, failure to plan, aggressiveness, irritability, irresponsibility, and a reckless disregard for their own safety and the safety of others. But they make good stories.

Chapter 1

The spinning bishop:
Myler Magrath

Myler Magrath was a proper rogue. One could even say that he was the quintessence of roguery, a weathervane that spun around as the wind blew. He loved women, drink and money, but not necessarily in that order. In an age when O'Neills were killing O'Donnells, Highlanders were killing Lowlanders, Tír Chonaill was raiding Connacht, and James Fitzmaurice Fitzgerald and Donal McCarthy Mór were massacring English settlers, Magrath was, essentially, devoted to the quiet and civilised accumulation of capital. He was a capitalist rather than a gangster.

Nonetheless he had a theatrical streak and rode around 'like a champion in town and country in doublet of proof buff leather, jerkin and breeches, his sword on his side, his scull and horseman staff with his man on horseback, after which a train of armed men to the great terror and bad example now in a most quiet time,' and when there were 'any matters of controversy with his neighbours' he was well able to assemble 'an army of horsemen and footmen to win his demands with strong hand.'

'Myler' is a corruption of Maolmhuire (devotee or servant of Mary), and Mary took care of him in spite of his behaviour. In an age when it was the rule rather than the exception that public figures should lose their heads and that the life expectancy of Catholic priests was short, Myler died in bed, a centenarian.

He was born in what is today County Fermanagh in or about 1522 to an ecclesiastical family, in the sense that his father, Donncha Magrath, was the *coarb* or guardian of church lands, called Termon Magrath and Termon Imogayne, in present-day Counties Fermanagh, Tyrone and Donegal. Termon Magrath was not an ordinary holding: it included St Patrick's Purgatory on an island in Lough Derg, one of the three entrances to the Underworld and a place of pilgrimage that rivalled Santiago de Compostela in the sixteenth century and even earlier.

Myler's eye for the main chance was inherited. When King Henry VIII's dissolution of the monasteries came into effect, Myler's father obtained a grant of the local Augustinian monastery with an assurance that it would pass to his son. Many years later, when Myler had won Queen Elizabeth's favour, he would obtain confirmation of his father's surrender of the territory only to have it regranted to him with letters patent from the queen.

Myler entered the Franciscan order when he was eighteen and took Holy Orders in 1549. He had been fostered with several influential families, among them the powerful O'Neills, and, no doubt because of this connection, he was sent to Rome in 1565 to lobby on behalf of the brother of the great Shane O'Neill, who wanted to become Bishop of Down and Connor. Somewhere along the way Magrath decided that he himself would be a more suitable occupant of the post. He convinced the papal entourage that he was a blood relative of Shane O'Neill, Prince of Ulster, and won golden praise for recovering papal letters of credence from the Pope attesting to the consecration and granting of the archiepiscopal pallium to Richard Creagh, Archbishop of Armagh. These letters of credence had been confiscated from Creagh when, on his journey home from Rome to Ireland, he had been arrested in England and thrown into the Tower of London.

The Vatican issued him with documents stating that the 'application and exceptional efforts' of the new Suffragan Bishop of Down and Connor and his 'great energy and enthusiasm' had accomplished, through his 'care and diligence,' something that the papal proctor could not achieve, and Archbishop Creagh was requested to assist Magrath's worthy efforts in his diocese, since he would be of great use in promoting the welfare of the Armagh church and its flock. It was decided that it was best that the recovered letters should be committed to the care of the 'resourceful bishop', who would shortly be following Creagh back to Ulster.

One wonders if John Le Carré's George Smiley would not have wrinkled his nose at Magrath's ability to remove valuable documents so easily from the clutches of the English secret service. Could it be that he was already playing a double game?

Unfortunately for Myler, his machinations in Rome did not generate any personal profit. Shane O'Neill was called Seán an Díomais—Seán the Proud—but *díomas* also means spiteful and vindictive. It is not to be wondered at, therefore, that when Myler returned to Ireland Shane took enough time off from plundering Dundalk, burning Armagh Cathedral and repulsing Sir Henry Sidney, Lord Lieutenant of Ireland, to make sure that none of the revenues of the see went to the new bishop.

Certain civilities must have been observed, because Bishop Magrath accompanied Archbishop Creagh some time later when the archbishop met Shane O'Neill on the island of Inishdarrell on a lake in County Armagh.

In the following year, without formally renouncing Roman Catholicism, Myler Magrath submitted to Queen Elizabeth I and took

a corporal oath upon the evangelist that the Queen's highness was the only supreme governor of [the] realm, and of all other her Highness dominions and countries, as well in all spiritual or ecclesiastical things or causes, as temporal, and that no foreign prince, person, prelate, state or potentate [had], or ought to have any jurisdiction, power, superiority, pre-eminence, or authority ecclesiastical or spiritual within [the] realm; and [he] utterly [renounced and forsook] all foreign jurisdictions, powers, superiorities, and authorities, and [promised] that from henceforth [he should] bear faith and true allegiance to the Queen's Highness, her heirs and lawful successors, and to [his] power [would] assist and defend all jurisdictions, pre-eminences, privileges and authories granted or belonging to the Queen's Highness, her heirs and successors, or united and annexed to the imperial crown of [the] realm.

Myler knew when swearing this oath that

if any archbishop, bishop, or other ecclesiastical officer or minister . . . shall peremptorily or obstinately refuse to take the said oath, that he then so refusing should forfeit and lose, only during his life, all

and every ecclesiastical and spiritual promotion, benefice and
office . . . which he had solely at the time of such refusal made; and
that the whole title, interest, and incumbency, in every such promotion, benefice and other office . . . should clearly cease and be
void, as though the party so refusing were dead,

but he went ahead and swore.

Two years later, in 1569, Magrath was seized in England and imprisoned in London, where he may have been tortured and would
certainly have been offered compensation if he would renounce his
entitlement to the See of Down and Connor. Like the hero of the
Czech novel *The Good Soldier* [and scamp] *Švejk*, Magrath did not see
any sense in being a hero and decided that if the Queen of England
was so keen to make him an Anglican, it would be churlish to refuse.
Accordingly, he did what she wanted, conformed to Anglicanism in
his own way, and was released from prison.

Having allowed sufficient time to pass to earn full appreciation of
the enormity of his sacrifice, he sent a letter to the Privy Council in
Ireland asking them to kindly inform him what Her Royal Majesty
and Their Excellencies had decided to grant him. Could it be the
dignity that he had formerly held? Could it be another, or could it
be—Heaven forfend—no dignity at all? It would make admirable
sense to return him to Down and Connor (or rather return it to him),
because he knew the place and could serve Her Majesty much better
and more effectively than if he was living in any other part of Ireland.
All of which made good sense.

However, Myler took pains to prove that he was not a greedy person.
If Her Majesty would not change her mind, he would be happy if she
granted him whatever she thought suitable for him, with one reser-
vation: he would prefer some safe place where her rule was observed,
because he had no desire to live among those rebellious and lawless
Irish. Now, if Her Majesty could see her way to giving him some
modest little bishopric in the English part of Ireland, he begged to
draw it to her attention and to the notice of the noble members of the
Council that the Diocese of Cork and Cloyne had been vacant for a
long time, and he would gladly accept it. Of course he would prefer
Down and Connor, because he could serve Her Majesty better there.

Did they know that there and in the neighbouring districts he had
many friends and relatives? He admitted that some of them were

rebels, but he would hope that, by his advice and persuasion, he could bring them back to peace and submission to Her Majesty. He would also publicly speak the true doctrine to the best of his ability, and no monk or Papist would stop him.

He had no intention of being pushy, but it was a good opportunity to remind Her Majesty that it would make sense to grant him those minor benefices—priories, simple rectories and chapels in Clogher—that the Bishop of Rome had given him. Their rent or taxes would provide him with a modest living. It would be no bother to Her Majesty to write to Lord Conor Maguire to release them completely and effectually to him. After all, they had been usurped by Papists and the Queen's rebels.

Myler then added a sad postscript reminding Their Excellencies that he was 'bereft of all human help' in that 'renowned kingdom' (England) and that there was no-one from whom he could hope to obtain a gift or a loan to get him back to Ireland. He would be very grateful if they requested Her Highness to grant him in some way the money that he needed for his journey home. He signed his letter, which was written in Latin, *Milerus Magrath, Irishman*.

His approach was successful. On 18 September 1570 Magrath was appointed Bishop of Clogher by Elizabeth; within six months he had been upgraded to the Archbishoprics of Cashel and Emly in the south. No doubt it helped that he had offered to hand over Shane O'Neill, his foster-brother, to prove the genuine nature of his conversion.

I do not know if Myler ever met Elizabeth, but at a distance he was certainly a favourite or had influential friends at court. He was obviously able to charm people, because the Queen, in a letter to Sir Henry Sidney in March the same year, recorded the opinion of the Anglican Bishop of London and others that Myler was esteemed a fit person to return to Ireland and, 'if no contrary thing might be found in him,' should be appointed to some ministry. She ordered Sidney to have some bishops and other learned men confer with Myler; and since, in her opinion, he would be found right and serviceable for the church, he should be 'used with more favour because of his conformity' as an example to persuade other clerical gentlemen who had gone astray— i.e. had remained faithful to Rome—to 'leave their errors.' She pitied poor Myler and wanted Sidney to ensure that the bishops would look after him 'for his relief and sustenance and to be thereby comforted to continue in the truth.' Our hero appreciated being comforted.

In spite of this kind letter, Elizabeth was not totally taken in and requested Sidney to have the formidable Adam Loftus, Church of Ireland Archbishop of Armagh and eventually Lord Chancellor, to investigate, together with the Bishop of Meath, Magrath's ability and judgement in Protestant doctrine.

After the collapse of the Berlin Wall many centuries later, the files of the East German Ministry for State Security, the Ministerium für Staatssicherheit or Stasi, were opened up in the former German Democratic Republic, and people were astonished to learn who and how many had been supplying the Stasi with information about their neighbours and families over many years.

Towards the end of the twentieth century the Hungarian writer Péter Esterházy wrote a novel about his family, *Harmonia Caelestis*. A few years later he was given access to Stasi documents in which he recognised his father's handwriting and discovered that his father, under the code-name Csanádi, had been giving information to the Hungarian secret police from 1957 to 1980. He republished the book, now entitled 'corrected edition', and inserted corrections, in red print, that revealed what he had discovered in the secret files.

Elizabethan Ireland was not unlike the GDR or Hungary in this respect. Informers supplied Dublin Castle and London with secret reports, and Magrath was one of those informers. He contacted the Lord Deputy, frequently denouncing rebels and active Catholic bishops and priests. His reports are still preserved in the English State Papers collection at the Public Record Office in London.

Such denunciations could have serious effects, because failure to take the oath that recognised Elizabeth's supremacy could lead to imprisonment or even death, on charges of treason and disloyalty. A typical report described Redmond O'Gallagher, Bishop of Derry and Pope's legate, who attended the Council of Trent (1545–63). Ironically, it accused him of riding from place to place with pomp and ceremony as in the times of Catholic Queen Mary (as if Myler would ever do such a thing).

In a typical letter Magrath noted that the clergy were using the new Gregorian calendar, registered a complaint about Cornelius MacArdle, Bishop of Clogher for forty years, who, in spite of being hauled up before various inquisitors, had not switched over to the new allegiance, and denounced Tadhg O'Sullivan, a Franciscan who was preaching from house to house in Waterford, Clonmel and

Fethard, and James O'Cleary, who acquired a dispensation for the town of Galway as a reward for killing some holy Spaniards.

Magrath also provided lists of priests who had been ordained by Bishop Dermot Creagh or MacGrath, Bishop of Cloyne and Cork, and others who had been 'seduced from their loyalty [to the Queen] and reconciled [by Creagh] to the Pope's laws.' He also informed the authorities that there were still sixteen monasteries functioning in Ulster, and that Bishop Creagh was living openly 'without pardon or protection' and exercising his jurisdiction as Pope's legate.

Magrath described Creagh as 'one of the most dangerous fellows that ever came to Ireland, for such credit that he draws the whole of the country to disloyalty and breaking of the laws.' Simultaneously Magrath, in a letter to his wife, described Creagh as his cousin 'Derby Kragh' and in letters to friends told them to send Creagh 'out of the whole country for there is such a search to be made for him that unless he is wise he shall be taken.' Indeed at a later point Magrath would be accused of sheltering and giving warning to Creagh when the government had plans to capture him. A commission report stated that Magrath was a 'notorious papist' who would rather die than capture Dermot Creagh.

It is interesting that much of the criticism of Myler came from Protestant sources. Obviously envy must have played a part in this and also puritan begrudgery of a flamboyant rascal. It would have stuck in the throat of many that this colourful Irishman collected church livings like stamps and at one and the same time was Bishop of Cashel, Emly, Waterford and Lismore—all prosperous livings. His enemies accused him of 'whoredom, drunkenness, pride, anger, simony, avarice and other filthy crimes.' He was not helped by the fact that the Lord Deputy from 1588 to 1594, Sir William Fitzwilliam, did not like him; but then the list of Fitzwilliam's 'not favourite' people was long, and the Lord Deputy himself would be accused of partiality to bribery and corruption.

One can imagine Fitzwilliam rubbing his hands when he read that Magrath was a dissembler and, even worse, a man 'of no standing religion who purposes to deceive God and the world with double-dealing,' that he had received large gifts from the Pope and owed more to him than most men in Ireland, that he hoped that if the Protestant cause was overturned, he would get more from the Pope than the people who had suffered, that he sheltered bishops from Rome in his house and had them baptise his children as Catholics and then denounced one of them when what he was doing became known, that he imposed severe cash charges on his (Protestant) clergy, which drove some of them out of his dioceses, and then collected this money for himself, and that he beat people cruelly, and once, when a poor tiler was looking for unpaid wages, cut all the flesh from the man's forehead to the crown of his head and then slapped it back on the bare bone, telling him to take that for reward. (In this case the witness could not testify to the 'This is your reward' part of the story.) Definitely roguish behaviour, if true.

Apart from informing on people, Magrath kept in favour by supplying intelligent analyses of the political tendencies in Ireland and the role played by the different discontented parties: the 'old Irishry, which greedily thirst to enjoy their old accustomed manner of life, as they call it,' the 'remnants of rebels whose ancestors were worthily executed, or forced into banishment with loss of lands and livings,' and 'the practising papists, which under pretence of religion will venture life and living, and do daily draw infinite numbers to their faction.' He described this third group as 'very dangerous and crafty, being the strongest, the richest, the wisest, and the most learned sort.' Obviously what they might lose, Myler would gain.

His tongue must have been in his cheek when, himself the husband of a Papist wife and father of Papist sons, he wrote that 'the lack and use of the right knowledge of God's word is the chiefest cause of rebellion and undutifulness against the Queen.' He was also shrewd enough to recommend the translation of the Bible into Irish, a revolutionary step when writing to people who despised and ignored the barbarous tongue. His own tongue had definitely moved over to the other cheek when he advised his readers that the Irishry were weary of the Romish bishops, seminary priests or friars for their sinful and evil examples.

A Catholic historian, Philip O'Sullivan Beare, writing in 1618, implied that Myler, having been given his bishopric in Rome, deliberately exposed himself to discovery and arrest in England by carrying his apostolic letters in a large and beautiful pyx that he hung around his neck. He also complained that no sooner had Myler been given Cashel than he married a woman called Áine Ní Mheára. Some years later Áine met a Franciscan friar, Eoghan Ó Dubhthaigh, who warned her about the risk she was taking with her faith. On the following

Friday, Myler was settling down to a dinner of beef, but Áine refused to join him. When he asked her 'Why is it, wife, that you will not eat meat with me?' she replied, 'It is because I do not wish to commit a sin with you.' 'Surely,' said Myler, helping himself to another slice, 'you committed a far greater sin in coming to the bed of a friar.'

It cannot be said of Myler Magrath that he did not know what he was doing. On another occasion he found his wife in tears and asked her what was troubling her. She replied, 'Because Eoghan, who was with me today, assured me by strong proof and many holy testimonies that I would be condemned to Hell if I should die in a state of being your wife, and I am frightened and cannot help crying if this be true.' Myler's cold comfort was to respond, 'Indeed, if you hope otherwise your hope will lead you astray, and not for the possibility but for the reality should you fret.'

O'Sullivan Beare admitted that, at the time of writing, Magrath did not hunt priests or endeavour to detach Catholics from the true religion but was nearly worn out with age. By this time he was ninety-six years old—an incredible age for the sixteenth century.

Although there were, as there always are, Catholic begrudgers who spread rumours that Myler hounded priests and lured Catholics from the 'true religion', in fairness to our rogue we must say that they were not many, and there seems to be scant evidence that he ever hunted a priest or made serious endeavours to detach the faithful from their Romish practices. The majority of the complaints concerning Magrath and his little ways continued to come from his Anglican brethren, particularly those born in England. The 'mere Irish' would appear to have restricted themselves to satirical poems promising him fire everlasting for feasting in Lent and for having a wife to kiss.

> To the friar whose religion is false,
> To Myler Magrath, the apostate,
> Until he submits to God's word, the boor,
> Give him your fist on each big jaw.

Sir Robert Cecil, second son of Lord Burghley, Queen Elizabeth's Secretary of State—no angel himself—said that Magrath had 'irreligiously suffered his church to lie like a hog sty.' Of course Magrath was not the only incumbent who diverted church funds to his own uses; it was the scale on which he did it that shocked his critics.

However, it would require the death of Elizabeth to ensure that a commission was set up under the Archbishop of Dublin, Thomas Jones, to visit Magrath's four dioceses of Cashel, Emly, Waterford and Lismore. The rapporteur was much grieved that a man 'so much graced by her late Majesty . . . should so far neglect his pastoral charge, or rather quite pervert it, against a good conscience and without regard of his own reputation.' Surely Myler would have laughed if he had read this report, which went on to charge him with participation in simony and granting livings to his sons and allies (for which they paid him his share), all of which caused 'havoc of the church'.

It was discovered that there were only six churches in two of the dioceses in any state of repair. The cathedral church of Cashel was in decay, and its sister church in Emly was 'quite ruinous'. The yearly profits of Cashel cathedral were leased out. The college of vicars-choral at Cashel, which should have had eight vicars-choral, an organist and a sexton to attend the daily service for £8 per annum each, had been reduced to two poor vicars. The whole income of the college had been leased to Redmond Magrath, one of our rogue's sons, for £24 per annum. The mansion house of the church in Cashel was leased by a dean who happened to be dead. The chauntership of the church was leased by another son, James, for a very small rent. The chancellorship of the cathedral was leased to Redmond, and the treasurership was possessed by one Dermott Ultagh. The archbishop received the profits.

The commission found that there might be other Anglican livings in Cashel and Emly, but the poor men were priests in name only and had little learning or sufficiency, being 'fitter to keep hogs than serve in the church.' The rapporteur was surprised that, in a province under English control, there was not one preacher or good minister to teach the subjects their duties to God and His Majesty (the clever but horrible James I). The records also show that another son, Marcus, a Roman Catholic, held the archdeaconry of Cashel and received the entire profits, worth £30 per annum. Altogether, Myler and his sons held thirty money-making posts in his dioceses.

The Attorney-General, Sir John Davies, noted that church services in Cashel were attended by only one person, 'for even the Archbishop's own sons and sons-in-law were obstinate recusants, persons who did not comply with the laws directing them to attend the services of the Church of Ireland'—in other words, Roman Catholics.

Knowing what we know today about agents, double agents and triple agents, one wonders how much of Magrath's undoubtedly profitable exploitation of church revenues and his neglect of both the physical fabric of the church and the spreading of Protestant doctrine was, in his own opinion, stealing from thieves, with perhaps the added bonus of sabotaging the new doctrines. At the same time we must take into account the fact that when, as they did, Catholics boycotted Protestant services, this meant a loss of income for him. We shall never know.

Myler lived through the Nine Years' War and was taken prisoner by Hugh O'Neill's son, Conn, but even then was treated as one of their own rather than as an enemy. The Catholics never criticised his simony or avarice; it was only his apparent public apostasy that upset them.

On the other side of the coin, Myler often gave sensible political advice to Elizabeth I and kept the English supplied with information while she was on the throne. But when she died things changed. The court of James I introduced a new rigidity, and Myler became yesterday's man. It appears that the prosecution of Myler was seriously considered, and rumours circulated that he intended to return to the Roman fold; but, as with everything about him, none of this can be proved.

It is a fact that the officials in Dublin Castle denounced Myler as a traitor, a drunkard and a despoiler of the goods of the church. They claimed that he sold or leased the property of his dioceses, that he kept a large number of benefices in his own hands solely to enjoy their revenue, that he appointed his own sons, his daughter and his daughter-in-law to parishes to provide them with an income, that he built no schools and made no attempt to maintain Protestant churches, with the result that many became ruins. There may be some basis for these accusations, for Myler's children made no secret of the fact that they were Papists, and he himself seemed to think that, though Protestantism had been useful to him in life, the old religion would be preferable at death. What is certain is that, while pretending to be scandalised by the toleration shown to Catholics, and especially to Catholic officials, and to be keen that the laws should be enforced with the utmost rigour, Myler took measures to warn the Catholic clergy whenever there was a danger of arrest. On one occasion when he was in London, having learnt that a raid was contemplated against the Catholic priests, he wrote to his wife to warn Bishop MacCreagh of Cork to go into hiding at once and to send away the priests who had taken refuge in his own palace at Cashel lest he should get into trouble.

In 1608 faculties had been granted to Archbishop Kearney of Cashel for absolving Magrath of the guilt of heresy and schism, and some years later Myler asked a Franciscan friar to procure his reconciliation with Rome, promising that for his part, if the Pope required it, he would make a public renunciation of Protestantism. This request was recommended warmly to the Holy See by Monsignor Bentivoglio, inter-nuncio at Brussels; but Myler's fondness for the revenues of Cashel and his other bishoprics and benefices seems to have proved stronger than his desire for pardon. He continued to enrich himself and his friends at the expense of the state church until he died in 1622. It was believed by his contemporaries that on his deathbed he abjured his errors and was reconciled with the old church by one of his former religious brethren. Another mystery.

The final twist in this enigmatic life is to be found on Myler Magrath's tombstone in Cashel. Unlike the surrounding Protestant monuments, it shows the effigy of a man wearing full Roman vestments and a mitre and carrying a cross. The final lines of his epitaph, written by himself in Latin, read:

Here where I am placed, I am not, and thus the case is,
  Nor am I in both places, but am in each place.

This has been interpreted as meaning (a) that he is not buried in that grave, (b) that the soul and the body have separate existence, or (c) that his true bishopric was Down and Connor, to which the Pope had appointed him, and that his role in Cashel and Emly had therefore been a charade.

Chapter 2

Eighteenth-century rogues: Garrett Byrne, James Strange, John M'Naghtan

Roguishness was such an integral feature of society in seventeenth and eighteenth-century Ireland that it is hard to single out individual rogues. They included abductors of heiresses, agrarian rebels (Ribbonmen and Whiteboys), banco men (who created confusion in a busy bank and availed of the disorder to pick up money left lying on the counter), buccaneers, bucks, card-sharps, cheats, clerical rogues, confidence men, counterfeiters, fortune-hunters, fraudsters, highwaymen, lechers, privateers, rakes, raparees, seducers, soldiers of fortune, spongers, swindlers, tories and trick-o'-the-loop merchants.

These can be broken down into Dublin rogues—Liberty Boys, Ormond Boys, the roguish staff and students of Trinity College, bucks, bullies and chalkies—and 'social bandits', familiar to many peasant societies and often depicted as Robin Hood-style figures of gentlemanly birth who were launched on an outlaw career as victims of official injustice. These colourful characters may have been robbers but they were invariably friends to the poor. Criminals in the eyes of the law, they were often folk heroes. A typical example was Redmond O'Hanlon, an Ulster bandit and 'son of a reputable gentleman' who 'frequently [gave] a share of what he got from the rich to relieve the poor' and preyed on Anglican settlers but left local Presbyterians and Catholics unmolested. Other highwaymen may be found in the classic text of Irish social banditry, *A Genuine History of the Lives and Actions of the Most Notorious Irish Highwaymen, Tories and Rapparees,* by John Cosgrove.

Jonah Barrington, in his *Personal Sketches and Recollections of His Own Times,* which covers the eighteenth and early nineteenth centuries, immortalised a fine collection of notable rogues, including the following.

Lanegan (first name not known) was not totally a rogue but was involved in the murder of his lover's husband, was betrayed by her, was hanged and quartered but appeared to Barrington as a 'ghost' who revealed that he had not died. He ended up in the monastery of La Trappe in France.

John Fitzgibbon, Lord Clare, a nasty piece of work, was heartily loathed by Barrington and all right-thinking people. Barrington claimed that Fitzgibbon was his 'most inveterate enemy' and attributed to him 'a vicious littleness of mind scarcely creditable . . . [and] implacability of temper [which] never exists without its attendant faults; and, although it may be deprecated by cringing, is seldom influenced by feelings of generosity.' Henry Grattan also had stinging words to describe Fitzgibbon when the latter manoeuvred to have Grattan's name as a hereditary freeman removed from the rolls of Dublin Corporation.

The roguish Sir Francis Gould, in the second decade of the nineteenth century, arranged that the delivery of a Papal Bull of absolution would be delayed until he had returned from a ten-day visit to Paris in the company of his landlady's daughter.

John Beresford, another vicious rogue, tortured suspects during the Rebellion of 1798 but lost an electoral contest with Barrington some years later because the man with the decisive votes at his command turned out to be one of Beresford's former victims.

Lord Aldborough got his revenge on Lord Clare by making a laughing-stock of him in the Irish House of Lords.

The Marquis of Ely was a typical member of the aristocracy and magistracy whose arrogance, tyranny, oppression and disaffection fitted Henry Grattan's definition of a 'regal rebel' and a typical member of a class that 'goaded the peasantry into a belief that justice was banished, and so driven into the arms of the avowed rebels.' Ely got his just deserts when he broke the windows of a house in which he heard a young maidservant singing what he took to be a rebel song. When the case came to court, the young woman's ready wit exposed Ely for the fool that he was.

A Mrs Cuffe, in a splendidly roguish way, manoeuvred her husband into a separation agreement that earned her a very handsome annuity.

James Fitzpatrick Knaresborough, who was sentenced to death for seducing the daughter of a magistrate, was transported to New South Wales instead. Many years later he turned up in London in suspicious circumstances and was locked up with Lord Aldborough in Newgate jail, where he had a love affair with a 'young person' who was Lady Aldborough's dresser and tea-maker. This young person, Barrington tells us, 'produced sundry young children of her own in prison, and was amply provided for.'

The company of these and many others can be enjoyed in Barrington's roguish settling of accounts, one of the most readable books ever published in Ireland, perhaps because one should savour it with a large pinch of salt.

———

A great source of rogues was the class of 'squireens', the younger sons or connections of respectable families, of whom Ireland had no shortage. They had no land and no prospects of their own and were not ready to demean themselves by sinking to the level of any useful or profitable pursuit. They could be recognised at fairs and markets, races and assizes, by their red waistcoats, lined with narrow lace or fur, their tight leather breeches and top-boots, and 'the bit of blood' (i.e. horses) on which they were mounted but that had been loaned or given to them from the stables of their wealthy relatives.

Both gentry and peasantry participated in hurling in those days, and the squireens were the local champions. The rules (where they existed) were very different from those enforced today, and the squireens were above all, in the words of Judge John Edward Walsh, 'generally addicted to a base and brutal advantage sometimes taken in this noble exercise.' It frequently happened that, in pursuit of the *sliotar*, two players crashed into each other, and as they collided one of them would thrust the handle of his hurley under his arm and, like a lance in a tournament, stab the point into his antagonist's side. Sometimes the victim was killed instantly; at other times his ribs might be crushed and he was left maimed and disabled for life. Not only was this a common ploy but it was applauded as a 'good stroke'. Usually, when districts or counties challenged each other, the teams were led by the squireens, a bonding exercise that identified them and united them to the peasantry. Their sporting exploits, the prestige of their family connections and their claim to the rank of gentleman made the squireens the popular favourites of the Catholic tenantry, who were ready and delighted to assist in any of their exploits.

Another type of rogue, and, it would be fair to say, the most popular, was the abductor. The custom of abducting or forcibly carrying off heiresses was celebrated symbolically in ancient Rome, lingered in Tory Island in County Donegal, and is still not unknown in Pakistan and Sicily. It boosted a man's reputation for daring and gallantry and was a matter of pride for the woman who was judged to be worth the risk. Patrick Sarsfield—the seventeenth-century hero of the ride to Ballyneety, where he and his troops destroyed the siege guns that were being transported from Dublin to Limerick for the siege of 1690—as a young man helped a friend in an abduction in London.

Once the rumour spread that a woman was likely to come into a fortune, she represented a challenge to the playboys of the district where she lived. No gentleman or farmer who had a daughter entitled to a fortune could sleep easily: until he had her safely married, he lived with the threat that she would be carried off, with or without her consent. It was the boldest and most notorious young scapegraces who were likely to make the attempt, and naturally they were more attractive to romantic teenagers than boring old worthies in their thirties, who might even be widowers.

Age-old Irish customs were of course barbaric in English eyes, and as early as 1634 a statute had been passed to punish those who 'carried away maydens that be inheritors,' but the statute was ignored, and as a result 'forcible abduction' was made a capital crime in 1707; and even those who carried off an heiress with her full consent were deprived of entitlement to their wife's property. In practice the women (who might, in any case, have been coerced by the parents into arranged marriages) became, 'like the Sabine women,' reconciled to their kidnappers, and successful prosecutions were as rare as convictions for motoring offences are alleged to be today.

The rakes and the consenting kidnap victims were not to be thwarted, however. It was common belief that a man could not be convicted if he were abducted by a woman, so to suggest that it was the man who was being carried off against his will, the woman would be put on the horse in front of him, and he became a defenceless pillion passenger. An example of such an arrangement occurred in the case of the daughter of a Captain Edgeworth (a relative of the novelist Maria Edgeworth). A widower with one son, he married a widow, Mrs Bridgeman, who had a daughter. When the son and the daughter were sixteen and fifteen, respectively, they fell in love and innocently informed their parents of this development. The new Mrs Edgeworth was not at all pleased, and refused her consent. The young Miss Bridgeman was an heiress, and she knew what the penalty would be if young Master Edgeworth were convicted, so she was the first to mount the horse and sit in the saddle. She then gave the young fellow a hand-up and he clung on behind her. They galloped off to the church and were married. It was Romeo and Juliet with a happy ending.

The squireens were a great source of abductors. In the absence of cricket, tennis or golf clubs, what other choice had the poor fellows but to found 'abduction clubs', in which the members took an oath to assist in the carrying off of any young woman on whom a fellow-member had his eye. They had a network of spies in the local houses who reported back on the extent of a woman's fortune, the state and circumstances of her family, the layout of the house, the parents' marriage plans for their daughter, and the details of the domestic arrangements and movements.

When a suitable target had been identified, the members would draw lots, or toss a coin, for her, and everybody would help the winner to carry out the operation. No class of society was exempt from these raids, and rich farmers, as well as the gentry, were the victims of the clubs.

Catherine and Anne Kennedy were the daughters of Richard Kennedy of Rathmaiden, near Kilmacthomas, County Waterford. Their father was dead and they lived with their mother. Each girl was entitled to £2,000 under their father's will—a very tidy sum, which local gossip had multiplied tenfold. It followed that they were looked upon as co-heiresses of immense wealth and, therefore, as fair game.

Lots were drawn, and the winners were Garrett Byrne from County Carlow, and James Strange (pronounced Strang) from Ullard, County Kilkenny. They were both popular, dashing and dissipated young men. Their temperaments, however, differed. Strange was irritable, impetuous and tyrannical, sacrificing everything to accomplish his ends, with little regard for the feelings of others—a casebook sociopath. Byrne was amiable and, allowing for his squireen behaviour, polite and gentle, particularly in his dealings with women, many of whom would have welcomed abduction by him.

Byrne had chosen Catherine Kennedy, who was also a gentle soul; Strange wanted Anne, whose determination and haughtiness matched his own. The young men had met the sisters at race balls, hunt balls and other events from time to time and had managed to make such an impression that word came back, through the sisters' confidential maids, that there was no possibility that their mother or relatives would consent to their marrying men with neither money nor employment and that the girls would be pleased if their suitors came to take them away as soon as possible. It should be noted that Catherine was fifteen and Anne fourteen. They were both considered very attractive but Anne, in particular, promised be a great beauty.

On 14 April 1770 the girls went with their mother, aunt and some friends to see a play in Graiguenamanagh; but before the performance ended a message was passed to them that Byrne and Strange had formed a plan to carry them off that night, and that the house that was used as a theatre had been surrounded by their henchmen.

The girls had indulged in adolescent dreams, but this was raw reality and it terrified them. With their mother and aunt they escaped from the room in which the play was being performed and took refuge elsewhere in the house. They were joined by several men, friends of their mother, determined to protect them. The door was bolted and barricaded.

Two hours passed and nothing seemed to be happening. Then, suddenly, there were loud noises as something thudded persistently against the door. There was a curtained bed in the corner and the women clambered into it, in the hope that the rioters would believe that they had escaped and were no longer in the house. Finally, the door gave way, and the mob invaded the room. Everybody froze as if paralysed. The hostages were barely breathing. The intruders stood looking at Mrs Kennedy and her friends. It was as if everyone was too frightened to move. Nobody spoke. This stalemate lasted for what seemed an hour until finally one, then two, then all the intruders rushed the bed, pulled back the curtains and dragged out the girls. It was only now that they began to brandish weapons, swords and pistols, and attacked the men who were trying to defend the girls. They threatened to kill the defenders and the girls and dragged the latter into the street, where they were surrounded by more than a hundred armed men with white nightshirts or smocks covering their clothes—the Whiteboys.

Two horses were saddled and ready. Catherine was forced to mount one, and Byrne got up behind her. Anne was lifted forcibly onto the other horse in front of Strange, who was already in the saddle. Surrounded by the ghostly army in their white smocks, the girls were carried off. To alleviate their terror, they were told that women would be coming to take care of them. The sisters' first feeling of relief at this proposal was quickly dashed when the women proved to be sisters and near relatives of the abductors, and part of the plot.

The four rode all night, surrounded by a strong armed guard of Whiteboys, to Kilmacshane, fifteen Irish miles from Graiguenamanagh. During the journey Byrne and Strange repeatedly asked the sisters to agree to marriage. These pleas were interspersed with threats that if Catherine and Anne did not give their consent they would be transported to a distant country and would never see their mother or friends again. The kidnappers' molls also pressured them and threatened to abandon them if they continued to be so stubborn, warning them that they would be left at the mercy of the men to do whatever they wanted with them.

Food was served in Kilmacshane, but the psychological torture did not let up. After several hours of this treatment, a man was introduced to them as a priest, before whom Byrne and Strange took a solemn oath that they would harass the women night and day by riding through the country with them till they should be exhausted with fatigue and suffering, but that if they agreed there and then to be married by the priest, they would be immediately restored to their family.

Whether the brainwashing had finally worked or the women were by now too tired to resist, they listened in silence to the reading of a short form of marriage ceremony and repeated words of agreement. The worst had now been done and they mustered enough courage to demand that they be allowed to return to their family, as had been promised, but this did not happen. When night came the women refused to go to bed until the kidnappers' female accomplices had solemnly assured them that one woman should sleep with each of them. The women did come to their beds but left them at midnight, and Byrne and Strange took their places. History has no record of what followed.

In the morning they left the safe house and the whole party rode on to Borris on the road to Castlecomer, where they passed the next night. The exhausted women begged to be allowed to sleep with the women 'companions' but their request was refused. They continued to complain about their violent treatment until they were silenced, first by the threat that they would be carried to Castlecomer and buried for ever in the coalmines there and then when Strange, in a fit of anger, struck Anne in the face with a pewter pot. Romance and fascination with the young daredevils disappeared with that blow, to be replaced by hatred and inextinguishable resentment.

The girls' ordeal continued for five weeks, during which they were paraded before onlookers, night and day, accompanied by terrifying bodyguards and their camp-followers, resting at miserable houses in Counties Waterford, Kilkenny, Carlow and Kildare and on to north County Dublin, where they stopped at Rush, then a fishing village. They were put on board a vessel, accompanied by the whole party, and sailed south to the town of Wicklow.

The kidnappers felt so secure in Wicklow that the ringleaders went on shore; but while they had been dragging their victims around the country, the friends of the girls' mother had not been idle. They had traced the cavalcade's movements, with the result that while Byrne and Strange's supporters were drinking in a tavern in Wicklow, their vessel was boarded by the girls' cousin, a Mr Power, at the head of an armed party, and the traumatised girls were rescued.

Unfortunately the principals, Byrne and Strange, had been warned of the attack and had escaped to Wales, but their pursuers followed them, captured them at Milford Haven on 6 July and had them locked up in Caernarvon at the opposite end of the country. This action did not assuage the anxiety of the girls' relatives. There was a genuine risk that the men would insist that the girls were their legal wives and that outsiders had no right to interfere in their domestic affairs. So real did this possibility seem that it was the common belief that the men would never be prosecuted.

Had the matter been left to Catherine Kennedy, this could well have been so. In spite of everything she still had feelings for Garrett Byrne, who, before the horror of the abduction, had always been gentle and affectionate. But Catherine did not have the final say: Anne's opinion had to be taken into account, and her detestation of Strange was absolute. The shame to which she had been exposed, and his brutality when he struck her, could be wiped out only by his death. She may have been the younger sister but her will was stronger, and her mind was made up. Her reaction was supported by a man called Hayes, a well-known duellist, whose obstinacy and views on honour matched her own. It was Hayes's determination and reputation that brought the two men to trial.

The girls' joint depositions were taken before Lord Chief Justice Annaly, and Byrne and Strange were tried at the Kilkenny Assizes on 24 March 1780. At the trial their defence counsel introduced letters that, he submitted, were from the girls. These letters, written in flowery terms, were an effusion of tenderness and longing, declarations of love that went beyond what might be expected from respectable girls. Not only did the letters say that the sisters would welcome their abduction but they actually begged to be carried off. However, a prosecution witness gave evidence that Byrne's sister had forged the letters. The witness swore that she had heard the sister boasting how she could perfectly imitate Anne Kennedy's handwriting. The defence produced other letters that referred to the men in an affectionate manner and called them their 'dear husbands'. The prosecution did not deny that the girls had written these letters but produced evidence that they had been written under duress.

The jury found Byrne and Strange guilty and they were sentenced to death, but it was taken for granted that the sentence would never be carried out, because of their social standing. In their favour were their connection with all the gentry in and around Rathmaiden, the fact that they were apparently lawfully married to the girls (the small matter of consent seems to have been ignored), and the common acceptance of abductions. The general view was that their action, however resented by the family, was not a criminal matter. Powerful friends were induced to make submissions on their behalf, among them a foreign aristocrat who was introduced as a 'Minister from the Court of Vienna'.

The Attorney-General led the prosecution and advised the judge and the jury that if this heavy-handed abduction were to go

unpunished there would be no safety for any girl and no protection
for the domestic peace and happiness of any family. This was enough
for judge and jury, and Byrne and Strange were hanged, to the great
astonishment of their numerous friends and admirers.

It was not only among the gentry that Byrne and Strange had
supporters. The small tenants, farmers and labourers were shocked.
(After all, the girls had been carried off with the backing of the
Whiteboys.) The degree of local unrest was so great that the authorities expected a rescue attempt, and an unusually large force of horse
and foot soldiers surrounded the gallows in Kilkenny. There was no
rescue attempt; but when the hangings were over, all the shops were
closed and all business suspended in Kilkenny and the neighbouring
towns as a gesture of mourning.

The episode brought no luck to the unfortunate sisters. Whenever
they appeared in public in Counties Waterford or Kilkenny the
people in the street cursed, hissed and abused them. Their situation
was not helped by the fact that the government granted them pensions, as compensation for their sufferings and a reward for bringing
the felons to justice. This was commonly interpreted as blood money
and made the Kennedy sisters doubly unpopular.

However, in spite of the hostility of the lower classes, they both
found husbands. (Whether or not one is entitled to say they 'married
again' is a moot legal point.) Catherine married a man named
Sullivan; but the past could not be wiped clean. He was a gentle man
who suffered from his nerves, and the horror to which his wife had
been subjected (and possibly the shame) tormented him. He was
haunted by Byrne's ghost and would wake up at night, shouting for
help and, shivering and sweating, would describe nightmares in which
Byrne was standing before him. He was frightened of the dark and
always kept a light burning in his room. Catherine became obese and
lost her good looks. It was said that she 'sought the indulgence of
smoking' to distract her from brooding on the past.

Anne had a rougher time. Though she grew to be a 'dignified and
magnificent beauty' who married a man named Kelly, the marriage
was unhappy and she died 'an object of great commiseration—sunk,
it was said, in want and degradation,' of what kind we do not know.
She got no sympathy from the plain people of Waterford and
Kilkenny, who interpreted her unhappiness as a judgement and continued to execrate her even after her death. From their point of view,

it had been a noble act on the part of Strange to risk his life in order to carry her off, and therefore to collaborate in his prosecution had been base ingratitude. Anne Kennedy's subsequent misfortunes were obviously the visible manifestation of Heaven's vengeance.

———

The records tell another, even sadder story of roguery gone wrong. This time the place was the seat of a family called Knox in the townland of Prehen, about two miles from Derry. The main actor was a young man from Derry, John M'Naghtan. His father was a wealthy merchant who gave his son all the advantages of a liberal education. John graduated from Trinity College, Dublin, most probably in the early 1740s, but when he inherited a large estate from an uncle and had no need to take up a profession, he embarked on a career of dissipation—not an uncommon pursuit in Ireland for young men of means. He married early and it was not long before he ran into considerable debt, so much so that that the sheriff arrested him in his own parlour in the presence of his pregnant wife. The shock brought on premature labour, and wife and child died.

The new widower was 'a man of address and ability', and his friends in Dublin Castle arranged a lucrative situation for him in the revenue service. In the course of his duties he became friendly with the above-mentioned Knox, whose daughter, a lovely and amiable girl, was heir to a large fortune, independent of her father. At this time M'Naghtan was thirty-eight years old and the Knox daughter was only fifteen, but this did not prevent him from paying her 'assiduous court'. Even for those days she was too young to marry, but he persuaded her to promise that she would marry him when she reached seventeen. In all innocence she told her father about their intentions, but the father would not even consider such an arrangement and barred M'Naghtan from his house. This prohibition was regarded as such a slight on M'Naghtan's good name that Knox was persuaded to withdraw it, on the strict condition that any notion of paying suit to his daughter was to be forgotten.

One day the two found themselves alone, apart from the presence of a child, a cousin of Miss Knox. M'Naghtan took a prayer book from his pocket, read the marriage ceremony aloud, and persuaded young

Miss Knox to answer the responses. However, every 'I do' that she pronounced was followed by 'provided my father consents.' M'Naghtan immediately 'took advantage of this ceremony' (not, one imagines, in the physical sense, given the presence of the young cousin), and when he next met her at the house of a mutual friend he openly announced that she was his wife. Shock and horror! Once again he was barred from the Knox house. His next move was to publish notices in newspapers stating that Miss Knox was now Mrs M'Naghtan.

The family took the matter to the ecclesiastical court, and the alleged marriage was declared to be null and void. At this point M'Naghtan seems to have lost control of himself. While the proceedings were still going on, he wrote a threatening letter to one of the judges of the Court of Delegates and, it was said, lay in wait to have him murdered when he came on circuit; but nothing happened, because the judges did not take their usual road on that occasion.

True or not, the story was out and M'Naghtan was obliged to flee the country; but not for long. These setbacks had increased his obsession, and in spite of the risks, he returned to Ireland and hid in the woods of Prehen. In such a small area absolute secrecy was impossible, and Knox was warned that M'Naghtan had been seen skulking on his land. However, he dismissed the story. A blacksmith, whose wife had nursed Miss Knox, lived near the Knox home, and he, with the known attachment of such a connection in Ireland in those days, always followed his foster-daughter, as her protector, whenever she left the house.

Eventually Knox realised that this state of affairs could not continue and he decided that the only thing to do was to take his daughter away from danger and bring her to Dublin, where she would meet civilised people. Accordingly, at the beginning of November 1761, the party prepared to set out for Dublin.

All this time M'Naghtan's informants were keeping him up to date with events at Prehen, and accordingly, with some friends, he set up headquarters in a cottage close to the Dublin road and brought a sackful of firearms with him. Once installed, one of the friends was dispatched, ostensibly to buy yarn, to the house of an old woman who lived by the side of the road. He was to wait there until Knox's carriage appeared.

When finally it arrived, the woman pointed it out, named the travellers it contained—Mr Knox, his wife, his daughter, and a

maidservant—and described the positions in which they were sitting.
Another servant, and the blacksmith, were walking on either side of
the carriage. The scout ran back and briefed M'Naghtan. Within
minutes the carriage was surrounded by M'Naghtan and three companions. M'Naghtan and one of the accomplices fired at the smith
and disabled him. The blinds of the carriage were drawn to prevent
the passengers from being identified, but M'Naghtan rode up to the
carriage and, either by accident or design, discharged a heavily loaded
blunderbuss. A shriek was heard inside. The blind was raised, and
Knox discharged his pistol at M'Naghtan. At the same moment
another shot was fired from behind a stack of turf by one of Knox's
servants. Both shots hit M'Naghtan, but his associates held him on his
horse and rode off with him.

The passengers then took stock. Miss Knox was dead, weltering in
her own blood. On the first alarm she had thrown her arms about her
father's neck to protect him and had received the contents of the
blunderbuss intended for him. All the fireballs from the weapon had
hit her. The other three people in the carriage were unharmed.

An alarm was raised immediately and a reward of £500 offered for
the apprehension of the murderers. A company of light horse scoured
the district and, among other places, were led to search the house of a
farmer named Wenslow. The family denied all knowledge of
M'Naghtan, and the party were leaving the house when a corporal said
deliberately to one of his companions, in the hearing of a man who
was digging potatoes nearby, that the discoverer would be entitled to a
handsome reward. The man immediately pointed to a hayloft, and the
corporal, running up a ladder, burst open the door and discovered
M'Naghtan lying in the hay. In spite of his wounds he made a desperate resistance but was ultimately taken and lodged in Lifford Jail.
Some of his accomplices were arrested soon after. They were all tried
before a special commission at Lifford, and one of them was persuaded to turn king's evidence.

M'Naghtan was brought into court wrapped in a blanket and laid
on a table in the dock, being unable to stand or to sit, but in spite of
his acute pain and weakness he defended himself vigorously.

What was described at the time as 'a singular trait of Irish feeling'
was demonstrated during the trial. One of M'Naghtan's men, named
Dunlap, had remained faithful to his master, and M'Naghtan was more
concerned to save Dunlap's life than his own. With this intention,

M'Naghtan insisted that he had no knowledge of Dunlap or of who he was. 'Oh, master dear,' said the chivalrous idiot beside him in the dock, 'is this the way you are going to disown me after all?'

M'Naghtan and Dunlap were sentenced to be hanged. On the day of their execution M'Naghtan was so weak that he had to be supported in the arms of attendants. He praised Miss Knox, told the spectators how much he loved her, and declared that he mourned her as his wife. As witness to his state of mourning, the cap covering his face was bound with black, his jacket was trimmed with black and had jet buttons sewn on it, and he wore large black buckles on his shoes.

In spite of his weakness, when the attendants lifted him up the ladder he broke away from them and exerted all his remaining strength to throw himself off with such force that the rope broke and he fell gasping to the ground. His generous nature, his escapades and bravery had made him highly popular, and the crowd opened an escape lane for him, through which his supporters tried to push him. He fiercely repulsed their help, however, and shouted, in a manner characteristic of his proud nature, that 'he would not live to be pointed at as the half-hanged man.' He called to Dunlap to give him the rope that was around his (Dunlap's) neck. In an instant the knot of this rope was slipped and the noose was placed round M'Naghtan's neck. Once again he was assisted up the ladder and, collecting all his energies, he flung himself off the scaffold and died without a struggle. His unfortunate but faithful follower stood by wringing his hands as he witnessed the sufferings of his dear master and begged the hangman to hurry up, so that he might soon follow M'Naghtan and die by the same rope.

The murder and execution took place on the road between Strabane and Derry, and for many years afterwards the scene of the ambush was pointed out to passengers.

Abduction was so common that the death of anyone who opposed it was considered a venial offence and the natural result of their unreasonable obstinacy. A victim of the eighteenth-century zeitgeist, M'Naghtan, in spite of his 'soft, gentle, and insinuating manners, his generous and humane disposition,' was said by the premature Victorians to have been destroyed by his 'most fierce and uncontrollable' passions. As often happens with extreme individuals and some rogues, his death was better than his life.

Chapter 3

Fighting Fitzgerald: George Robert Fitzgerald

Although his family's lands were in County Mayo, George Robert Fitzgerald, born in 1748, was descended from the Norman Fitzgeralds of Munster and was excessively proud of his ancestry. Whatever nobility he inherited from his paternal line was warped by his connection with the colourful Frederick Hervey, Bishop of Derry, his mother's brother. His mother had separated from her husband five years into the marriage and had taken George and his brother to England. George went from Eton to the British army. (His father had served the Austrian emperor.) Although in general he was a popular member of society, he soon became known for his volatile temper, which earned him the sobriquet of Fighting Fitzgerald.

One day, in his favourite coffee house, one of the habitués was urged to challenge him for a bet. The rash young man brushed past Fitzgerald and said *sotto voce*, 'I smell an Irishman.' He had not taken two steps before Fitzgerald drew a knife and cut off his nose, while telling him and the company, 'You shall never smell another!'

Fitzgerald returned to Ireland when his regiment was posted to Galway, and he liked what he found there. The main activities of the

bucks of Connacht were gambling and duelling. This was a country
that Fitzgerald could appreciate.

One of his early duels in Galway was almost his last. He was shot in
the skull and the bullet had to be removed by trepanning: part of his
skull was cut off with a circular saw. It is quite possible that this
wound made Fitzgerald's already unstable temperament even more
capricious and could well have been the cause of his future, often outrageous, behaviour. For the rest of his life he went out of his way to
provoke confrontations. When he visited Dublin, or even at home in
Galway, he would punch passers-by or try blatantly to steal their rings,
watches or other valuables. If he could not find anyone brave enough
to react in crowded places, such as theatres, he would plant himself in
the middle of a narrow lane so that anyone who tried to pass him
would inevitably bump into him and be challenged.

Apart from this unattractive hobby, Fitzgerald was a charmer, fond
of and attractive to women, and it was not long before he met and fell
in love with a beautiful young woman, Jane Conolly, the sister of
Thomas Conolly of Castletown House in Celbridge, County Kildare,
and grandniece of the famous Speaker. Though the father of their
great-granduncle had been a shebeen-keeper in Donegal and possibly
a Roman Catholic, Jane's brother, Thomas, had married the daughter
of the Duke of Leinster and was one of the wealthiest men in Ireland.
The match, therefore, could be considered a good one.

This, however, was not how Thomas Conolly saw it. He knew about
Fitzgerald's famous temper and was determined to prevent the marriage. Fitzgerald persevered, was charming and flattering in Conolly's
company and eventually obtained the latter's consent. The marriage
took place in 1772, and the newly-weds went on their honeymoon to
France, where Fitzgerald's maternal connections provided an entrée
to the court of King Louis xv in Versailles. However, you can take the
man from Turlough to Versailles but you can't take Turlough from the
man. Fitzgerald may have had his hat and sword-knot studded with
diamonds, may have been dressed in the finest French brocade and
velvet, may have worn two emerald watch-chains across his stomach,
hung with lines of seals, but he was too much a west of Ireland landlord to scrape and bow in accordance with the court etiquette of
foreigners or even to play by their rules.

His first mistake was to use loaded dice (and to be caught) when
playing hazard with the Comte d'Artois, who had taken him under his

wing. His second blunder was, when taking part in the royal hunt, to behave like a typical Galway rider to hounds. He rode in front of the king and brought the stag to bay by himself. At a royal ball, in the presence of the queen, he slapped the face of a creditor who was nagging him. If a Frenchman had done such a thing, he would have been dragged straight to the dungeons.

It was not only in the court that Fitzgerald broke the rules of French etiquette. In the centre of Paris he ran his rapier through a Frenchman who had accidentally stepped on his dog. More than a decade before the Bastille was attacked, an outraged Parisian mob chased Fitzgerald through the city.

In 1775, a year after Louis XVI became king, Fitzgerald returned to his estate, three miles north of Castlebar, but without his wife, who refused to go further than Dublin and rapidly went into a decline brought on by her husband's outrageous behaviour. She never recovered and died after a short illness. There is no hint that he was ever unfaithful to her, and indeed his display of grief at her funeral was regarded by onlookers as immoderate and not the behaviour of a gentleman. He was now twenty-seven and owed £120,000.

The Castlebar of the late eighteenth century was inhabited by a cock-fighting, dog-spitting, gaming, gossiping population. Fitzgerald went native very quickly.

In fairness to him, it should be said that his life at this time was not wholly given over to playing the rake. He improved his estate and lived on it, unlike the majority of his peers, who were absentee landlords. Connacht in those days could be compared only to the Russia of Catherine the Great. The Russians were drawn to St Petersburg, the Irish to London, but Slavic or Anglo-Irish, both groups had vast estates in which, according to Jonah Barrington, the landlord's word was law; 'their nod would have immediately collected an army of cottagers and colliers or whatever the population was composed of.' The great difference was the absence of serfdom, at least officially. Legally the tenants were not tied to the land; in practice they probably had little choice in the matter.

Fitzgerald considered himself to be superior to his illiterate squireen neighbours, whose pastimes were hunting, dog fights, gambling and drinking. They belonged to a world that certain Irish politicians sought to emulate in the twentieth century. In 1778 he stood for Parliament, and his election campaign would make present-day politicians squirm with envy and provide months of work for tribunals of inquiry. The distribution of parcels that Fitzgerald undertook, each containing fifty guineas of eighteenth-century currency, would certainly merit a hearing in Dublin Castle today.

Much has been written about Fitzgerald by W. H. Maxwell, the nineteenth-century author of *Wild Sports of the West*. He noted particularly Fitzgerald's prowess and antics as a Protestant on a horse. 'His desperate riding was the theme of fox-hunters for many a year. No park wall or flooded river stopped him—and to this day, leaps that he surmounted and points where he crossed the Turlough river are pointed out by the peasantry.'

For a wager, Fitzgerald jumped a wall with a fourteen-foot drop on the other side, killing the horse. He hunted at night, surrounded by his henchmen carrying burning torches. Like the Hound of the Baskervilles, this Wild Horde terrified local people, and the parish priest was called in to exorcise the ghost riders of the night. In time the local population discovered the truth, and thereafter, whenever a stranger was terrified by the midnight hunt they would comfort him, saying that it was 'only mad Fitzgerald out hunting in the night.'

This was the time when the Boston Tea Party took place and Britain's American colonies had risen in rebellion. They were assisted by France, and rumours that the French were on the sea were an excuse for Fitzgerald to form his own militia, the Turlough Volunteers, which was in essence a vigilante group 'who knew no will but his, and had no desire but his pleasure.' He fortified an old ring-fort and armed it with six cannons rescued from the wreck of a Dutch ship in Clew Bay.

None of this activity hindered Fitzgerald's propensity to 'blaze', i.e. to fight duels. Everywhere he went he continued to pick quarrels, even at his own dinner table. It was dangerous to catch his attention on the hunting field. If you were a gentleman you ran the risk of a bullet; if he judged you to be of a lesser breed, he would lash you with his whip and drive you away.

He tried to shoot Denis Browne of Westport House, without success, but did not miss when he shot at Browne's wolfhound. He then left a note on the hound's corpse saying, 'Until Lord Altamont shows more charity to the poor, who up until now had only come to his door to be barked at and bitten by the overfed monster I have just shot (which ate all the broken meat due to them) I, George Robert Fitzgerald, cannot allow any such beast to be kept at Westport.'

Fitzgerald's quarrels were not limited to strangers. He developed an insane hatred of his father, who had squandered his inheritance and was unable to pay him the allowance of £1,000 a year that, at the time of George Robert's marriage, the father had undertaken to give him. George's first shot was to apply to the Court of Exchequer to have himself made custodian of his father's estate until the debt was paid.

Neither father nor son had good relations with their neighbours and were accordingly thrown back on each other's company. The result was a constant dog fight. On one occasion, when George Senior refused yet again to change his will in favour of his son, the latter punched him in the mouth, knocking out three of his teeth. Fitzgerald had several bears, which he had brought from France, together with foxes and vicious dogs, and on the next occasion that he quarrelled with his parent he chained the old man to one of the bears.

At about this time Fitzgerald was travelling back from Dublin with an attorney. There were three people in the coach: George, the attorney, and a 'friend' wrapped in a blue travelling-cloak and scarlet cape and wearing a white cloth around his head. On the long journey to County Mayo it was customary for coaches to leave Dublin before dawn, and it was not until they arrived at Kilcock, County Kildare, that it was possible to see who were one's travelling companions. On this occasion it took the light from a tavern to reveal to the attorney that he was sharing his carriage with a Russian bear. The attorney did not appear to appreciate his unorthodox travelling companion, which prompted Fitzgerald to hand him a stick, saying, 'Just welt him a little, my good Harry, and keep him quiet until we reach Kinnegad, where we breakfast.' In less than thirty seconds the attorney had scrambled out of the coach and was running for his life.

Chaining his father to a bear was not enough for Fitzgerald. On one occasion he imprisoned George Senior in a cave; but this time he had gone too far. His younger brother, Charles Lionel Fitzgerald, was outraged and had him arrested while sitting on the bench at Ballinrobe Assizes, from where he was taken to Castlebar, charged with extreme cruelty, fined £500 and sentenced to two years' imprisonment; but a rowdy protest by Fitzgerald's followers and admirers outside Castlebar Jail forced the terrified authorities to release him.

Fitzgerald was determined to avenge this ignominy, and it was his father whom he blamed. He kidnapped George Senior, dragged him to a boat in Clew Bay and sailed for one of the bay's many islands. He had chosen a truly deserted island, without even the usual few scrawny sheep grazing it, dragged the old man ashore, cursing him and threatening him. He then gave his father three choices: he could be murdered on the spot; he could be abandoned to the winter's cold (it was now October); or they could both remain there and starve to death together. Several hours of mutual abuse and increasingly inclement weather were needed before a bargain could be struck. George Senior would drop all charges against his son, and the latter would pay his ancient parent £3,000.

They sailed back to the mainland, but Fitzgerald Senior proved himself to be a true father to the child. As soon as he was back in Turlough he not only reneged on their agreement but had George Robert charged with abduction.

By this time Fitzgerald and his Volunteers were more than an embarrassment to the powers that be. Their behaviour was flint striking against steel when all Connacht was a powder keg. Sensing this disapprobation, and convinced that there was a plot against him, Fitzgerald fled to Dublin, but within a short time the authorities found him, arrested him and put him behind bars in Newgate Prison. Once inside, he began a one-man public relations campaign and arranged to have pamphlets distributed by his supporters and read with delight by the scandal-loving Dublin public. These declared that he was 'a staunch Protestant and firmly attached to the Hanoverian succession,' whose father kept 'open house and [entertained] at free cost all the unprincipled gambling swindling young fellows of the neighbouring towns who in their mad frolics had either broken all furniture in his [George Robert's] best rooms, or utterly spoiled it with their dressings and powderings, or what was still worse, with the filthy disemboguings from their over-gorged stomachs.'

As for his younger brother, the pamphlets claimed that 'his conduct in Dublin was, if anything, more scandalous and outré, wantonly and wildly squandering every guinea he could rap or rend upon the lowest and most infamous prostitutes of the town, like another Macheath, bedizening his Chapelizod Seraglio with silk gowns, stockings, and other glaring, gaudy, silk-suited apparel . . .'

These pamphlets may have been popular but they did not keep Fitzgerald out of court or prison. They did, on the other hand, earn the cheers of a host of curious onlookers when they saw him being led out, deliberately dressed in beggar's clothes, with a diamond band worth £1,500 around his tattered beggar's hat.

Fitzgerald did not stay long in prison, which was not surprising, given that his uncle was the colourful rogue Frederick Augustus Hervey, fourth Earl of Bristol, fifth Baron Hervey of Ickworth, fifth Baron Howard de Walden, and Bishop of Derry. On his release he went home to County Mayo and in the blink of an eye was fighting a duel with an old enemy, 'Humanity Dick' Martin, no mean duellist himself, who was kind to animals but always ready to blaze (for which he earned a second nickname, 'Hairtrigger Martin'). Both duellists suffered superficial wounds, and another duel would have been in order, but Martin was disgusted with Fitzgerald and accused him of being 'appallingly unsportsmanlike' because 'his body [was plated] in order to make it bullet proof.'

In spite of Martin's public denunciation, Fitzgerald's public image improved for a while, thanks to his uncle the earl-bishop, who came to Dublin for the Volunteer Convention in October 1784 and won the applause of the mob for his triumphant displays and of society for his lavish entertainments in George Robert's house, which he had rented for a thousand pounds. (Peter Somerville-Large, in his excellent book *Irish Eccentrics*, revealed that the thousand pounds had been appropriated from the See of Derry.)

Following this triumph, Fitzgerald sailed for Derry, where he was given the freedom of the city. After all this glory he returned to Castlebar, where the majority no longer found him entertaining and his entourage was reduced to a Scottish huntsman and a Welsh attorney, Timothy Brecknock. These new circumstances did not prevent him from acquiring a new grievance. A Catholic, Patrick Randal McDonnell, had been elected colonel of the Mayo Legion of Volunteers. Encouraged by Brecknock, Fitzgerald had McDonnell arrested by a gang of his Turlough Militia and shot while allegedly trying to escape. Brecknock had advised Fitzgerald that such behaviour would be within the law. But it was not so, and the murder of McDonnell became the straw that broke the Mayo camels' collective back. Fitzgerald was arrested by soldiers who found him hiding in a chest covered with blankets. When he was brought to Castlebar, McDonnell's enraged supporters attempted to lynch him. The loss of his popularity and the fury of the mob put paid to Fitzgerald's former arrogance. He stayed in prison from February to June 1786, when his trial finally took place in Castlebar.

The prosecution was conducted by that rogue of all rogues, John Fitzgibbon, Attorney-General, future Earl of Clare and the most hated man in Ireland, and the trial was a magnet for the gentry of the province. It was assumed that Fitzgerald would get away with it once again. Nonetheless, heavy bets were made about its outcome, and there was shock and horror when he was found guilty and condemned to death.

A bottle of port on the morning of his execution restored Fitzgerald's old flair, but his ragged clothes were a far cry from the Dublin finery of his better days. He jumped bravely off the ladder, but the rope broke and, though he fell from the height of the scaffold, he was still alive. He acknowledged the cries of the spectators. 'You see I am once more among you unexpectedly,' he called out. Still confident, he advised the sheriff that the rope was faulty and that a new one should be fetched, but not from the same shop.

Hours passed while a rope was being acquired and a search was made for another hangman. By this time George had sobered up and was not as cocky as he had been in the morning. He shouted for more time, and a contemporary account stated that 'even after he had mounted the ladder, [he] thrice downed the cap and thrice raised it again, beseeching each time some minutes for prayer.'

Chapter 4

This wicked prelate: Frederick Hervey, Bishop of Derry

G
iven the uncomfortable twinning between Ireland and England for at least four hundred years, it is not to be wondered that many 'Irish' rogues were English. They lived in and off Ireland and were given (or took) carte blanche to practise their roguery in John Bull's other island.

A supreme example was Frederick Augustus Hervey, the son of Lord John Hervey, second Baron Hervey of Ickworth, who was described by Peter Somerville-Large as 'the painted courtier, philanderer, father of eight children and [Alexander] Pope's enemy, Sporus.'

On the face of it, Frederick Augustus had a brilliant career. He was born on 1 August 1730 and was educated at Westminster School, London. Admitted to Lincoln's Inn in 1747, by 1753 he had become Clerk of the Privy Seal, a post he held until 1767. In 1763 he became chaplain to King George III. In 1767 he not only became a bencher of the King's Inns, Dublin, but also Bishop of Cloyne and a privy councillor for Ireland. In the following year he was appointed Bishop of Derry and the year after that, as a result of a lucky series of deaths among his siblings, succeeded on the same day to the titles of Baron Hervey of Ickworth and Earl of Bristol. In 1782 he was invested as a

fellow of the Royal Society and finally, in 1799, succeeded to the title
of Baron Howard de Walden.

Jonah Barrington tells us that he was

> . . . a man of elegant erudition, extensive learning, and an enlight-
> ened and classical, but eccentric mind: bold, ardent, and versatile;
> he dazzled the vulgar by ostentatious state, and worked upon the
> gentry by ease and condescension: he affected public candour and
> practised private cabal.

Lord Chesterfield stated that 'at the beginning God created three
different species, men, women, and Herveys.' Lord Charlemont added
that

> . . . his genius is like a shallow stream, rapid, noisy, diverting, but
> useless. Such is his head, and I fear it is much superior to his heart.
> He is proud and to the last degree vindictive; vain to excess, incon-
> sistant in his friendships . . . fond of intrigue in gallantry as well as
> politics, and sticking at nothing to gain his ends in either . . . A bad
> father, both from caprice and avarice; a worse husband to the best
> and most amiable of wives; a determined deist, though a bishop,
> and at times so indecently impious in his conversations as to shock
> the most reprobate. His ambition and his lust can alone get the
> better of his avarice.

As we shall see, there appears to be no evidence that the accusation of
lust has any substance.

A man who inherited so many titles must have been well connected,
and this was confirmed at his christening, which was attended by the
Prince of Wales, the Duchess of Marlborough and the Duke of
Richmond. He may have been an aristocrat but he was also a younger
son and accordingly had little means. Unlike many of his peers,
Hervey did not marry an heiress but chose the penniless daughter of
a baronet, Elisabeth Davers. The only avenue open to him was ordi-
nation in the Church of England and the hope of a living. The couple
scraped along until Frederick's brother, Lord Bristol, was appointed
Lord Lieutenant of Ireland. The appointment was a short-lived one but
was long enough to allow Lord Bristol to appoint his brother Bishop
of Cloyne, to make another brother a baron in the Irish peerage and

to be paid £3,000 in travelling expenses, even though he never set foot in Ireland. That is how things were done in those days, and indeed it is a wonder that the automatic succession to hereditary peerages survived until the rebellion of Anthony Wedgwood Benn in the twentieth century.

The Bishopric of Cloyne solved Hervey's more immediate financial problems but was small beer and did not match his ambitions. He kept himself busy by having the bog drained, insinuating himself into the Privy Council and looking around for richer pickings. It did not take long. The Bishop of Derry, Dr William Barnard, was rapidly approaching his final elevation to another world, and this set Hervey to work. Within two days of Barnard's death, as a conclusion to lobbying that had evidently begun earlier, Lord Bristol was writing to his successor, Townsend: 'My Lord, I am persuaded it is unnecessary for me to remind your excellency of the promise you made me to recommend the Bishop of Cloyne for Dr. Barnard's successor.'

It took a mere three weeks for the *fait* to be *accompli*. A story went the rounds that Hervey was playing leapfrog with other clerics when the news of his appointment came through. He stopped the game and called out to the others: 'Gentlemen, I will jump no more. I have surpassed you all. I have jumped from Cloyne to Derry!'

Wherein lay Hervey's roguishness? It depends on the critic's viewpoint. Churchmen were suspicious of his theology, or lack of it. His political views were hardly mainstream. Otherwise, his taste for travel, his obsessive collection of works of art and his interest in geology were pastimes that differed little from the interests of his fellow-bishops. It was perhaps the unashamed flaunting of his worldly interests that annoyed his low-key fellows. As for his flock, it had cause to complain that the Grand Tour was not an isolated indulgence but would become a regular feature of his life. He spent more time on the Continent than he did in Derry, and for the last thirteen years of his life he was the eighteenth-century equivalent of the nineteenth-century absentee landlord: an absentee bishop.

Combined with his supercilious attitude, arrogant self-esteem and tendency to act according to his whims, there was another failing that was more than his congregations and the Anglo-Irish ruling class could stomach. If we link 'roguery' with the greatest crime that a member of an elite can commit—the breach of the group's codes and solidarity—Hervey was certainly a rogue. His 'crime', like that of

Roger Casement and Erskine Childers, was to become an Irish patriot and, horror of horrors, a defender of Catholic emancipation.

Like many men of flawed genius, Hervey was capable of a good start; it was staying the course that evaded him. When he went to Derry in 1769 the diocesan stipend was £7,000 a year—a goodly sum. Within a short period he increased this to £20,000 by inventing a different system of rating and a more efficient means of collection. This new method, incidentally, was not dependent on rackrenting (though it should be remembered that tithes were still being collected from the Catholic majority). He did not necessarily squander the money but spent it on improvements and, in his own words, 'Though so few choose to live in it, I would fain make the County of Derry look like a gentleman; and nothing can give it that air better than a strutting steeple and spire with arms akimbo.'

New roads were built and mines explored. (One road from Downhill Strand across the Sperrin Mountains was called the Bishop's Road.) He assisted in the plans for the first bridge across the Foyle and encouraged new methods of farming. He also introduced a very neat kind of gate, the bars of which were oak rounded (which presumably means smoothed or dressed). Hervey was also interested in architecture and built three formidable houses, two in Ireland and one in England. One of the Irish houses, Downhill, commanded a stunning view from a cliff overlooking Lough Foyle. Hervey claimed that it was as big as Blenheim Palace in Oxfordshire and had as many windows as there are days in the year. He filled it with sculptures and other works of art from the brushes of Rubens, Murillo, Correggio, Raphael, Tintoretto, Perugino, van Dyck and Dürer.

The second house, Ballyscullion, was at Lough Beg, a few miles from Downhill. It took sixteen years to build, and even then was not quite finished, and cost £80,000. Unusually for the period, it was domed. It also boasted a double corkscrew staircase and two art galleries. He planned to fill the galleries with Flemish and Italian paintings, but it never happened.

His third, even more extravagant, house was in Ickworth, Suffolk, but he died before seeing the completed masterpiece.

All this may have given employment to labourers and artisans, but a price was paid by his immediate family, whom he kept in reduced circumstances because his income was simply not enough to feed and clothe them and to finance his building activities, his foreign travel and his obsessive collecting of works of art.

Hervey loved to visit Rome, where he dressed in red plush breeches and a broad-brimmed white hat, which annoyed the clerics in the Vatican, whose costume this was. On one occasion in Siena, having had his luncheon disturbed during a procession of the Host by the ringing of hand bells (which he could not abide), he opened his window and threw a tureen of spaghetti at the marchers.

In 1778 he returned to England from a two-year stay in Italy to learn that, on the death of another brother, he had become an earl, with an annual income of £20,000 and full ownership of the family estate in Suffolk. Shortly afterwards he and his wife went for a carriage drive together and for the rest of their lives never spoke to each other. Nobody knows what they said to each other on that drive. She stayed in Ickworth and he returned to Derry.

In spite of his travels, Hervey obviously enjoyed Derry. Shortly after his return he wrote to his daughter:

I am writing to you   with an eastern sun dawning upon me and the magnificent ocean roaring in the most authoritative tone . . . How does my day pass? In acts of beneficence to the poor, of society with the rich and benevolence to all. I improve my lands, enrich my tenants, decorate the country, cheer my neighbours, acquire health and good humour for myself and communicate wealth and comfort to others.

That was his view of things. A French traveller of the period exclaimed, 'Oh, what a lovely thing it is to be an Anglican bishop or Minister!' Whatever others might think of Hervey, Jeremy Bentham was complimentary.

To dinner came a singular person, who . . . may be termed a double man. I mean the Earl of Bristol, also Bishop of Derry. He is a most excellent companion, pleasant, intelligent, well read, well bred and liberal-minded to the last degree. He has been everywhere and knows everybody. Everyone seems to be agreed about two things, that he is touched in the middle and that he draws a long bow.

Peter Somerville-Large explains that 'touched in the middle' is the eighteenth-century version of 'a bit touched,' not all there. 'Drawing a long bow' means telling tall tales.

Hordes of guests passed through Downhill House at Lough Foyle, and Hervey did not discriminate. He invited rich and poor, Catholics and Dissenters, as well as Church of Ireland clergymen; and though his detractors accused him of atheism, he performed his religious and liturgical duties in a manner that impressed even John Wesley when his travels brought him to Ulster. A group of guest rooms was called the Curates' Corridor, and Hervey organised races between Presbyterian ministers and Church of Ireland divines at Magilligan Strand, lending his own splendid horses for the occasion. An account of one such race stated:

> The established clergy being generally rather portly men, who were more accustomed to drive in their carriages than to ride on horse-back, tumbled from their horses . . . while the Presbyterian ministers, being leaner men, kept their seats.

On another occasion a very desirable living fell vacant, and Hervey decided that the award should be the result of a foot race. He then selected the most rotund clerics in his diocese and gave them a very generous dinner. The race track was across a bog; not one of the contestants finished the course, and none of them got the living.

Hervey's roguishness in the eyes of his co-religionists can be said to have begun with his programme of refusing to appoint English clergymen to Irish livings. This extended to opposition to the Penal Laws and the tithes system and, finally, his recommendation of repeal of the Test Act, a piece of English legislation applied to Ireland in 1691 that excluded from public office and from Parliament those who would not take the Oath of Supremacy, which denied the Pope's temporal and spiritual authority, or who would not make a declaration denouncing the Catholic doctrine of transubstantiation, the sacrifice of the Mass, and the invocation of the Virgin Mary and saints. Such behaviour was not playing the game, and for an English-born bishop to ask, 'Can any country flourish where two thirds of its inhabitants are still crouching under the lash of the most severe illiberal penalties that one set of citizens ever laid on the other?' was akin to treason.

Jonah Barrington had his own view of Hervey and wrote, in relation to a Volunteer meeting in Dungannon:

Brought to notice a most singular personage, Frederick, Earl of Bristol, Bishop of Derry, who altogether adopted the view and avowed himself a partisan of the rights of Ireland. He was given a special vote of thanks by the five hundred Ulstermen present, who resolved that a Grand General Convention of the Volunteers of all Ireland should be held in order to prepare the way for Parliamentary Reform.

Hervey's reputation was not helped by his behaviour at the Volunteer Convention when it was held in Dublin. He came down from the north, in his triple role of earl, bishop and colonel, surrounded by dragoons commanded by his nephew, Fighting Fitzgerald (whom we have already met). His servants, in extravagant livery, surrounded his open landau, drawn by six horses, while the dragoons, in gold-and-scarlet uniforms, rode before and behind. Hervey's purple coat was faced with white, and the hat he wore as colonel of the Londonderry Corps was hung with gold lace and surmounted by a cockade. He wore white gloves fringed with gold tassels and had diamonds on his knees and shoes. He 'never ceased making dignified obeisances to the multitude like royalty and it all went down well with the Dublin citizenry who cried out "Long life to the Bishop".'

He stopped in front of the Parliament building in College Green. His band sounded a fanfare and then played the Volunteer March, a tune that did not please Dublin Castle. Things could have got out of hand but in fact, in the words of Jonah Barrington, 'all was peace and harmony and never did there appear so extraordinary a procession within the realm of Dublin.'

Hervey stayed in Fitzgerald's house in Merrion Square and continued to parade in Dublin to satisfy the public, who could not get enough of him. This was not just showmanship but was also to thwart the conservative commander-in-chief of the Volunteers, Lord Charlemont, who opposed reform. It was also a method of canvassing for the desired post of President of the Convention and, it was rumoured by some, the Lord Lieutenancy of Ireland.

In spite of Hervey's display, Charlemont conducted a successful blocking campaign against all liberal motions, above all votes for Catholics. Dirty work won the day. A letter was produced, purportedly written by Lord Kenmare, a Roman Catholic, stating that Catholics were satisfied with what they had and were not looking for any further relief. Charlemont circulated copies of the letter and vouched for its authenticity and the value of its contents. It was only later that it was found to have been a forgery.

While all this was going on, Hervey was the leader of the opposition and doing his best to make Charlemont's role a 'seat of thorns'. 'Things are going well,' he thundered at Charlemont. 'We shall have blood, my lord, we shall have blood.'

Hervey was not a politician or a lobbyist in the sense of someone who could be all things to all men, giving something to one applicant, promising something else to another. His heart was in the right place, but he lacked the cunning and duplicity of the true intriguer. Nevertheless, when he returned to Derry he continued the struggle and thundered, 'Tyranny is not government and allegiance is due only to protection.'

He tried to convince doubters of the commonality of the interests of Catholics and Protestants, which in the eyes of a Protestant government was treason and could have led to prosecution and imprisonment. The new Lord Lieutenant, the Duke of Rutland, wrote to a friend: 'I shall keep a vigilant eye on Lord Bristol's conduct.'

Unfortunately (or perhaps fortunately for him) Hervey's attention span was short. He gradually shed his liberal skin and by the end of his life had reverted to the reaction of his forefathers. In a letter to his daughter he confessed: 'My common course is a circle and, like a planet, a vagabond star, I almost turn round my own axis while I make another revolution around the sun.'

He had dabbled in politics and architecture, but it was now time for new horizons, civilised companions and art collections. He left for the Continent and, apart from two short trips home, never returned. Many hotels in Europe have been named the Bristol Hotel, and no doubt many still are. This was not necessarily because Hervey had stayed in them but because of his reputation as a traveller and extravagant guest.

Having been a devotee of France, he now turned his back on it, which was perspicacious, given that revolution would soon break out. Not that there was peace elsewhere: Russia was at war with Turkey; Poland was about to be partitioned yet again; Napoleon was shortly to fight the Austrians and take Rome. Back home, 1798 came and went, the Act of Union was passed and Robert Emmet would be executed in 1803, five months after Hervey's death.

Hervey's first love had always been Italy, but on this new excursion he developed an interest in Prussia and became besotted with the King's mistress, Countess Lichtenau. He began to wear a miniature of the countess framed by diamonds. The French tutor to the royal children, Count Dampmartin, took a poor view of this display. He wrote:

> A fatal destiny made the countess meet with Lord Bristol, Bishop of Londonderry, who was remarkable for a revolting combination of witty knowledge, pride, ostentation, *mœurs libres* [loose morals], causticity, contempt for *les convenances* [normal behaviour] and irreligion.

The tutor had put his finger accurately on another facet of Hervey's roguery: the naughty schoolboy who cannot help disrupting the class, whose delight it is to shock and whose own interests and fads come first. Guilt does not seem to have plagued Hervey. Like many rogues, he was amoral rather than immoral.

For the record, it is important to note that Peter Somerville-Large takes the view that, although the bishop admired many women and flirted with them in the extravagant eighteenth-century way, the majority, if not all, of Hervey's flirtations were nothing more than that: admiration without touching. He flirted with the widow of Bonnie Prince Charlie in Florence and with Emma Hamilton, presumably before she met and fell in love with Lord Nelson, but the verdict would seem to be that these these addresses were nothing more than extravagant gallantry.

The sociopathic aspect of Hervey's nature can be identified by the fact that, though he had an annual income of £60,000 (which would probably make him a billionaire in today's terms), his treatment of his wife and children was worthy of Scrooge. While his family in England were scraping by, he was entertaining lavishly in Rome in rooms decorated with paintings of his female friends, three of whom had posed as Juno, Minerva and Venus. Could he have been the model for Paris, who had to chose between them?

In 1797 he tried to persuade Countess Lichtenau to sail up the Nile with him but, luckily for him, the death of her protector, Frederick William II of Prussia, put paid to his plans. The Battle of the Pyramids was to make Napoleon Bonaparte master of Egypt in the following year, and a British lord and a Prussian countess would not have been welcome in the land of the Pharaohs. He did not escape the French, however, but was arrested when they invaded Italy and was imprisoned in Milan for nine months.

Hervey died in Albano, Italy, from 'gout of the stomach' (possibly a stomach ulcer) on 8 July 1803, aged seventy-two. Eight hundred artists attended his funeral in Rome. Sent back to England, wrapped appropriately 'as a piece of antique statuary', he was buried on 21 April 1804 at Ickworth.

Rogues often get the best lines, and an obelisk was erected in Hervey's honour in Ickworth Park. The money for the monument was contributed by the citizens of Derry, including the Dissenting minister and the Catholic bishop. Inscribed on it was:

Sacred to the Memory of
Frederick, Earl of Bristol, Bishop of Derry,
who during 35 years that he presided
over that see, endeared himself
to all denominations of Christians
resident in his extensive diocese.
He was a friend and protector of them all.
His great patronage was
uniformly administered upon the purest
and most disinterested principles.
Various and important public works
were undertaken at his instigation
and completed by his munificence.
And hostile sects which had long entertained
feelings of deep animosity towards each other
were gradually softened and reconciled
by his influence and example.

One cannot help feeling that this eulogy was not totally tongue in cheek.

Chapter 5
Tiger Roche and the giant wheel

The story of Tiger Roche is quintessential film fodder. It calls out for the big screen, with an anti-hero, adventure, exotic locations, colourful costumes, echoes of James Fenimore Cooper, and tragedy at its heart. The main character could not be played by any old action hero: the actor would need to combine derring-do with the tormented nature of a lost soul. Who could play Tiger Roche? Neither Johnny Depp nor Colin Farrell. Gabriel Byrne could cope with Roche's aggression and bewilderment at injustice, but Daniel Day-Lewis, who has already run through the woods with the Mohicans, could dig up his multiple personalities and give his all to revive the Riesenrad, the giant Ferris wheel in the Prater amusement park in Vienna (immortalised by Carol Reed and Orson Welles) on which Roche was condemned to live all his life.

Many years ago an English writer summed up the Irish for the benefit of his compatriots: 'In short, if they are good, you will scarcely meet a better; if bad, you will seldom find a worse.' Was he suggesting that the Irish are bipolar? It is certain that Tiger Roche displayed all the symptoms of manic depression: today brave, generous, kind and extravagant; tomorrow depressed and cowardly, or treacherous and brutal. There were no straight lines in his life. His chart climbed and dropped faster than the stock exchange: now the darling of the masses, now in jail on capital charges. Whenever he celebrated or indulged himself, everybody was his guest; when he was at odds with the world, he was more lethal than a tiger; when the wheel dragged him down into depression, he became a snivelling coward.

Roche was born in Dublin in 1729. He came from an old Norman family and was educated not only in the academic sense but, perhaps more importantly, in all the necessary arts that in those days confirmed the rank and character of a gentleman. He was the younger brother of the better-known Sir Boyle Roche, famous for such alleged 'spakes' as 'Posterity be damned! What has posterity done for us?' and 'I smell a rat: I see it floating in the sky: I'll nip it in the bud.'

At sixteen the younger Roche left home and applied to the Lord Lieutenant, Lord Chesterfield, for a position. Against the odds, he was offered a free commission in the army. It was at this point that he made his first mistake—the first of many. Though the army was the perfect career for him, friends persuaded him that he could do better elsewhere. It is impossible to guess their motives. Did they want to keep him in Ireland so that they could enjoy his company and his money, or were they jealous?

He must have kept contact with his father's friends, because he was offered other positions that were suited to a gentleman in the eighteenth century, but he arrogantly refused to consider any sensible proposal. Instead he spent the next few years in the company of the 'dissipated idlers of the metropolis'. Idle and indulgent, he and his friends became involved in all the outrages and excesses that then disgraced Dublin.

Binge drinking was not invented today or yesterday. Tiger Roche and friends were adepts. Pouring out of a tavern one night, the gang attacked and killed a Watchman, who, with others, had been trying to break up a fight that Roche's followers had started. As the most prominent of these gentlemen-hooligans, Roche became a wanted man.

He escaped to Cork and stayed in hiding until he could board a ship for North America. This must have been before 1756, as some say he fought the Indians on behalf of the French before volunteering for the British army when the French and Indian War (the nine-year North American chapter of the French-English Seven Years' War) broke out. Roche joined one of the provincial regiments and, like Leather-Stocking, became famous for his exploits in hand-to-hand encounters with the native allies of the French. As they would have been his comrades in arms a short time before, he was bound to know their fighting techniques, for he acquired not only woodcraft and tracking skills from them but also their alleged 'fierce and cruel qualities' and forest tactics, which were certainly not those of recruits fresh out of England. No doubt he also learnt more from his new Six Nations fellow-combatants.

His officers and in particular Colonel Massy, his commanding officer, quickly noted Roche's courage and ability; but Roche's line of fate was never straight. One of the officers in Massy's regiment had a valuable gun, a fowling-piece. It disappeared from his tent, and though he searched high and low it could not be found, until someone reported that Roche had been seen with it. His baggage was searched and the gun was found. When Roche was questioned he claimed he had bought it from an Irish soldier, Corporal Bourke. When Bourke was interrogated he swore on oath that Roche was lying and that he had not sold the gun to him. Roche was court-martialled and convicted of theft, but because of his record he was ordered to quit the service under a cloud of disgrace and ignominy—a lenient punishment.

This was the sort of insult that woke the sleeping tiger in Roche. He immediately challenged the officer who had conducted the prosecution. The latter refused to meet him, on the grounds that, as a degraded man, Roche was no longer entitled to the rank and consideration of a gentleman. Berserk with rage, Roche ran to the parade ground, showered the officer with the choicest examples of Dublin obscenities, then raced to the picket-guard, attacked Bourke with his sword, all the time shouting his intention of killing him. Bourke managed to defend himself until other soldiers leaped on Roche and disarmed him. Deprived of his sword, Roche crouched like an Indian, then sprang up and seized Bourke by the throat with his teeth. By the time the soldiers had pulled him off, not only had Bourke almost choked but Roche had bitten off a mouthful of his flesh. He was to say afterwards that this was 'the sweetest morsel he had ever tasted.' This was how he earned the name 'Tiger'.

A few days later the British army advanced to attack the French at Fort Ticonderoga, on the southern tip of Lake Champlain, at the borders of the present-day states of New York and Vermont. Roche was left alone in the wilderness, an outcast from society. In spite of this, or perhaps because of the challenge presented by his new solitude, the

Ferris wheel turned and brought him up again to its highest point. He trekked through the forest until he fell in with a party of friendly Indians and, by extraordinary exertions and forced marches, arrived at the fort with them to join the attack in a battle fought mainly with muskets, bayonets, hatchets, tomahawks and knives. Owing to the incompetence of their general, James Abercrombie, the English did not use their artillery, and their attack failed. Once again Roche's military abilities and the sort of bravery that would be shown in the next century by Meagher of the Sword in the American Civil War came to the fore, and he was seriously wounded four times. Abercrombie took note of this heroism, but the brand of 'thief' was on Roche, and no daring deeds, however brilliant, could remove it.

The wheel began to turn again, dragging him down to earth. Pain, poverty and ill health made his life a misery but, doggedly, he made his way to New York. There he had only one defender, Governor Rogers, who was not satisfied by the charges against him. An appeal was made on Roche's behalf, but few of his former friends rushed to his aid. Those who did collected enough money from his former drinking companions not only to enable him to sail back to England but also to purchase a commission.

Whenever Roche ran out of luck, there was no question of half-measures. Just as the deal was about to go through, someone told the regiment about the charge of theft in America, and the officers refused to serve with him. One more insult.

Roche was not going to take this lying down. All the concentration and determination of his upswing became devoted to ascertaining the source of the rumour. It was a Captain Campbell, who lived at the British Coffeehouse in Charing Cross, London. Roche ran him to earth in the public room and accused him of a gross and false calumny, which Campbell vehemently denied. A duel followed, in which both men were seriously wounded.

Roche did the rounds of all the places in London frequented by his peers and announced that, since he could not get satisfaction from the villain who had traduced his character in British North America, he would personally chastise every man in England who spread the slander. He learnt that his former colonel, Massy, and another officer had returned to London and very quickly ran them to earth in Green Park. He begged them to remove the stain from his character, but when they contemptuously rejected his appeal, he thumped both of them. They immediately drew their swords and disarmed him. A crowd of onlookers made a circle and they thrashed the unfortunate Roche.

He had not given up, however, and bided his time until he heard that one of the officers had gone to Chester. Roche set out after him with what a contemporary chronicler called the 'indefatigable perseverance and pursuit of a bloodhound,' caught up with him in Chester and attacked him. Once again Roche got the worse of the encounter and received a severe wound in his sword-arm, which disabled him for some time.

He was at his lowest ebb, but Justice removed her blindfold and rescued him in the unexpected way that Justice can do occasionally. Corporal Bourke, Roche's accuser, was mortally wounded by a scalping party of Indians and on his death-bed made a solemn confession that he had stolen the fowling-piece and had sold it to Roche, without telling him how he had come by it. He admitted that Roche had innocently bought it from him and had no idea that it had been stolen. This declaration of the dying man was properly attested and was immediately broadcast. Roche's name and character were restored.

As often happens in such cases, those who had been foremost in slandering him fell over each other in making friendly offers to serve him. He was rewarded for the injustice and injury he had suffered with a lieutenancy in a newly raised regiment, and he soon returned to Dublin a hero. The story of the injuries he had received, his bravery and his romantic adventures among the Indians in the woods of North America were the talk of the salons and coffee-houses. Convivial parties were held in his honour. Wherever he appeared he was the lion of the night. A handsome man, made still more attractive by the wounds he had received, a graceful form in the dance, in which he excelled, and an accomplished teller of the tales of the hairsbreadth 'scapes' with which he was never too shy to entertain the company made him 'the observed of all observers' in Dublin.

But Roche did more to sustain his new reputation than boast to mesmerised ladies. He added to it by physical action. Dublin was plagued by notorious gangs of thugs, called 'sweaters' or 'pinkindindies'. It was not safe to go out at night. One late evening an old gentleman and his son and daughter were returning home from a friend's house when they were attacked on Ormond Quay by a gang of these pinkindindies. Roche, who happened to be going the same way at the time, heard the shrieks of a woman crying for assistance and rushed to her aid Single-handedly he rescued the daughter from the lout who was holding her and then attacked the other brawlers, severely wounding some and putting the rest to flight.

The feat increased his reputation and inspired others to follow his example. He formed a body consisting of officers and others of his acquaintance to patrol the dangerous streets of Dublin at night, and these vigilantes gave a protection to the citizens that the inadequate and underfunded Watchmen—who, before the establishment of a police force, were supposed to protect the city's inhabitants—could not afford.

As with everything in Roche's life, this honeymoon was not to last. His uncontrollable temper and a weakness for slow horses and fast women, wine and song made him the prey of every possible ill wind. The ending of the Seven Years' War in 1763 meant cut-backs in the army, and in his newly reduced circumstance Roche made for London, where it did not take much for him to live beyond his income. Something had to be done and, being a man of action, he did it. He wooed and won a Miss Pitt, who had a fortune of £4,000. Unfortunately his 'anticipatory extravagance' grossly exceeded the marriage portion. He was arrested and thrown into the prison of the King's Bench.

Yet again the giant wheel began to turn and brought him down to cruel earth. The courageous hero and Indian-fighter disappeared. His fellow-inmates smelled his weakness. He was mocked but bore the insults without protest; it was as if he could not even feel what was happening to him. On one occasion he had a small disagreement with a fellow-prisoner, who kicked him and punched him in the face. There had been a time when only the blood of the offender would have washed away the offence. Instead, Roche sat down and cried like a child.

On another occasion a fellow-Irishman, Buck English, who was also locked up in the King's Bench, quarrelled with Roche and, seizing a stick, thrashed him savagely. Roche made no attempt to retaliate or resist but crouched under the punishment, his hands over his head.

He accepted the chastisement from men but took out his frustration on his wife, to such an extent that she had no choice but to leave him and abandon him to his fate. How long he might have stayed in prison is not certain, but eventually he was freed under an act of grace. The wheel had started to move, and hardly had he come out of confinement than he inherited a small legacy from a relative and was able to take his place in the world once again.

By now Roche's seat on the wheel had passed eleven o'clock. He became a frequenter of billiard tables, was overbearing and, instead of a sword, used sarcasm as a weapon. One day when he was idly driving the balls about with the cue, a companion complained that his hogging of the table was hindering other gentlemen from their amusement. 'Gentlemen!' said Roche. 'Why, sir, except you and me, and two or three more, there is not a gentleman in the room.' His friend afterwards remarked that he had grossly offended a large company and wondered that none of them resented the affront. 'Oh!' said Roche, 'there was no fear of that. There was not a thief in the room that did not consider himself one of the two or three gentlemen I excepted.'

The wheel had reached midday, and the man who shortly before had been the miserable, spiritless, flogged and degraded prisoner of the King's Bench was called on to stand as a candidate to represent Middlesex in Parliament. He was nominated in April 1769, with a good chance of winning, but, to the surprise and disappointment of his friends, he withdrew his candidature. The common gossip was that the opposition had promised him something better.

To keep his hand in, as it were, he fought another duel, this time with a Captain Flood, who had offended him in a coffeehouse. If anything, Roche was more outgoing, daring and generous than he had been since his return from America. Returning one night to his lodgings in Chelsea, he was held up by two thugs who rammed cocked pistols into his chest. He sprang back and drew his sword. One of them fired, and the ball grazed his temple, but he went into the attack. While he was pinning one man to the wall, the other ran away. Roche tied up the man he had caught and handed him over to the authorities. The second robber was caught the following day. The two men were tried at the Old Bailey and sentenced to be hanged, but Roche pleaded for leniency on their behalf and the punishment was mitigated to transportation, presumably to Van Diemen's Land (Tasmania).

Unfortunately, it was time for the wheel to start its downward roll yet again, and from that time Roche's Hyde character began to dominate. Shortly after his adventure with the two robbers he saw a young woman walking with her mother in St James's Park and was immediately captivated by her. He insinuated himself into their acquaintance, and she more than returned his affection. It is possible that they became engaged, because Roche was given control over the considerable fortune the young woman possessed; but once again his extravagance and dissipation soon swallowed it up, and mother and daughter had to leave London because of the morass of debt into which he had plunged them.

It was time to move on, and Roche got himself an appointment as captain of a company of foot in the East India Service. In May 1778 he embarked in the *Vansittart* for India but had not been many days on board before he had quarrelled with all the passengers, including a Captain Ferguson, who called him out as soon as they arrived at Madeira. Suddenly, Roche was seized with an unaccountable fit of terror and made cringing apologies to Ferguson. This strange combination of arrogance and cowardice revolted his fellow-passengers, and they insisted that the captain expel him from the common table. Roche's only company now was the ordinary sailors and soldiers. He tried to ingratiate himself with them by treating them as equals and swearing vengeance against every gentleman and officer on board ship, particularly Ferguson, whom he blamed for his latest disgrace.

When the ship arrived at Cape Town, Roche went ashore in the evening after all the other passengers had disembarked. He was seen near the door of the house where Ferguson was lodging. A message was delivered to Ferguson, who went out. He did not return, and he was found soon afterwards round the corner of the house, covered in blood, with nine deep mortal wounds, all on the left side. It was immediately assumed that this had been an ambush when he was off his guard, because the left was the unprotected side in sword-play.

Suspicion immediately fell on Roche, who had fled during the night and taken refuge with some black Africans. The Cape was at that time a colony of the Dutch, who, vigilant and suspicious of strangers, did not let them settle but allowed them merely to call for provisions and sail on. A rumour went out that the authorities had demanded that Roche be given up to them and that he had been seized, handed over and broken upon the wheel—the penalty in the Dutch criminal law of the Cape for atrocious murders.

He had indeed been found by the Dutch authorities at the Cape of Good Hope and put on trial, but he was acquitted. He then took a passage in a French vessel to Bombay, but the *Vansittart* had arrived in India before him. Information had been given to the British authorities, charging Roche with Ferguson's murder, and Roche was arrested as soon as he landed. He asked to be discharged, or at least bailed, on the grounds that there was not enough evidence against him and that he had already been acquitted. He also argued that since the offence, if any, had been committed outside British dominions, he could be tried only by special commission, and it was not certain whether the Crown would issue one or not, or when or where it would sit. He argued his own case with the skill of a practised lawyer. The authorities, however, declined either to bail or discharge him, and he was sent back to England as a prisoner.

He was charged with murder, and a commission was issued to try the case at the Old Bailey on 11 December 1774. Counsel for Roche refused to rely on the acquittal at the Cape of Good Hope; instead he argued that the fact of the killing was undisputed and that from the peculiar nature of the proceedings there could not be, as in a common indictment for murder, a conviction for manslaughter.

There were good grounds for an acquittal, in that a valid doubt had been raised. On the evening of their arrival at the Cape, Ferguson and his friends were sitting at tea in their lodgings when a message was brought into the room. Ferguson rose, went to his own rooms and, having put on his sword and taken a loaded cane (one weighted with lead at one end) in his hand, left the house. A friend, named Grant, followed him, glimpsed Roche and Ferguson at the side of the house round a corner, and heard the clash of swords, but refused to interfere. It was too dark to see exactly what was occurring; but in a few moments he heard Ferguson falling and Roche going away. Ferguson was carried in and died immediately. It was accepted that bad blood had existed between the two men and that Roche had threatened 'to shorten the race of the Fergusons.'

It is interesting that two versions of the message were produced in court. The first was 'Mr Mathews wants Mr Ferguson,' the second 'A gentleman wants Mr Mathews.' The case for the prosecution was that, whatever the wording, it was a trap to draw Ferguson out of the house, and that when he went out Roche attacked him. This could have been confirmed, firstly by the improbability of Roche's going out in the dark on the night of his landing for an innocent purpose, not only in a strange place but also in the neighbourhood of Ferguson's lodgings, and secondly by the wounds on the left side, which could not have happened in a fair fight with small swords.

Roche's defence was that on the evening of his arrival he went out to see Cape Town, accompanied by a boy, a slave of his host, that they were watched by some person until they came near Ferguson's house, when that person disappeared, and that immediately afterwards Roche was struck with a loaded stick on the head, knocked down, and his arm disabled. It took him some time to get to his feet but when he did succeed in rising he recognised Ferguson, drew his sword and, after a struggle, in which he wished to avoid bloodshed, killed his assailant in self-defence.

This account had been corroborated to some extent by the boy at the Dutch trial and backed up by a sailor in England, even though both witnesses were a little shaky in their testimony. According to the defence, the message was a signal to Ferguson, who had set a watch on Roche, intending to assassinate him. The position of Ferguson's wounds was accounted for by the agreed fact that he had fought with cane and sword, using the former to parry. It was also agreed that if the second version of the message was correct it would strongly confirm this hypothesis. There was no proof that Ferguson knew any-one named Mathews.

The judge directed the jury to acquit the prisoner if they did not believe the killing to be malicious and deliberate, and the jury accord-ingly acquitted him.

It is not known what happened to Roche next, or where and when his life ended. At least one source has claimed that he returned to India to die.

That was the life of Tiger Roche—in the words of John Edward Walsh, 'one day exposed to the foulest charges and narrowly escaping ignominious punishment, the next day the object of universal esteem and admiration.'

Chapter 6

The jewels in the crowns: Colonel Blood and Francis Shackleton

Back to the seventeenth century and forward to the twentieth century: a thief and a possible thief whose stories are linked by precious baubles.

In spite of his close links with England, Thomas Blood, son of an ironmaster, has more right to be included among the Irish rogues than most of the Roses of Tralee have to that title. His father had land-holdings in Counties Clare, Meath and Wicklow. One source claims that Blood was born in County Clare in or about 1618 and came from a relatively prosperous family. Another and perhaps more authoritative source maintains that he was born in Sarney in the parish of Dunboyne, County Meath. In a survey of Ireland made in 1654–6 Blood Senior was listed as a Protestant with 220 acres, which he had held since 1640.

Some historians have questioned Thomas's right to call himself Colonel Blood, but the fact that he married a young Englishwoman of good family, Mary Holcroft, the daughter of Lieutenant-Colonel John Holcroft of Holcroft Hall, Golborne, Lancashire, suggests that he must have been able to convince the father that he held an appropriate rank in the army. It is claimed that he served in General Monck's

campaign against Irish rebels in 1642/3. Other sources have it that
he was an officer in Oliver Cromwell's army in Ireland and was
rewarded with grants of land for his services to the Commonwealth.
This could have been in 1649. Yet other historians claim that he had
earned his new holdings as a spy for the Parliamentary cause during
the Civil War.

In 1660 Good King Charles II was on the throne and the Blood
lands were forfeited. Not a man to take slights easily or to wring his
hands in the face of setbacks, Blood decided in 1663 that he would kidnap the Lord Lieutenant of Ireland, James Butler, Duke of Ormonde.
With a group of fellow-conspirators he tried to break into Dublin
Castle, but they were discovered and taken into custody. Blood managed to escape but, not surprisingly—given that daring, even fool-
hardy, exploits were his forte—did not desert his companions, one of
whom was his brother or brother-in-law; instead he returned to the
scene of the crime with more men in an attempt to rescue the prisoners. Once again the castle garrison were too strong or too well
informed and the sortie ended in failure, with the arrest of most of
Blood's followers.

Ireland had now become too hot for Blood, so in disguise, first as a
Quaker and later as a priest, he left Dublin and, in spite of the price
on his head, found a ship to take him to Holland. His unfortunate
brother or brother-in-law was convicted of high treason and executed.

In spite of his willingness to take risks, Blood's greatest gift was his
sense of survival. Though he mingled with anti-Stuart malcontents
and conspirators, he had access to the Stuart government councils. It
is now accepted that he was most probably a double agent. He is said
to have supported the Parliament in the Great Rebellion, and in 1666
he turned up in Scotland, where he fought for the Protestant
Covenanters at Bullion Green.

The following year he was back in England and taking part in
another rescue attempt. This time the object was an old friend of his,
a Captain Mason. Mason was being escorted by government forces to
York. Shots were fired and there was swordplay. Blood was wounded
but succeeded in rescuing Mason. Several troopers had been killed in
the ambush, and for the second time a price of £500 was put on
Blood's head and once again he found himself on the run from
government forces. He called himself Thomas Allen and lived a quiet
life in Kent until the heat was off.

Nonetheless, three years later, on the night of 6 December 1670, when the Duke of Ormonde had come over to England, Blood made another attempt to kidnap him. Ormonde was seized in his coach outside London, and Blood's intention was to hang him at Tyburn, but somehow Ormonde escaped unharmed. Various hypotheses circulated about this new attempt at abduction. Ormonde's son was convinced that Blood was acting on behalf of George Villiers, Duke of Buckingham. Others believed that he was avenging the death of his brother or brother-in-law. Yet another story was that our rogue intended to keep Ormonde as a prisoner until the latter returned his Irish estates to him.

The high point of Blood's contribution to popular English history came about a year later with the theft of the Crown Jewels from the Tower of London. There was nothing slipshod about this adventure. Dressed as a clergyman, Blood visited the Tower and became friendly with the Keeper, Talbot Edwards. One thing led to another until the reverend gentleman was agreeing to arrange a marriage between his nephew and the Keeper's daughter. During their visits and in the course of their conversations Blood and men in his employ familiarised themselves with all the security arrangements and the coming and going of the staff and Beefeaters.

When everything was ready, Blood asked the Keeper to show the Crown Jewels to some friends. No sooner had the exhibits been taken out for the viewing than Blood's gang seized Edwards, bound and gagged him and made for the entrance with the jewels.

Once again a Blood coup was abortive. Edwards raised the alarm and all the robbers were caught. Blood was locked up in the Tower more securely than the jewels but refused to speak to anyone except the King. For reasons best known to monarch and man, Charles II, at the instigation of the Duke of Buckingham, visited Blood in prison, and two months after the temporary theft of the Crown Jewels our rogue was pardoned and instead of having his head chopped off not only walked out of the Tower a free man but was accepted at court. This was not all: his Irish estates were restored to him, and he was granted a pension of £500 per annum.

Some believe that the Duke of Buckingham may have had some hand in the leniency shown to Blood, but nobody knows for certain what the latter had done to gain the King's pardon: perhaps he had secrets that were best unknown. Given the role of Monck (who had died in 1670) and his army in the restoration of the monarchy, it may be that Blood's service in Monck's army had a part in the leniency of his treatment.

Thomas Blood died in his bed in Westminster, London, on 24 August 1680. Some time later rumours circulated that, given his reputation for trickery, his body had been exhumed to confirm that he was truly dead.

————

We now move forward 220 years and cross the Irish Sea to consider the successful theft of another set of jewels, this time the so-called 'Irish Crown Jewels', which were not in fact crown jewels but the regalia of the Order of St Patrick, a chivalric order founded by the British government in 1783 as the Irish equivalent of the Order of the Garter. The members of the order were leading peers, called knights companions; the first Grand Master was the third Earl Temple, who was Lord Lieutenant of Ireland. The Ulster King of Arms, the heraldic and genealogical officer in charge of the Office of Arms, was made responsible for registering the order's membership and caring for its regalia.

King William IV had presented the regalia to the order in 1831, and they are believed to have been made up from diamonds belonging to Queen Charlotte, wife of King George III. They were manufactured by Rundell, Bridge and Company of London and consisted of a star and a badge composed of rubies, emeralds and Brazilian diamonds, mounted in silver, which were to be worn by the Lord Lieutenant as Grand Master on formal occasions.

In 1905 it became mandatory that the jewels, including the collars and badges of the members, should be kept in a steel safe in the strongroom of the Office of Arms, which had moved two years earlier to new premises in Dublin Castle. The Ulster King of Arms was Sir Arthur Vicars, who had held the job for fourteen years. There were other office-holders under Vicars, but their role was largely honorary. These gentlemen were Pierce Gun Mahony, Cork Herald; Francis Shackleton, Dublin Herald; and Francis Bennett Goldney, Athlone Pursuivant (the lowest rank in an Office of Arms). Mahony was a nephew of Vicars; Shackleton, brother of the Antarctic explorer Sir Ernest Shackleton, was his close friend.

Unfortunately, the statutes of the order had not taken into account the fact that the safe in which the jewels were to be kept was too large to fit through the door of the strongroom in the new premises. It was decided to leave the safe where it was until a smaller safe could be acquired. This never happened. While Vicars and his staff had among them seven latchkeys to the door of the Office of Arms, there were only two keys to the safe. Both were in Vicars's custody.

On 11 June 1907 Vicars opened the safe and showed the jewels to John Hodgson, librarian of the Duke of Northumberland. This was the last occasion on which they were seen. On the morning of 3 July the office cleaner, Mrs Farrell, found the entrance door unlocked and told William Stivey, the office messenger, about it. Stivey passed the message to Vicars, who did not appear to take the news very seriously.

On the morning of 6 July, Mrs Farrell found that the door of the strongroom was open. Stivey reported this disturbing phenomenon to Vicars, who once again answered offhandedly, something like 'Is that so?' or 'Did she?' and did nothing about it.

In the early afternoon of the same day Vicars gave Stivey the key of the safe and a box containing the collar of a deceased knight and asked him to put the box in the safe. As can be imagined, such an action was not only unusual but was contrary to normal practice. In fact this was the first time that Stivey had ever handled the safe key. Stivey went to the safe and found, to his surprise, that the door was unlocked. He rushed back and told Vicars, who returned with him and opened the safe. When he looked inside he found that five knights' collars and some diamonds belonging to Vicars's mother had disappeared. The police were called immediately, followed by lock experts, whose judgement was that the lock had not been tampered with but had been opened with a key.

The police inquired into the movements of the other personnel and established that Mahony had been in the Office of Arms from April until 4 July but that there was no record that Shackleton or Goldney had visited the premises, or even been in Ireland, between those dates.

The theft of the jewels caused a furore at the highest level. King Edward VII took the whole matter as a personal insult, as it had been arranged that he would visit Ireland shortly and invest a knight of the Order of St Patrick. He called for instant changes, and it was decided to get rid of Vicars and appoint a new Ulster King of Arms. Vicars, however, was not going to play the game and become a scapegoat. He refused to resign. His refusal to be the whipping-boy was supported by Mahony's father, Pierce Mahony (who called himself 'the O'Mahony'), who would become the most prominent figure in a campaign for a public inquiry to clear Vicars's name.

A Viceregal Commission of Inquiry was appointed but did not have the power to subpoena witnesses. Its first session was held on 10 January 1908 in the Office of Arms. When Vicars learnt that the commission was to carry out its business *in camera,* he refused to co-operate and demanded a public hearing. Francis Shackleton, on the other hand, came home from San Remo in Italy to give evidence. The commission got through its work with what might be called unseemly haste and published its report within fifteen days. The report was a damning indictment of Vicars, but his angry supporters protested that the sins of others were being laid on his grey head.

The report noted that the safe was not in the strongroom as required but had stayed in the library, to which the public had free access during business hours. Much was made, not without justification, of Vicars's seeming dismissal of the breaches of security that had been brought to his attention. In a similar vein, the report stressed that the only way to open the safe was with one of the two keys that he held. The only other possibility was that one of his keys had been copied. The summing up was decisive: Vicars had not exercised 'due vigilance or proper care as the custodian of the regalia.'

The superfluity of one pronouncement in the report makes one wonder if there was not a hidden agenda. This was a blunt statement that there was no evidence that Francis Shackleton had stolen the jewels. No-one in the office had accused him of the theft, so why the need to stress his innocence? It is true that the rumour machine had been busy throughout Dublin and that Shackleton's name had been bandied about, but he was only one of many possible culprits who had been named. Certain facts were agreed. Shackleton shared a house with Vicars in Clonskeagh and was up to his neck in debt. The commission knew this and was rigorous in questioning him about his income and his outgoings.

Shackleton's riposte to the inquisition was to remind the commission that the name of Lord Haddo, son of the Lord Lieutenant, the Earl of Aberdeen, was also being passed with the port among the chattering classes. This revelation was seen as a little warning that if they were too severe in their questioning he could open a nasty can of worms.

A letter from Vicars to Shackleton, dated 25 August 1907, was read into the records of the inquiry. It was plain from this letter that both Vicars and Goldney believed that Shackleton knew of the whereabouts of the jewels.

Why was the commission so insistent on emphasising Shackleton's innocence, and so determined to place the blame on Vicars? The olfactory organs of many quivered at the presence of a large rat. Their suspicions were confirmed by the failure of the commission to mention Captain Richard H. Gorges, one of Shackleton's many seedy friends, who was generally believed to have had a role in the disappearance of the regalia.

An Irish-American nationalist newspaper, the *Gaelic American*, was not so discreet. Bulmer Hobson, a member of the secret Irish Republican Brotherhood, gave the world a full account of the fiasco, which he reported as yet another example of British corruption, an early example of low standards in high places. The article stated that riotous parties were frequently held in the Office of Arms (later versions would hint at homosexual orgies) and that on one occasion, as a drunken prank, someone had borrowed the key of the safe from a sleeping Vicars, took the jewels out of the safe and returned them by post a day or two later. It was alleged that Shackleton and his friend Captain Gorges had decided to repeat this splendid jape, but dropping the bit about return post; instead they sold the jewels to pay for their gambling and other debts. The staff of the Office of Arms were either not present or too drunk to know what the pair had done. The article also claimed that the Dublin Metropolitan Police had carried out their own inquiry, operating in parallel with that of the commission, and had subjected Shackleton to a severe grilling but without success.

Many years later Bulmer Hobson recalled that he had interviewed Gorges in 1912 when the latter was acting as an *agent provocateur*. Hobson stated that Gorges assured him that the *Gaelic American* article was essentially correct but that, though the authorities knew who had stolen the jewels, they could neither gather sufficient hard evidence to convict the culprits nor persuade them to say where they had hidden the jewels. Frustrated, and anxious to avoid further scandal, their only recourse was to tell Shackleton to get out of Ireland immediately. Gorges added that poor Vicars continued to hope, against all the odds, that Shackleton, as a gentleman, would return the jewels; but Shackleton's code turned out to be that of the cad.

Gorges may have had an axe to grind, but many commentators feel that his account carries a certain amount of conviction. On the other hand, the trail may be even murkier than the Gorges version. Another person who could have had access on the fateful evening was Francis Bennett Goldney, who had been appointed Athlone Pursuivant only six months before the theft and who was revealed years later to be a regular thieving magpie. When he was killed in a motoring accident in France in 1918, the executors of his will found a treasure trove of stolen goods in his house, among them ancient charters and documents belonging to the city of Canterbury, a painting belonging to the Duke of Bedford and two communion cups from Canterbury Cathedral.

Vicars was sacked on 30 January 1908, and Captain Neville Rodwell Wilkinson was appointed Ulster King of Arms. However, Vicars refused to hand over the keys to the Office of Arms strongroom, and Wilkinson had to break into it. Vicars retired to County Kerry and, in spite of the allegations about his sexual orientation, married Gertrude Wright in 1917. On 14 April 1921 he was shot by a local IRA unit, which also burned down his house. In his will he condemned both the Irish executive and King Edward VII for making him a scapegoat and shielding 'the real culprit and thief, Francis R. Shackleton.' Because of the risk of legal action, the will was not made available to researchers until 1976.

Whatever about the 'Irish Crown Jewels' episode, Shackleton's reputation was conclusively sullied when he was convicted of fraud in 1913. On his release from prison he changed his name to Mellor and stayed in England, where he died in Chichester in 1941. Pierce Gun Mahony was found shot through the heart in 1914 in what appears to have been a hunting accident, though suspicions of murder were voiced. Captain Richard Gorges killed a policeman in 1915 and was convicted of manslaughter. While in prison he let it be known that he could tell the authorities what had happened to the jewels, but they would not believe him.

One thing is certain about the stolen baubles. It has been confirmed, in a history of Irish heraldic offices, that the authorities in Ireland and England systematically destroyed all records relating to the 'Crown Jewels' scandal. The rest is silence.

Chapter 7

The Sinn Féin irreconcilable: Robert Erskine Childers

There is nothing in nature more removed from the imaginative boy than the grown man who has cut himself apart from life, seems to move entirely by his own inner light, and to face his doom with equanimity . . . And yet again and again, in my own imagination, I have had to go through those terrible moments with him almost as if I were there: see the slight figure of the little grey-haired Englishman emerge for the last time into the Irish daylight, apparently cheerful and confident but incapable of grandiose gestures, concerned only lest inadvertently he might do or say something that would distress some poor fool of an Irish boy who was about to level an English rifle at his heart.

This is how Frank O'Connor transcribed the words of David Robinson, a prisoner held next door to the death cell of Erskine Childers in November 1922.

Childers was undoubtedly a rogue in the sense of someone who breaks away from the herd and who could be blind to the reality of others. He served causes rather than people and adhered obstinately and blindly to his own judgement. The British regarded him as a man who was betraying his native land; many of the Irish were convinced that he was a British spy. As Andrew Boyle says in his masterly biographical work *The Riddle of Erskine Childers,* his enigmatic spirit had always led him bit by bit to extremes; and if others shrank from accepting the conclusions of his hair-splitting logic he did not, or could not, draw back and did not hide his disdain for those who could not meet his standards. In the words of a contemporary, Frank MacDermott, referring to the seeming arrogance of Childers's logic, 'It was his sniff that got him killed.'

His father, Robert Childers, came from a landed Yorkshire family whose fortunes had been improved by marriage with a wealthy Sephardic family, refugees from Portugal in the seventeenth century. Robert Erskine Childers's great-great-grandfather, Thomas Erskine, had been the defence counsel of eighteenth-century radicals, became Lord Chancellor of England in 1802 but rapidly grew tired of the woolsack and retired at the age of fifty-six. A cousin, H. C. E. Childers, was Chancellor of the Exchequer from 1882 to 1885 in Gladstone's second government. He was not a thin man, like the future Irish patriot, but was so fat that his nickname was 'Here Comes Everybody', a term seized on by James Joyce for *Finnegans Wake.*

Erskine's father, Robert Childers, was an oriental scholar and compiler of the first dictionary of the Pali language. He died of tuberculosis in 1876, when Erskine was six. In those days TB was regarded with as much fear and superstition as leprosy. Erskine's mother, who had nursed her husband, also contracted the disease, and her five children were immediately taken from her. She was consigned to a home for incurables, and the children were sent to Glendalough House, County Wicklow, the home of their uncle and aunt, Charles and Agnes Barton, parents of Robert Barton, who would take part with Childers in the Treaty negotiations in London forty-four years later. Barton was a double cousin, because his mother was a Childers, the sister of Erskine's father. The new home was within walking distance of Lough Dan, where Erskine's passion for sailing would begin.

It is interesting that when still a young man Childers wrote to an aunt: 'I believe I want action more than anything. It has always been best for me . . .' Could this have attracted him to Michael Collins? If that was so, the riddle of Childers is why he followed de Valera rather than Collins. It is arguable that the contorted logic of the former was more attractive to his own convoluted mind than the bluff humanity of the latter.

Childers did not fraternise with the other boys in school. A contemporary wrote: 'He was peculiar in liking to go for long runs by himself.' When he was nineteen he contracted sciatica from a solitary hike in foul weather from Glendalough to Connemara and back, with a target of thirty miles a day. It left him with a limp for the rest of his life. At school he developed, or increased, a taste for Tennyson, in particular his poem 'Ulysses'.

The long day wanes: the slow moon climbs: the deep
Moans round with many voices. Come, my friends,
'Tis not too late to seek a newer world.

Childers was to write:

These lines always send a strange thrill through me and are half responsible for any longing I ever have to desert civilisation and 'wander far away—on from island unto island to the gateways of the day'—and so on. If ever I disappear for a year or two, you will know what sent me.

In a sense he would spend his life seeking this newer, better world. Such a feeling may also have been part of the *zeitgeist*, as the admission above could also have been written by a younger man and another maverick, T. E. Lawrence, of Arabia fame.

For the moment the real world intruded, and in 1894 Childers passed the competitive examination for a clerkship in the House of Commons, which he saw as a stepping-stone towards a career in politics. About this time also he bought his first yacht, the *Sheila*.

Two years after Childers had taken up his post in London, the disastrous Jameson Raid—an attack on the independent Boers in the Transvaal by migrant miners, the Uitlanders—had taken place in an attempt to overthrow the President, 'Oom' Paulus Kruger. The businessman and imperialist Cecil Rhodes had organised and financed the attack, which led inevitably to the Boer War. At this stage of his life Childers was still an ardent imperialist but was emerging as a Jekyll and Hyde. The Jekyll was the House of Commons clerk, working contentedly within the confines of a conservative system; the Hyde was a young man who could write in his diary long eulogies of solitary sailing and who in 1897 began his famous voyages through the channels of the Frisian islands to the Baltic Sea, voyages that would produce rich literary fruit and make his name known to many who might not link him with the Irish patriot who died the victim of a bloody civil war. One can wonder if this temptation to push oneself to the extremes might not be the same lure that compelled Tennyson's Ulysses to leave the sceptre and the isle to his son, Telemachus, and set sail for the Pillars of Hercules.

In relation to the Jameson Raid, Childers wrote:

I am so excited about the African business that I can hardly think about anything else . . . Lloyd-Jones is here and we spend the day in telegram-hunting and Emperor [Kaiser] cursing and expressing sublime confidence in the tenacity of the Anglo-Saxon race.

He volunteered to join the Battery of the City Imperial Volunteers and in 1900 sailed for Africa. However, a few months in South Africa convinced him that the Boers had a case, caused him to admire their chivalrous, brave and clever conduct of the war and to develop doubts about the rationale of the British cause. He objected to the burning of farmhouses and the description of the Boers as rebels and not belligerents, as well as the unilateral abolition of the Transvaal and the Orange Free State and their annexation as colonies. In his private notes he protested that the Orange river had never been conquered.

At the same time, when John Dillon MP, who supported the Boers, was accused by Joseph Chamberlain of being 'a good judge of traitors,' Childers followed suit by describing Dillon as 'very rabid'. When, some time later, Childers was introduced to Dillon as 'the Mr Childers who defended de Wet' he was, in his own words, 'frightfully annoyed as it was as good as stamping me as a fellow pro-Boer of Dillon's.'

In 1903 Childers visited New England, where he met and fell in love with Mary (Molly) Alden Osgood, of an old American family. Molly, like Erskine, walked with a limp. He proposed to her within three weeks and was accepted. The wedding took place in Trinity Church, Boston's largest Episcopalian church, though Childers was not a normal member of the Church of England or the Church of Ireland. In a letter to an elderly relative, the widow of a canon, he stated that his faith had been deepened, not undermined, by love.

My belief, in the orthodox sense, in Christian tenets . . . was shaken and finally overthrown long before I met Molly . . . While I was dissatisfied with the old faith, I had not the backbone and character to carve myself a new one, which should really represent me, my inmost spiritual nature . . . I have a spiritual life such as I never knew before; and I love good, in its widest sense, as, to my shame, I never loved it . . .

This was perhaps the first example of the influence that Molly was to have over him. She was a devotee of the Eastern sages and no doubt in a later era would have been a meditator and a reader of Khalil Gibran. Childers regarded himself as an 'eclectic', choosing the best values of every religion to create a ramshackle pantheon of his own.

The second example was in 1908 when Childers, encouraged by Molly and by Robert Barton, was won over to the concept of home rule for Ireland and, with all the enthusiasm of the convert, began to work on a book called *The Framework of Home Rule*, which was published in London in 1911.

As late as 1912 Childers's background and social circle still prevented any close contact with the Catholic middle class or even the Irish Party in Westminster. Sir Horace Plunkett seems to have been his only filter to the other Ireland, and Plunkett had little time for Arthur Griffith and no knowledge of Sinn Féin or the IRB. At one point Childers's name was on the list of Liberal parliamentary candidates but he withdrew it, which was a wise move, because one thing is certain about Childers: he was not a natural politician. He was a hopeless impromptu speaker, too honest, too simple, to endure the twisting and turning, the compromises and crowd-pleasing that are the politician's lot, and he was disgusted when he attended a political meeting in Ulster. He wrote to his wife:

I had a sickening experience yesterday, a sermon by one Patterson, a Presbyterian, in a big church here—a howling tirade against Catholics and the beastliest appeal to bigotry I have ever heard. Like a Mad Mullah and only fit for the Congo, calling them heathen and as good as goading his people to burn them at the stake.

On 25 April 1914 eight hundred members of the Ulster Volunteer Force invaded the harbour at Larne, County Antrim. It was not a surreptitious operation under cover of darkness but a blatant demonstration of strength, led by Sir William Adair and Major James McCalmont MP. They cut off telegraph and telephone communication, drew a cordon around the harbour, excluded the police and the customs officers and waited for two steamers to come in and unload arms and ammunition. This was the forerunner of the violence that was to come.

The Cabinet called a conference, which proposed that the Irish problem be solved by carving out chunks of Ulster and separating the severed counties from the rest of the country. This marked Childers's breaking point. If the unionists could smuggle in armaments, so could the nationalists. His justification was based on two events and one non-event: the British decree banning all importing of arms and ammunition into Ireland 'for warlike purposes', and the unionists' defiance of the ban and the British government's failure to do anything about it.

It is one of Ireland's recurring paradoxes that it was a group of Anglo-Irish gentry who got together in May 1914 to even the odds, possibly because they had the financial means and the contacts. This group was made up of Sir Roger Casement, Alice Stopford Green, Erskine and Molly Childers, Lord Ashbourne, Sir George and Lady Alice Young, Sir Alexander Lawrence, Captain George Fitzhardinge Berkeley, Conor O'Brien and Darrel Figgis.

Figgis, a poet and politician who had a short and tragic life, had already been in contact with an arms dealer in Hamburg, Moritz Magnus Junior. The committee was ready to put its money where its minutes were and produced £1,523 19s 3d for the purchase and transport of the weapons. It was decided to use Childers's yacht, the *Asgard*, and Conor O'Brien's boat, the *Kelpie*.

An interesting interpretation of Childers is to be had from Colonel Robert Henry Pipon of the Royal Fusiliers, whom Childers invited to take part in the adventure.

Childers asked us both to come and help him on his yacht to meet a German ship off Terschelling where, at sea, cases of arms would be transshipped. He was then going to land them at Howth Bay for the Irish Nationalists to show they could do what the Ulster people had done. He promised us there was no intention of using them other than as a gesture of equality. I refused. I recognised Childers as a crackpot. Something always happens to crackpots. Something always goes wrong . . . Shephard and I knew the Childers well . . . [They had] a little boy of nine whom they—chiefly she—wouldn't allow to be told any word of religion of any sort until he was old enough to decide freely which he considered the best religion . . . Poor little devil! Crackpot, of course. It always comes out somewhere.

The crew of the boat was finally Erskine and Molly Childers, Captain Gordon Shephard of the Royal Flying Corps (a sailing companion of Childers), Mary Spring Rice, and two Donegal fishermen, McKinley and Duggan. They met the tug carrying the arms off the mouth of the Scheldt by the Ruytigen lightship. Conor O'Brien took 600 rifles and 20,000 rounds of ammunition on board the *Kelpie,* which had sailed from the Shannon, past the Fastnet and up the English Channel. On board with O'Brien was the writer Diarmid Coffey. The crew of the *Asgard* worked non-stop until 2 o'clock in the morning to bring on board and stack away 900 rifles and 29,000 rounds of ammunition, and the German ship then towed them to the cliffs of Dover.

When one is considering what the venture achieved, it is important to remember that this portage of a heavy load of arms and ammunition was done with a yacht propelled by wind power only. It sailed past the Royal Navy and around Lambay Island in wild weather, then, not receiving an all-clear because of the weather, risked landing at Howth, where Eoin MacNeill, Michael O'Rahilly ('the O'Rahilly') and Bulmer Hobson would be waiting for them. Cathal Brugha and Arthur Griffith (both of them in Volunteer private's uniform) were also there.

While this adventure was coming to a successful end, Austria was sending an ultimatum to Serbia, and the Great War was about to begin. Four days earlier King George V had summoned British and Irish party leaders to a crisis conference at Buckingham Palace. This led to accusations (quite justified) from Liberal, Irish and Labour MPs that he was indefensibly partisan and was siding with the Ulster Unionists. Speaking for the Labour Party, James Keir Hardie claimed that the king had precipitated the most serious constitutional crisis since the seventeenth century.

King George is not a statesman. Born in the ranks of the working classes his most likely fate would have been that of a street-corner loafer. He is being made the tool of the reactionary forces to break the power of democracy.

Meanwhile, having done his illegal bit for the Irish cause, Erskine Childers was back in London and within a few months would be a naval lieutenant in the Admiralty building in Chatham, drawing up a plan for the invasion of Germany from the Frisian Sands so familiar to him. Fact had imitated fiction.

Though Childers was now forty-five, he obtained permission to fly on missions in seaplanes over the North Sea. This was an extremely dangerous activity, and the danger did not necessarily come from the enemy but rather from the primitive nature of the planes. He described them as 'tractors with propellers in front, the passenger's seat forward, next the engine.' This was an 'enterprise new in war: an incalculable experiment.' His companions, and perhaps he also, existed in an

atmosphere . . . of cheerful optimism . . . So sanguine and jovial is the anticipation of a certain doom in our gimcrack pleasure boat with its popguns and delicate, butterfly planes.

On his second flight, engine failure forced their seaplane to land on a heavy sea in the middle of a minefield and to spend the night drifting, at risk at any moment of hitting one of the mines.

His public-schoolboy sense of fair play did not desert him even in what was going to be the bloodiest war in history. Before setting out to fly to Hannover in order to bomb Zeppelins, Childers was collecting survival gear to equip the seaplane when he 'found to [his] disgust that his revolver cartridges were flat-nosed dum-dums.' His reaction was immediate: 'I should like to see the responsible person shot and his carcase sent to the Germans as a proof of bona fides. I resolved to throw all away and go unarmed.'

He flew on a bombing mission on Christmas Day, 1914, which was a failure, in that they could not find their target, but to Childers it was of

extraordinary technical interest . . . a new era in war; the first regular battle between the ships of the sea and the ships of the air. We were fortunate to have witnessed this remarkable event which is but a foretaste of a complete revolution in warfare.

The more one knows about Childers, the more he emerges as a driven, multi-faceted enigma, with his propensity and ability to use every spare moment to record his activities and his opinions, whether in the form of letters or a diary (in itself extraordinary, as if his over-worked brain needed relief), his more than brave impulse to seek out dangerous situations, his addiction to hyper-accuracy and obsessive attachment to detail, his usefulness in the intelligence world, which could give justification to those who would later see him as a British agent in Ireland, and above all his tendency to go into a trance when thinking—his 'vagueness'—which shut out the external world. One cannot help feeling that at times he considered the means and the *modus operandi* as more important than the aims of any particular action—which could explain his behaviour during the Treaty debate. It could be said that an element of his rogue status, as one always out-side the herd, was the sensitivity and intensity of his reaction to events. In one sense it could be said that he never grew up.

In the midst of the global turmoil, his attention, like that of an observer homing in on one point below his plane, was jerked back from time to time to events in Ireland: the 1916 Rising and the savage British response, followed by the trial of Roger Casement and his execution. It was at this point that Carson and Redmond accepted immediate home rule exclusive of the Six Counties (until after the war, when the matter could be sorted out at an Imperial Conference); but the proposal was sabotaged by the Colonel Blimps.

The tragic riddle of Childers's life was that the man who in 1916 had teased Robert Barton for resigning his British army commission by saying that the next worst thing that could happen would be Barton's 'conversion to Sinn Féin' mutated into a militant (though unarmed) opponent of the Treaty, for which Barton would vote, and became de Valera's secret weapon during the Treaty debate.

Several contemporary commentators blame the influence of his wife. Early in their married life the only known breach between Childers and Molly arose over her sudden support of England and things English, which lasted until Barton put her wise. 'I don't believe you', he wrote, 'when you say that England has more gleanings of righteousness than any other nation. She has more hypocrisy.' Having pushed her husband in one direction, Molly was now finding that it was not possible to move him back to his former stance.

The strange twists of Childers's world view are revealed in a comment in his diary about a proposal to fly across the Netherlands in order to bomb Germany: 'It is utterly unsportsmanlike and immoral.' How does one get inside the mind of a man who, after four years of bloody carnage, is still using words like 'unsportsmanlike' about what at worst would be a breach of air space, at best sneakiness? Truly a knight *sans-pareil.*

This strange amalgam is also illustrated by the Childers's insistence that they and their children were English. Perhaps his motivation was an innate arrogance, with everyone with whom he allegedly co-operated, which told him that he, from his height, was helping the Irish, who were not willing or capable of helping themselves. He told his wife that he felt he should work in Ireland because it was 'far the less easy course in every way.' Later he was to record another very revealing sentiment.

I have been growing more and more to dislike compromise, which only builds on the work of the idealists, and to thirst for whole ideals where the creative work is accomplished and whence all the splendid inspirations of the past arise—all the great messiahs, earth movers.

Such sentiments could be blessed by Lenin, Stalin or Hitler.

It was Barton (an almost forgotten man) who introduced Childers to Michael Collins, who in turn introduced him to de Valera. De Valera was to say later that Childers was 'the model of all I had wished to have been myself'—an admission that speaks volumes about both men. Cynics might say that, apart from Childers's social position, his assured public-school lack of any feeling of inferiority, and his lack of a desire for, or need of, power, this was rather an admission of de Valera's regret that he lacked true altruism.

Another aspect of Childers's personality as a rogue can be seen in his rejection of the attitudes of his former English colleagues at the Paris Peace Conference in 1919.

Pressed, they care nothing about anyone's freedom in Europe and regard the whole thing as a means of curbing Germany. I have a kind of blind fury sometimes at seeing these cultured, cold-blooded, self-satisfied people making careers out of the exploitation of humanity and crucifying the Christs with a *bon mot* or a shrug. Meanwhile I smile and argue good-temperedly.

It would be interesting to conduct psychological profiles of de Valera and Childers, two men who had not known their fathers. De Valera was interested in power and in his own glorification. Childers was obsessed with doing the job in the correct way—which always happened to be his way. His tragedy was that he meant well. There was something of the colonial district officer about Childers, a character from one of Joyce Cary's African novels, the slave to duty determined to sort out the confusion of the well-meaning but incompetent natives. In his case it meant that the propaganda office should take control of the army's image. It may also be that, like many rogues, he was seeking an identity and a commitment and had now chosen Ireland. He became a judge in the Dáil courts (as did the fascist Charles Bewley) and was a director of the Land Bank, headed by Robert Barton.

When Childers moved definitively to Ireland to help the republican cause, he moved into the publicity department, which was his forte but would eventually contribute to his downfall. In one sense this was his natural homeland, a position where he had to make his way alone through sandbanks of mistrust and suspicion, both English and Irish, waiting to ground this decorated former British intelligence officer. He wrote articles for the *Daily News* of London that described the activities of the Black and Tans in Dublin on lines that would be recognised today as the behaviour of the Nazi soldiers in the Second World War, the American troops in Arab countries, and Israeli troops in the occupied territories of Palestine.

When Robert Barton and Desmond Fitzgerald, Minister of Propaganda, were imprisoned, de Valera appointed Childers to the latter's post, to the annoyance of Arthur Griffith. Perhaps this was a side-swipe on the part of Dev against his Vice-President, who had been running things successfully while Dev had been fomenting havoc and creating enemies and splits in the United States. There were objections to this appointment, but Childers, whatever his faults, was at heart a knight errant looking for dragons to slay and, above all, dangerous adventure—a twentieth-century small, beardless Quixote. In fact his later photographs remind one of the Knight of the Sorrowful Countenance. Childers and Quixote were both *knights errant* (which, like 'arrant', can also mean a notorious, unmitigated and erring individual).

The resemblance to the Sorrowful Don is supported by a book published in Dublin in 1922, *Free State or Republic?: Pen Pictures of the Historic Treaty Session of Dáil Éireann.* The book is made up of articles published in the *Irish Independent* while the debate was going on and gives a contemporary view of the drama. Erskine Childers is mentioned ten times. The first reference deals with the second meeting of the Dáil on 19 December 1921, when some people are chatting, some are reading from weighty documents and

> Erskine Childers is reflective in that pale, rather white, and keenly cold way of his.

Later in the day, when Griffith moved the ratification of the Treaty, the *Independent's* reporter described the scene as follows:

> De Valera was very busy with his papers . . . Mrs. Pearse was listening with calm intensity . . . Erskine Childers seemed always to be melancholy.

Towards the end of the day,

> A thin, slight figure arose. It was Erskine Childers. Every line of his face is illuminated by the pale cast of thought.

On 20 December the reporter recorded that Childers,

> looking more than usually melancholy . . . took his place beside his chief . . .

Finally, after eight days of prolonged and animated debate had placed imprints on the delegates' faces,

> Erskine Childers seemed even more gloomy than ever—if that were possible.

This does not mean that there were no dragons (or dinosaurs) to be slain. Winston Churchill, for one, while proposing stronger measures at a meeting of the Cabinet, called for the hanging of the 'rebels' and told his colleagues:

> What strikes me is the feebleness of the local machinery. After a person is caught he should pay the penalty within a week. Look at

the tribunals which the Russian government has devised. You should get three or four judges whose scopes should be instrumental and they should move quickly over the country and do summary justice.

How much, one wonders, did Churchill—another rogue—know about the ruthless barbarity of Bolshevik summary justice during and after the Russian Civil War? When the Attorney-General reminded him that the English judges had already rejected such a proposal for summary justice, the man whose mulish insistence in 1915 that Allied troops should force their way through the Dardanelles and join up with Imperial Russia, causing the death of 36,000 Commonwealth soldiers, of whom many were Irish, replied:

Shows all the more need for extraordinary action. Get three generals if you cannot get three judges.

Childers was useful to certain elements of the freedom-fighters, but he had his share of critics. Piaras Béaslaí, the army's director of publicity, was given an impression

of fussy, feverish futility. He displayed the mind, outlook and ability of a capable British civil servant, but no adequate appreciation of the situation with which he was dealing.

It was Béaslaí who said, in relation to the Treaty debate:

There was something particularly irritating in the spectacle of this English ex-officer, who had spent his life in the service of England and English Imperialism, heckling and baiting the devoted Griffith, with his livelong record of unselfish slaving in the cause of Ireland.

In June 1921 General Macready recommended that Éamon de Valera, Arthur Griffith and Erskine Childers be tried for treason and, presumably, hanged. Griffith was in prison, but for some reason neither de Valera nor Childers was taken in. Hamar Greenwood, on the other hand, while approving that de Valera should be left alone, agreed that Childers, who was 'very mischievous', could be arrested, possibly because, despite his public-school probity, he was not averse in his propaganda work to putting out false statements.

Such immunity for de Valera must have reflected either his unimportance or some sinister motive. De Valera had told General Smuts, the Boer soldier and politician, that he would not accept an invitation to negotiate through intermediaries. There would be no reply unless he received 'a written communication addressed to me directly.' Was this vanity, or a typical de Valera ploy to trap the British authorities into an implicit recognition of his standing as President *de facto* of the Irish Republic?

A letter that Childers ghosted for Arthur Griffith for the attention of the US State Department is unconsciously humorous. Recommending a reasonable Dominion Home Rule Act without oath of allegiance, tricks and traps and limited powers, it had this to say by way of illustration:

> The trouble is that England, like a nursery governess in a dispute, insists first of all in standing on her own dignity—and when there is no dignity to stay one, what must happen?

How many members of Sinn Féin, the US Congress or poor Arthur Griffith, for that matter, had experienced their nursery governess standing on her dignity?

It must have been very strange for Winston Churchill and Admiral Beatty to see across the negotiating table, countering their every point about naval matters, the author of *The Riddle of the Sands* and its plea for defence against naval attack. They must at least have seen him as a rogue, if not a downright traitor. It is significant that later, on 24 October, a private meeting was held between David Lloyd George and Austen Chamberlain on the one hand and Arthur Griffith and Michael Collins on the other. Lloyd George had insisted that Childers be kept out, because he was 'believed by Britain to be the most extreme.'

It is worth noting that Childers was so correct and so concerned to keep his distance from the British delegates seated across the table that he did not even acknowledge Churchill's secretary, Edward Marsh, who had been Childers's friend in Cambridge and later his fishing companion. Childers had definitely left the herd.

He was also in the process of running away from his new herd, the moderate negotiators, and began to irritate them with his pedantic editing of their proposals wherever he, with his experience as a clerk in the House of Commons, came across what he considered to be sloppy drafting that could give an edge to the British negotiators. Lloyd George summed him up as rigid and fanatical, and towards the end he handed preliminary drafts of proposals directly to the pleni- potentiaries, Griffith and Collins, so that they could weigh them up and, it was to be hoped, accept them before they 'got into the hands of Childers' (who would certainly send them back to de Valera). One can sympathise with the impatience of these horse-dealers.

Obviously, two factors were at work here: Childers's pedantic perfectionism and his by now all-or-nothing republicanism. In fair- ness to him it must be said that it takes a thief to catch a thief, and the blunt man of action (Collins) and idealist advocate of the dual monarchy (Griffith) could be outclassed easily by the seasoned drafts- man from the British civil service.

Another characteristic that could place Childers in the rogue cate- gory was his occasional lack of tact and 'un-Irish' insensitivity to the feelings of others when pursuing what he saw as the righteous path. When the London negotiations were almost at an end, Childers draft- ed a document that set out how many concessions the delegates had made without any *quid pro quo* from the British side.

> Ireland's claim is for a Republic, unfettered by any obligation or restriction whatsoever . . . Out of the ten paragraphs of the pro- posals, Nos. 1 and 7 are the only ones that do not make concessions from this position.

Such a statement reveals serious naïveté in someone who had been exposed to the give and take of the House of Commons and House of Lords for many years. Surely such a man should be aware that the point of negotiation is that everybody must walk away feeling that they have achieved something, at the price of a few concessions. When Griffith accused him of doing his best to make an agreement impossible, Childers got up on his high horse, like a good Anglo-Irishman, and demanded that Griffith put his words in writing.

The late Frank Pakenham, Lord Longford, in his book *Peace by Ordeal,* sums up the situation and draws attention to what might be called the 'awkwardness' of Childers:

> Childers, the old committee clerk of the House of Commons, was prone to a formalism, strange to Ireland and, in the eyes of Griffith,

ridiculous. It has been said, and not by enemies of Griffith, that behind these trifling exasperations lay a genuine and growing suspicion that Childers was no honest friend of Ireland. Be that as it may, there is no doubt that Griffith saw in Childers, with his rigid limits on the verbal scope of the bargaining, an obstacle not much less menacing than the British themselves to a satisfactory settlement.

The pride and self-esteem of the rogue crept into Childers's records of events. He complained of slights by the others and wrote in his diary of how, on one of the last nights, he 'thought of the fate of Ireland being settled hugger-mugger by ignorant Irish negotiators.' When it came to the signing of the final British document, under threat of immediate war, a telling occurrence took place. Childers's cousin, Robert Barton, was not going to sign, nor was Childers. They went out for a private discussion, and Childers told Barton that he was refusing to sign on a point of principle and that he felt that Molly was with those who would not sign. Barton reflected for a moment and then said, 'Well, I suppose I must sign.' Years later, Barton confessed that it was the mention of Molly's name that made him change his mind. He felt that Childers

had been acting throughout like a man under the spell of his absent wife, focussing his mind intently until it responded exactly as Molly's would have done, while damning the consequences for everyone else.

Lloyd George, in a newspaper article, has left a telling pen-picture of Childers at this low moment in his life.

Outside in the lobby sat a man who had used all the resources of an ingenious and well-trained mind, backed by a tenacious will, to wreck every endeavour to reach agreement: Mr. Erskine Childers. At every crucial point in the negotiations, he played a sinister part. When we walked out of the room where we had sat for hours together, worn with toil and anxious labour, but all happy that our great task of reconciliation had been achieved, we met Mr. Erskine Childers outside, sullen with disappointment and compressed wrath at what he conceived to be the surrender of principles he had fought for.

Principles before practicalities. A wretched pawn in the hands of de Valera, who ostensibly had kept those hands clean, Childers, like Dev, had been shielded from, or had blinded himself to, the reality, a reality admitted by Michael Collins to Hamar Greenwood after the signing of the Treaty:

> You had us dead beat. We could not have lasted another three weeks. When we were told of the truce we were astounded. We thought you must have gone mad.

Perhaps Childers had been taken in by his own propaganda. In any case he was seen as a rogue or worse by his opponents at the time of the Civil War. Kevin O'Higgins, who would himself be assassinated by Childers's former comrades, described the

> able Englishman who is leading those who are opposed to this Government . . . Steadily, callously and ghoulishly on his career of striking at the heart of this nation, striking deadly, or what he hopes are deadly, blows at the economic life of the nation.

On the other side of the Irish Sea, Winston Churchill described him as a 'murderous renegade'.

One must have pity on someone who inadvertently invoked such hostility. To understand some rogues it is important to take note of their personal philosophy. After Childers's death a sailing companion, Alfred Ollivant, described him as an agnostic mystic.

> Nobody could be with him and not feel his spiritual apartness. He lived in a cloud of dreams and ideals remote from the world. His intellect was the least of him and its limitations his ultimate undoing. Had his mind been as good as his heart was big he would have been one of the great world forces of our times . . . The good democrat had become merged in the dogmatic pedagogue. At last, it was no longer the will of the Irish people he sought but what he believed was good for the Irish people. In this final phase, his judgement proved as faulty as his purpose remained pure and his courage high. Some will-o'-the wisp seemed to possess his brain and lead him ever forward over bogey-haunted quagmires to his inevitable doom.

The relationship between de Valera and Childers is inextricable from any examination of Childers himself. When it comes to the question of Childers's stance on the Treaty, the chicken and the egg come to mind. Who influenced whom? Both were intelligent men. Francis Costello's book *The Irish Revolution and Its Aftermath* casts some light on both men. With masterly understatement the author states: 'Understanding what, in fact, De Valera's actual bargaining position was up to the onset of the Anglo-Irish Treaty negotiations continues to defy ready characterisation,' and he argues that de Valera's time in America enabled him 'to develop a nuanced approach to complex questions,' with the result that the question of the objective of the Irish struggle was 'met by his own brand of doublespeak. De Valera's finely honed skills in answering questions with half-answers, combined with his mathematician's brain, equipped him with a capacity for obfuscation.'

Costello makes the telling point that de Valera 'equated the title of President of the Irish Republic with the American presidential model—the strong executive in whom the aspirations of the nation were invested.' In addition, he is of the belief that the famous proposal of 'external association' was the brainchild of Erskine Childers. It is easy to see how de Valera and Childers could illustrate a meeting of minds, the former with his genius for never saying anything that could pin him down, the latter a civil servant trained in the production of documents littered with escape clauses that lend themselves to mixed interpretation. Both de Valera and Childers were followers of Humpty Dumpty and adhered to his policy: 'When *I* use a word, it means just what I choose it to mean, neither more nor less.'

Costello also confirms that Childers's role as secretary to the Irish delegation allowed him to act as de Valera's eyes and ears.

During the Dáil debate on the Treaty, de Valera was to argue that the plenipotentiaries had signed the Treaty under duress. This was supported by Robert Barton, who renounced his signature, saying that he had signed only because of British threats. Costello points out that Childers's diary (now in Trinity College Library) reveals that he did not attempt to prevent his cousin from signing but on the contrary eased Barton's conscience by giving him an escape route: if he did sign, he could always claim that he had done so under duress. As Costello points out tellingly, this suggestion was made before any of the Irish delegates had picked up their pen, and it should be noted that Collins's response to the duress plea was to declare in the Dáil:

> It has also been suggested that the Delegation broke down before
> the last bit of English bluff . . . England put up quite a good bluff
> for the last five years and I did not break down before that bluff.

As we know, in spite of his loyalty to his cousin, when the chips
were down Barton voted for the Treaty.

Childers' denigrators had accused him of being a British spy. He
wrote before his death:

> I have been held up to scorn and hatred as an Englishman who,
> betraying his own country, came here to lecture and destroy
> Ireland. Another and viler version is to the effect that so far from
> betraying England, I have been actually acting as the secret instru-
> ment of Englishmen for ruining Ireland.

It is the fate of many rogues to become the subject of legend, and
this was the case with Childers. Many of those on the pro-Treaty side
came to believe at the time that he was the military mastermind of
republican opposition and personally responsible for rebel outrages
and daring military exploits.

Other interesting contemporary reactions to Childers can be found
in Risteard Mulcahy's edition of the 'Family Memoir' of his father,
General Richard Mulcahy. The first example is General Mulcahy's
claim that when de Valera returned from the United States in
December 1920 he did not confide in the Dáil Ministry (government)
on the Truce or Treaty but kept things close to his chest rather than
share them with the organised Sinn Féin party. His only confidant and
adviser was Erskine Childers. Mulcahy also felt that it was Childers's
influence that saw Duggan and Barton appointed as liaison officers to
assist Cathal Brugha during the Treaty negotiations. Childers or Collins
may have proposed the mysterious appointment of Brugha as a pleni-
potentiary, but it is doubtful that it was Collins, given Brugha's lack of
co-operation with Collins, inspired by blatant jealousy of the hero.

Another example of Childers's influence can be seen in the case of
the fanatical Liam Lynch, who, in or about August 1922, told de Valera
that he would have to look in future to Childers as leader. Risteard
Mulcahy comments:

I assume that Dad means that, by August 1922, even Dev was not extreme enough in his opposition to the Provisional Government to satisfy Lynch. Lynch would look to Childers, the leading anti-Treaty propagandist, as his political leader. And Lynch was literally deserted when he died on the Knockmealdown mountains through the capture of many of his republican colleagues and the retirement of the rest as they saw their cause was lost.

Another insight into the contemporary common perception of Childers's role in the Civil War is to be found in Richard Mulcahy's annotations on Piaras Béaslaí's biography of Michael Collins, *Michael Collins and the Making of a New Ireland,* published in 1926. Commenting on Béaslaí's section on the split in the army after the Treaty debate, Mulcahy recorded the following:

The Volunteers, the army generally, were in a very different position [from the majority of the population, who were in favour of the Treaty]. They had heard from the highest possible level that the plenipotentiaries had, as it were, behind the backs of de Valera and other members of the government, broken their word in London and had done something which they should not have done; with the implication that they would not have been allowed to do it if, having obeyed what were alleged to be their instructions, they had consulted their colleagues before taking action; they [the Volunteers] were told that in future they would be the King's army, and that the King himself or his Governor General in Ireland would be the person who would permit and sign all their commissions; and that, while the British Army could go out now, it had every legal right to return where and whenever it pleased. They had all this painted to them by a person [Childers] who knew all about the King and the inside of British Government working and he was supported by de Valera and other members of the cabinet and other members of the Dáil, in the contention that the King had power over every scrap of legislation in Ireland . . .

The binding and immobilising influence of the oath to the Republic was pressed home on them; and the inflexibility of any possible interpretation of that word in practice, except in accordance with some brainwave of de Valera's or some aspect of de Valera's conscience was pushed home.

The implication is that this stemmed from Childers's propaganda, the power of which can be found in the fact that Austin Stack, another anti-Treaty militant, 'had said that he would commit suicide if he thought Dev would do anything wrong.' Mulcahy held the view that

> Childers's inflammatory attack on the Treaty was an important factor leading to the intransigence of the IRA, and particularly may have influenced those members of the army in Munster. Perhaps it is little wonder that the leaders of the Provisional Government were so bitter about Childers's intervention and his subsequent inflammatory publicity campaign on behalf of the Irregulars in the civil war.

The belief overrode the facts.

Childers was tried by a military court on 17 November 1922, but no sentence was pronounced at the time. The sentence was debated by the Ministry and, ironically, it was Kevin O'Higgins, apparently unforgiving in Dáil debates, who argued for a lesser sentence. In any case W. T. Cosgrave, first President of the Executive Council of the Irish Free State following the death of Arthur Griffith in 1922, considered a reprieve, and a message was sent to Childers the night before the execution, telling him that if he 'would agree to cease all further opposition to the democratically elected parliament of the Free State' the government would cancel his death sentence.

Childers replied that he would make a decision after he had spoken to his wife. Some time later he sent a message that he could not give such an undertaking—another example of what some called the malign influence that Molly Childers and her 'particularly extreme and rigid . . . views had on her husband.'

Everybody is agreed that Childers died bravely on 24 November. Despite his unorthodox religious views, he asked for Bishop Gregg of the Church of Ireland to attend him. The bishop spent the night with him and was seen to weep several times. Before the fatal moment Childers walked down the line of the firing squad and shook hands with them. He did not want a bandage on his eyes, but when it was put on he called out, 'Take a step or two forwards, lads. It will be easier that way.' He then gave the arranged signal and was shot. Many of the riflemen were wiping away tears before they marched back to Beggar's Bush Barracks.

The papers of Archbishop Byrne in the Dublin Diocesan Archives have revealed that Molly Childers wrote to the archbishop on 27 November to tell him that her husband's body would be released on the following day and asking permission for the remains to be received at Whitefriars Street, a Catholic church. She claimed that Erskine had asked for one Catholic priest first and then another before his execution. She said she believed his intention was clear, and she wished to see it carried out. She asked to meet Archbishop Byrne so that she could convince him. There does not seem to be any record of such a meeting taking place.

Risteard Mulcahy's account of Childers's participation in the bloody events of those years and the Big End v. Little End disputes over oaths and Documents 1 and 2, which cost the new Free State so much in lives and the destruction of the economy, sums up the sad and unnecessary outcome:

> The tragedy of Childers's death is a sad reminder of the consequences where principle conflicts with pragmatism, where passion over-comes all sense of realism, and where a man will die for what others may perceive to be an empty formula.

Childers was the victim of people like the fanatical sister of Terence MacSwiney, who told the Dáil: 'No physical victory can compensate for a spiritual surrender . . . This fight has been a spiritual fight.' This raising of political problems to a vague metaphysical level could be said to be the cleverest trick of C. S. Lewis's devil, Screwtape: the inveigling of well-intentioned people into bloody disaster.

Erskine Childers was a tragic rogue, a good man whose inflexibility doomed him to disaster. The final word can be left to his friend Alfred Ollivant:

> This is how I shall always see him now—a tussling wisp of human-ity, high overhead, and swirling with the slow swirl of the mast against a tumult of tempestuous sky.

Chapter 8
Speak some good of the dead: John DeLorean

As we have pointed out already, an essential quality of many rogues is that, no matter what havoc they wreak, it is never their fault: they can always produce irrefutable evidence that *They* (malign persons or forces) were responsible.

John DeLorean, one of the hottest properties in the United States and Europe forty years ago, set up a revolutionary car manufacturing business at Dunmurry, a suburb of Belfast, in 1975. The British Labour government supported the endeavour, but everything collapsed in 1981 when a Tory government under Margaret Thatcher pulled the rug from under him.

A lot of money was lost, particularly by the British taxpayer. Who was to blame? Obviously not John DeLorean, a well-meaning Jack on the Beanstalk who was crushed by Giants.

It is only fair that both sides should be heard, and it is for readers to make up their own mind. The prosecution case was made by an obituary writer in the *Guardian*, Christopher Reed, on 21 March 2005. DeLorean will conduct his own defence.

The heading of the obituary described DeLorean as a car-maker and conman whose victims included the British and American governments. Reed claimed that the majority of those who dealt with DeLorean suffered money losses, which amounted to millions, and stated that an irate English judge thundered that he would like to sentence DeLorean to ten years for 'barefaced, outrageous and massive fraud.' He failed to mention that some English judges are not free from bias, or that their judgements are notoriously the children of their prejudices.

Reed charged DeLorean with fraud, embezzlement, tax evasion and defaulted loans and listed his victims, in particular the governments of Britain, the United States and Switzerland, but admitted that creditors in the United States received 91 cents to the dollar in bankruptcy proceedings, which money did not come from DeLorean personally but from the accountancy firm Arthur Andersen, because the latter had failed to discover the flaws in DeLorean's activities.

The obituary ends with the writer scratching his head in bewilderment because, in spite of DeLorean's naughtiness, he maintained till the end a host of dedicated fans. It happened that the majority of these faithful ones were the owners of DeLorean's stainless-steel cars, which are now valuable collectors' items!

The details of DeLorean's downfall at the hands of big business and evil politicians make fascinating reading. Much of the progression of his tragedy can be found in a document that he submitted to a Californian court on 22 August 2000. Is this a fairy-tale?

The Industrial Development Authority is an Irish state-sponsored agency with the responsibility for securing new investment from overseas in manufacturing and internationally traded services. More than 1,050 companies have chosen to invest in Ireland as their European base and are involved in a wide range of industries and services.

Normally the IDA was only too eager to welcome new enterprises, provided that a company was prepared to respect certain requirements, that its solidity and liquidity were confirmed and, particularly, that it undertook to create an agreed number of jobs in Ireland. The IDA, like any national body, is always secretly pleased when it snatches something from under the nose of its main rivals. When, in the days before the birth of the Celtic tiger cub, those competitors were England, Scotland, Wales or Northern Ireland, the discreet chuckles were clearly audible. There was, however, one operation that was turned down on a hunch and that went up to Belfast. Within a few years the executives of the IDA would have reason to be smug. The business in question was the DeLorean Motor Company, and its founder was John DeLorean.

DeLorean was born in 1925 in east Detroit, the motor capital of the United States. Though his father was a Romanian immigrant and his mother was born in Austria, he claimed to have Irish ancestry, which permits him to feature in this book.

He was creative as a child, and his teachers reported that his projects at Cass Technical High School showed vision and ingenuity. He enrolled in the Lawrence Technical College, where he studied engineering. From there he moved on to an 'internship' (work experience) with Chrysler.

By the age of forty he was the youngest general manager of the Pontiac division of General Motors, and eight years later he had become a vice-president of General Motors and controller (financial director). During his time with General Motors he broke away from the stereotype of conservative Midwestern car executives and convinced the company to escape from its boring classic, heavy cars and to concentrate on smaller, more sporty models.

He was in the running to become president of General Motors but left the company and, with some friends from the industry, set up the DeLorean Motor Corporation. His partners were engineers and executives from large international manufacturers of exotic cars, rich in experience but not in cash. Their aim was to create a car that would attract sports car enthusiasts around the globe, not limited to the United States. The car would be the DMC-12 and would represent a revolution in car design. It would have a V-6 fuel-injection engine, gull-wing doors, super-sleek design and unpainted stainless steel skin, which made it very light and virtually rustproof. The engine compartment was in the back for better performance, and the design was made very similar to the Ferrari. The DMC-12's top speed was only 125 m.p.h. but it could go from 0 to 60 in 8½ seconds, an acceleration that today is comparable to the Mazda 626 or a Jeep Grand Cherokee V8.

However, it wasn't the speed that DeLorean was looking for but the style. The style and the angular design were to earn it a cult following, as did the doors, which opened above the body like a Viking helmet or an eagle's menacing outstretched wings. So enthusiastic were its fans that when the popular *Back to the Future* films were made in the late 1980s the producers insisted that Michael J. Fox's time-travelling machine should be a DMC-12. Of course there were begrudgers who dismissed the new car as 'flashy'.

DeLorean and his partners began a plausible and hard-selling campaign around the world and particularly in Europe. Ireland was one of their first ports of call in Europe, but they were to end up at Dunmurry, a 'struggling industry and port area' outside Belfast.

In spite of their concentration on foreign investment, they did not neglect the United States and received three million dollars from the Bank of America and $1.5 million from the talk-show host Johnny Carson. They established their corporate head office in Manhattan, their quality-control department in Michigan and their marketing and promotions department in California. Their largest investor, however, was the British government under Ted Heath, which invested $100 million, on condition that DMC's production plant be based in Dunmurry. The hope, shared by the Conservatives and their Labour successor, was to create employment in a deprived area, and to bring Catholics and Protestants together in a working environment. By 1981 the company had a work force of 2,600—an enormous figure for the region, then going through very difficult times.

As a good rogue should be, DeLorean was a colourful figure who was seldom out of the newspaper headlines, was not afraid to take risks and lived an extravagant life. He owned two estates, a twenty-room apartment in New York and a personal fleet of twenty-two trucks and several cars and motorcycles. He was photographed dining with Hollywood stars (his second wife was the actor Candice Bergen) and skiing in Colorado. He married for the third time in 1981. His autobiography, *DeLorean*, was published in 1985.

Unfortunately, things were not going smoothly back in Belfast. To begin with, it would be eight years before the first DMC-12 would be in the showrooms of the world, and even then over the following three years only 8,900 were produced. Furthermore, the model's closest rival would be GM's Corvette, which cost $15,000, as against the DMC-12's price of $26,000, which was $13,000 over target. Nevertheless it was received rapturously and the car reviews were full of praise. The public snapped up these new playthings, and the DMC-12 became the best-selling and only profitable car in Europe in 1981.

The scales tipped against DMC in 1982 when DeLorean realised that he needed more capital. In fairness to him, it must be said that he

increased the number of cars coming off the assembly line. This
added to the company's debts and, when combined with one of the
worst winters that Ireland had experienced for some time, worsened
rather than improved DMC's situation.

Some of the executives saw the writing on the wall and (to mix
metaphors) jumped ship. Customers started to complain, rather late
in the day, that they had been given no warranties to cover them if
they wanted a part replaced. An eternal optimist, DeLorean had not
taken into account such petty matters as warranties, a world economy
that was on the decline and the need for current cash flows.

In the British general election of May 1979 the Labour Party was
defeated by the Conservatives, led by Margaret Thatcher. Immediately
the new government stopped all payments to DMC, and demanded the
repayment of money due to the British exchequer for the previous
two or three years.

The death on hunger strike of Bobby Sands in 1981 resulted in riots
in Belfast, and parts of the production unit were damaged, but the
government refused to compensate the company, even though the initial contract between DMC and the British authorities provided for the
payment of compensation in respect of destruction caused by the
'Troubles'. DeLorean did everything he could to bring in more money,
including face-to-face discussions with possible investors, one of
whom was a James Hoffman, a confidential informant for the Drug
Enforcement Administration, which would later feature prominently
in DeLorean's life. The British government put DMC into receivership
in 1983, and 2,500 people were back on the dole.

On the same day that the plant was closed down by the British
government, John DeLorean was arrested in Los Angeles on a charge
of conspiring to import $24 million worth of cocaine in order to prop
up his failing enterprise and being involved in racketeering and fraud.
He would maintain that this sequence of events was not a coincidence;
but in any event the arrest of DeLorean sealed the fate of the
DeLorean sports car.

The prosecution was unsuccessful. The FBI had videotaped him
allegedly accepting a suitcase full of cocaine and stating 'It's better
than gold,' but lawyers proved that the man who was handing it over
to him was a government agent. They also discredited the prosecution's chief witness, a convicted drug dealer who had been 'persuaded'
to become a government informer. The court found that DeLorean

had been a victim of a 'sting' operation, which amounted to entrapment. He was acquitted of all charges.

He was also charged with defrauding his investors but was acquitted in that case also. However, as DeLorean said after his acquittal, 'I don't know, would you buy a used car from me?'

The reply to the question 'Where did it all go wrong?' will depend on who is giving the answer. DeLorean's defenders laid the blame firmly on Margaret Thatcher, claiming that, according to the former Arthur Anderson audit accounts, DMC in its first six months in business had made $26.5 million and was earning $5 million a month when the British government pulled the plug by putting the company into receivership on the spurious grounds that the company was unable to pay a debt of $800,000. The value of DMC's stock of unsold cars plummeted by more than $20 million in one day: nobody wanted to buy a car from a company in receivership, because their warranty would be void if the company went bankrupt. As a result, 2,500 jobs were lost in Belfast, and many of its suppliers went bankrupt almost overnight.

The DeLorean lobby claimed that information obtained under the Freedom of Information Act showed that the British government's chief motivation for investing in DMC had been an attempt to cripple the IRA, and when this did not happen Thatcher decided to cut her losses and destroy the company. The Tory government claimed that DMC could not pay the debt in question because it had no working capital. DeLorean's friends asked rhetorically why it had no working capital and answered that it was because the Thatcher government refused to give export financing to the company, even though there was a contractual obligation to give such financing and every other government-subsidised company in Britain was receiving it.

In a deposition sworn almost twenty years later DeLorean claimed that another motivation was Thatcher's determination to deny the Labour government any credit for its successful industrial development policies. He asserted that the Tories had also engineered the collapse of a successful aircraft plant, Lear Fan, and that in both cases the reasoning behind the government's actions had nothing to do with the prudent management of public resources but was a cold-blooded determination to cripple both companies.

It did not stop there. DMC and the British government had an agreement with regard to export financing that stated that the government was obliged, when cars left the Dunmurry factory and were loaded onto ships, to loan the company approximately 80 per cent of the money that the dealers would pay for each car. As soon as the dealers had paid DMC, the company would refund the advance to the Treasury, plus interest at market rates. The purpose of the agreement was to give DMC a cash flow for the payment of creditors and the purchase of materials. Instead, the British failure to meet its commitments deprived DMC of working capital.

DeLorean had about $9 million of his own money invested in the company, and on two separate occasions he went to the British government and offered his entire share in the company if it would undertake to keep the company alive. He had worked out a proposed merger with British Leyland, which would have made DMC very profitable, but the British government rejected this offer out of hand.

DeLorean's champions also claim to have unearthed evidence that the British government was not alone in its campaign to destroy DMC: it was aided and abetted by General Motors. The DeLorean party allege that a telex was sent to the State Department by Kingman Brewster, the US ambassador to England, stating that General Motors objected strongly to all the financial incentives being given to DMC and that these were a 'serious threat to their business.' As a result, DMC was forced to pay royalties of $400 per car—which was more than General Motors was earning on its own vehicles for most of the period in question. In addition, in 1982, when it was obvious that DMC would be a winner, GM suddenly shut off 'floor-plan financing' to DMC's dealers in the United States. The effect was that these dealers could no longer afford to buy from DeLorean's company.

It was also alleged at the time that not only was Denis Thatcher, the Prime Minister's husband, employed as a GM executive with a very substantial salary, in spite of his lack of automotive experience, but Thatcher's son, Mark Thatcher, was employed by Lotus as a highly paid executive in Texas. Lotus, of course, was owned by General Motors.

Four years after his acquittal on the drug-dealing charge, John DeLorean and Marvin Katz from Columbus, Ohio, who had bought most of the tooling and parts in the closed Belfast plant, made an attempt to resurrect DMC and to manufacture the car once again, this time in Ohio. They sent Gordon Novel to Belfast to purchase the master body-mould and body dies. He failed to do so, because, although the master body-mould had remained untouched since 1982, it was, according to the DeLorean camp, immediately cut into little pieces when Novel made himself known in Belfast. As for the body dies, they were sold (at a much lower price than Katz had offered) to a fisherman, who allegedly threw them into Galway Bay as anchors for fishing nets, ensuring that no more DeLorean sports cars would be built.

DeLorean left an interesting description of his trials (both emotional and legal) in a history of his 'harassment and persecution' set out in a written submission to the United States District Court of New Jersey. This submission was made in response to a motion proposed by his former legal adviser, Mayer Morganroth, to enable Morganroth to avoid paying debts due to DeLorean. This submission, made in August 2000, was stated to be 'on the basis that the Morganroth Judgement and many of the actions that preceded and followed it were based on . . . fraud and perjury.' It prayed that Morganroth's motion be denied (*a*) on the grounds of simple justice and truth, (*b*) 'to stop the unending clutter of these matters in the Federal Court system continuing without interruption for the last 18 years. It is time for finality,' and (*c*) on the grounds of 'proven fraud, bribery, perjury and criminal conduct on the parts of Mayer and Jeffery Morganroth and Malcomb Schade, it would be unjust to grant their motion. Enough is enough.' The affidavit was signed *John Z. DeLorean, Pro Se Defendant* [defendant representing himself].

The rogues' perpetual belief that alleged victims are the authors of their own destruction can slip over into paranoia and a belief in criminal conspiracies against them. However, because a rogue shows symptoms of such a persecution complex does not mean that he has no enemies who are determined to harm him. There is no doubt that DeLorean was badly treated by the British government and wrongfully prosecuted by the Drug Enforcement Administration and the FBI. In fairness to him it should be said that his presentation of the alleged corruption and wrongdoings of his own legal representatives and his cries of 'conspiracy' do raise significant questions.

Let John DeLorean speak for himself.

We built our plant in Belfast, Northern Ireland, in the expectation of providing jobs to truly needy people, which, indeed, we did. It was gratifying to see the impact on the Catholic community:

middle aged men who had never had a regular job were suddenly able to provide for their families. The beautiful, red haired, freckled faced Irish children got new clothes and some perhaps a shiny bicycle. Burned out, boarded up shops were reopened. We had a true spirit of comradeship between the 2600 Catholic and Protestant workers in the plant. A beautiful miracle!

Suddenly, in early 1982 the new Thatcher government, for no apparent reason, closed DMCL [DeLorean Motor Company Limited]. DMC did not fail but was deliberately closed for political reasons (as was Lear Fan). We later found, when Arthur Anderson subpoenaed the British Cabinet meeting minutes, that the DMC had been financed in Belfast in an effort to destroy the IRA. They put us in an impossible and dangerous political quagmire. We couldn't win.

In my various court trials, the British Government and her lawyers have been caught in many illegal actions. We all know that, if they had truth and justice on their side, the British Government would not need fabricated evidence, perjured testimony and threats to win their case. In the totally fake and fabricated narcotics trial in Los Angeles, I was found innocent without presenting one witness or one single word of defence. Not because of entrapment, but because the jury found that no crime had been committed.

DeLorean also claimed that the prospective buyer of his California ranch, which he was selling in order to cover legal fees, had received death threats if he persisted in the purchase, and that another witness, Joseph Cefaratti, was told that income tax charges against him would be dropped if he helped the government to entrap DeLorean or Barry Goldwater, the right-wing Republican candidate who in 1964 lost the presidential election to Lyndon Johnson. DeLorean added that charges made against him on the strength of an entrapment operation carried out by Cefaratti were later dismissed for 'outrageous government conduct'. He asserted: 'I was the victim of a sick frame-up created by publicity hungry prosecutors.' He also made a deposition that tapes used against him were faked *ab initio* or doctored, and that two FBI agents had destroyed their handwritten daily logs and had fabricated new logs to incriminate him. Unfortunately for them, one of the agents had mistakenly written seventeen of the dates as '1983' instead of '1982'.

The prosecutors were equally unfortunate. While they were illegally coaching the FBI agents in an attempt to cover up their errors, the courtroom microphone was switched on and everything they said was broadcast to the news room, to the delight of the assembled reporters. 'Real Keystone Cops,' commented DeLorean. 'Funny, if not so tragic. They destroyed my life and family.'

The affidavit did not stop there.

> David Raskin, the very top, world renowned polygraph [expert] in the United States, the leading consultant to Defence Intelligence and the Secret Service, conducted a lie detector test on me in Utah that proved that I was absolutely innocent with a 99.9 certainty. FBI Agent West used the entire resources of the FBI to try to destroy David Raskin and his business for daring the tell the truth. Outrageous!

It was in this affidavit that DeLorean made the allegations about the US ambassador's complaints concerning

> unfair financial incentives to DMC, the enforced car royalties, the shutting off of floor-plan financing and the jobs for the Thatcher boys.

He also outlined the 'GPD-Lotus-DMC transaction' prosecution instigated in Detroit by the British government but thrown out when it was proved that the prosecutors had not only withheld more than 600 pages of exculpatory evidence but had also introduced false evidence, much of it provided by the British. In DeLorean's words,

> Does this sound like the 'Birmingham Six', the 'Guildford Four' or the 'Stalker Case'? All gross miscarriages of justice based on false evidence fabricated by the British Government. The 'Birmingham Six' served 13 years in prison for a crime they did not commit because they had acetate from their playing cards on their hands. The British government beat and tortured confessions out of every one of them! So far that has not worked on me!

Later, following complaints about the refusal by the British government to provide export credit finance, he described the damage done to the plant.

When our Belfast office building was fire bombed 142 times with Molotov cocktails and burned to the ground during the martyr Bobby Sands' wake (next door), we filed the requisite Terrorist Insurance claim. They refused to pay DMCL (which would have kept the plant open) but later gave it to [our competitor].

Here he identifies the alleged payee and makes allegations about his private views on the transaction that it would be reckless to repeat. We can note, however, the further evidence of the vindictive behaviour of the Tories, which he submitted to the United States District Court of New Jersey.

The DMCL assets were owned entirely by the U.K. Government, every brick, every pencil; so there was no collateral for another loan. Without export financing, DMCL was forced to run on an instable basis. We bought parts from the suppliers on 60 day terms and tried to get the cars built, shipped and sold quickly enough that we could pay the suppliers and build more cars. An impossible balancing act without the Export Financing we were promised.

As it happened a minor shipping strike between the British mainland and Belfast killed us; it broke the unstable circle. When it became clear [that] the Conservative Thatcher Government was not going to honour the Master Agreement in regard to Export Financing, I twice went to Ken Bloomfield, the head of the Department of Commerce, and I offered to give them all of my shares in DMC for NOTHING if they would keep the company alive. They would have owned 92% of the company with their shares and mine. This offer is a matter of public record. Since the UK Government already owned British Leyland, a number of economies would be effected in overall management, sales, shipping, parts warehousing, service, etc. DMC profit would have instantly doubled to $10,000,000.00 per month.

How could they possibly have turned this offer down unless they just plain wanted to shut down the factory? With the British Government owning my shares there would have been no need for receivership and 15,000 jobs in Britain could have been saved (2,600 in Belfast). The British Government would have preserved their $200,000,000.00 investment! Even if they elected to stop building DMCs and built Rovers in our plant, they would have saved millions of dollars and the jobs of the workers. I asked NOTHING in exchange for the years of work and millions of dollars I had invested in DMC. I just wanted DMC and her workers to survive.

DeLorean then introduced the possibility of political manipulation and dirty dealing.

The prevailing wisdom in Ireland is that our Catholic workers were being forced to tithe to the IRA. So we were shut down. As the recent revelation of the British Cabinet minutes shows, they were trying to use DMC to cripple the IRA, when that failed they closed us up.

At this point he sailed again into more provocative and possibly libellous waters and accused some of his executives of wrongdoing. In the same breath he reminded the court that he was worthy of trust because he was a religious man.

I was raised a Catholic and it distressed me to see how badly Catholics were treated in Northern Ireland. The first time I stopped at the beautiful Catholic church in Hillsboro to pray, the surprised Protestant NIDA [Northern Ireland Development Agency] executives with me almost died of shock.

At the time of writing, DeLorean had become a member of the Church of the Unbroken Chain, and it was Elder Vincent of that church who warned him that the lawyer who was the subject of his complaints was in the pay of the British government. Another member of the Unbroken Chain worked in the office of a lawyer who represented British interests and knew of the bribes that were passing but 'would not testify for fear of being fired and destroying her career.' He then stated that not only were his own lawyer, the British government's advocate and an American judge conspiring to destroy him but that more dangerous methods had been used in the case of Gordon Novel, who had been too late to rescue the master moulds of the DMC.

The remaining dies went to British Steel. When Gordon Novel went to British Steel to see about them a car plunged up onto the sidewalk in an attempt on his life. He clambered up a chain link fence to save himself and the killers sped away.

The final paragraph of this unusual deposition concerns a lawyer who represented the object of DeLorean's complaint.

'Bilker' insisted on coming to New Jersey to take my son's deposition rather than by telephone. Despite the thousands of legal secretaries in New Jersey he brought his own court reporter from Utah, a tartish blonde. On my way to the men's room at his hotel one of the maids who recognised me told me that 'Bilker' and the court reporter slept together. Thus in addition to perjuring himself in court, 'Bilker' cheats on his wife.

DeLorean was never afraid of hitting below the belt.

The outcome was in DeLorean's favour. He was cleared of defrauding his investors, but continuing legal entanglements kept him on the sidelines of the car world, though his passion for cars did not abate. After declaring bankruptcy in 1999, to thwart his former counsel's claim for a fee payment of $3 million, he said he wanted to produce a speedy plastic sports car selling for only $20,000. He never did.

DeLorean's story would not be complete without a mention of at least one of the colourful and larger-than-life figures he attracted. The most colourful was the man to whom he owed his acquittal in Los Angeles, Larry Flynt, the pornographer and protector of the First Amendment of the US Constitution. In DeLorean's own words:

During the trial Larry Flynt, the publisher, somehow acquired an audio tape from the duplicitous government confidential informant, James Hoffman, a sleezebag who was playing both sides. In this tape, tested and authenticated by the top forensic tape agent at Stanford Research Institute, the Government agent threatens to "Kill and send my daughter's head home in a shopping bag" if I refused to go along or tried to escape them. I had refused to go to the infamous California meeting that was later video "faked". This tape was made in the LA hotel room during the "2½ hour gap."

Larry Flynt was a genuine American hero: he served a horrible six months in prison in his wheelchair rather than reveal his sources under the Second Amendment. That took real guts! The whole scenario was a fabrication. The marking on the dope used in the fake video proved it was confiscated by the DEA [Drug Enforcement Administration] two years earlier, in another case.

DeLorean then claimed that an important prosecution witness named Hetrick had taken a plea bargain to keep his drug-dealer sons out of jail and that while in prison he had obtained documents under the Freedom of Information Act that revealed that his lawyer had received $800,000 and had been made a judge for inducing Hetrick's plea bargain. Apparently, once this information was made public, Hetrick was released.

This defence was corroborated by two journalists, Jacob Isaacson and John Ashcroft, who published reports that undercover FBI agents had approached DeLorean and offered to ease his financial woes. They proposed that cocaine be loaded into the door panels of his cars as they were shipped overseas. Accordingly, DeLorean was arrested for conspiracy to traffic narcotics, and it was while he was fighting these charges that the DeLorean Motor Company went bankrupt.

Now back to Larry Flynt. How does he feature in the DeLorean saga? The only reason that John DeLorean avoided a long prison sentence is that the publisher of the pornographic magazine *Hustler* had the contacts and the cash to obtain tapes showing not only that the drug-trafficking idea was invented and proposed by the US government but that both the cocaine and the money were provided by the FBI and, most importantly, that DeLorean told the undercover agents that he wasn't interested and begged to be let go. The tapes, played in court, showed the agents actually threatening to kill DeLorean's daughter if he did not proceed with the drug deal.

In 1983 Flynt threatened to release these tapes in order to embarrass the FBI but still refused to reveal his sources. He was fined $10,000 and later $20,000 per day for every day that he refused to reveal his source. When questioned by the media about the nature of his actions, he stated: 'Yes, this is a publicity gimmick, and I thank God you all fell for it.' Flynt's mischievous behaviour in court became notorious. He shouted profane words, threw orange peel at the judge, and even wore an American flag as a nappy, claiming 'If they're gonna treat me like a baby, I'm gonna act like one.'

What, incidentally, has Ecclesiastes 9:10–12, the name DeLorean gave to Logan Manufacturing, to say?

Whatever work you find to do,
do it with all your might,
for there is neither achievement, nor planning, nor science,
nor wisdom in Sheol where you are going.
Another thing I have observed under the sun:
that the race is not run by the speediest,
nor the battle by the champions;
it is not the wise who get food,
nor the intelligent wealth,
nor the learned favour:
chance and mischance befall them all.
We do not know when our time will come:
like fish caught in the treacherous net,
like birds caught in the snare,
just so are we all trapped by misfortune
when it suddenly overtakes us.

Was he referring to himself, the British government, or his investors?

Chapter 9
The deadly charmer: James H. Lehman

A rogue may be a murderer, and a murderer may be a rogue, but neither connection is inevitable. James H. Lehman was not addicted to telling the truth—a good qualification for 'roguery'; and James H. Lehman (if that was his name) was indubitably a rogue.

Lehman was a man with a varied career and seven names: James Joseph Feeley, James Hiames, James Edward James, James Herbert Lehman, James McCaigue, William Martin and James Richman. Lehman was the name by which he became famous in Ireland, and we shall stick to that.

William Martin was found guilty of robbery in Ohio in 1919. James Edward James was found guilty of grand larceny in Minnesota in 1936. One of the seven named above was found guilty in Aldershot, England, of eleven offences of passing fraudulent cheques and obtaining goods and money by false pretences. The convictions are real, but many of the other 'facts' about his life are matters of probability only. What is incontestable is that he dominated Irish newspaper headlines in 1944 and 1945.

Although Lehman may have been Canadian by birth, born in Montréal in 1889 but educated in Pennsylvania, he claimed Irish ancestry, and the events recounted in this book took place in Ireland.

He may have served in the Canadian army and may have been discharged for 'brain fever', but this claim is dubious. It is fact that he joined the US army in 1917 and within the year was discharged with a disability pension of $62 a month. He claimed to have acquired a law degree in 1925 in Philadelphia, to have married in 1933 and to have been divorced by his wife in 1936.

With the outbreak of the Second World War in Europe, Lehman joined (or rejoined) the Canadian army, was sent to England and was stationed at Aldershot. There he met an Irish woman, Margaret Hayden, in the army canteen, and they were married within a few weeks. Shortly after this she fell ill and he took leave of absence to visit her. This made him a deserter. He surrendered himself after a few days and was given ninety days' detention. Some time in the next two years he injured his back on manoeuvres and in January 1942 was discharged as unfit. He did not malinger but enrolled immediately in the Home Guard.

Lehman was tall and good-looking, sported a 'ronnie' (a thin moustache made popular by the film star Ronald Colman) and talked convincingly. Everyone who met him liked him. Neither a braggart nor ostentatious, he left new acquaintances with the feeling that this was a man of substance, a shrewd, capable man in whom there were depths.

James and Margaret decided to go to Ireland and went with their two children to live in Margaret's home in County Kildare. His back continued to give him trouble, and later that year he was admitted to the British Military Pensioners' Hospital in Dublin. He was joined by his wife and children, and they moved from a hotel to furnished rooms, the property of the hotel-owner. Christmas came, and Lehman had run out of money. His wife was pregnant again, but he told his landlord's wife that the marriage was unhappy and that it had been a thoughtless war marriage. The woman in whom he confided was later to describe the wife as 'an unhappy little person.'

No money was coming in, so in January the couple did a runner, leaving behind a considerable debt. They found furnished rooms in Leinster Road, Rathmines: a bedroom on one floor, the kitchen on the next and a sink on the landing.

Lehman went looking for money, conned more than £200 from new friends and with this capital opened a baby-food shop in Ranelagh. This venture lasted for about a month until new debts forced him to sell off all his stock. He held on to the premises and, trading as 'Leigh', began to sell coffee in a period when for most households coffee, if it was drunk at all, meant coffee in bottles— Camp or Irel. When, after six weeks, his attempt at being a coffee merchant proved to be a failure he began to look for a venue in Dún Laoghaire but found nothing suitable.

In the meantime he had been keeping alive a friendship he had established with a nurse from the Military Pensioners' Hospital. Her name was McCaigue—a common name in County Monaghan. He told her he had married a woman in England but had separated from her when he discovered that she was already married to a man called Stokes. He told McCaigue that his wife had gone back to England when he discovered the truth but had returned to Dublin when he had gone into hospital.

Lehman and Nurse McCaigue met from time to time until she told him one day that she saw no point in their continuing to meet. He reacted badly but persuaded her to meet again, because he had bought her an expensive ring and would like to give it to her. McCaigue, a level-headed woman, was annoyed rather than pleased by the gesture. 'What did you want to do that for?' she asked. 'Aren't we only friends?'

'Well, maybe that's how it is,' he told her. 'But, you know, a woman made a fool of me once and that's not going to happen again. From the first time you and I talked, I knew that I had met a decent girl.'

Touched by the compliment, she agreed not to break off the relationship and was rewarded when Lehman let her into the secret that he had just completed the profitable sale of a business premises in Dublin, was engaged in negotiations for opening a chain of shops, and wanted to employ a competent and trustworthy person, like her, as his supervisor. She could use his car for work (this was a time when cars and petrol were both in short supply). McCaigue was tempted and gave him £25 to invest in the enterprise. When she asked him what his bigamous wife was doing, he told her that she had been joined by Stokes, her lawful husband, and that they were both living in Dublin. Later he told her that he had heard that 'Mrs Stokes' had taken an overdose of aspirins and was in hospital somewhere.

McCaigue had her own share of shrewdness, and when Lehman suggested that they combine their shares in the shops she backed off and told him that she would have to know more about him before taking such an important step.

While he was making these business proposals to McCaigue, Lehman was contacted by Anna Finucane, a woman he had employed in his short-lived baby-food shop. She was replying to a newspaper advertisement, inserted by Lehman, looking for staff. He told her he was the manager of a shop that was part of a chain operating in England and the United States. To get the job she would need to put down a security of £50, but when she told him she could afford only £40 he took it and told her not to worry, that he would persuade the directors to agree to her appointment because, after all, he knew her and could vouch for her.

His meeting with the 'directors' was obviously successful, because Anna Finucane got the job and came to work for him. They had plenty of time to talk and, increasingly, Lehman confided in her. The first big secret to which he made her a party was that Nurse McCaigue was in fact the owner of the business, having invested £300 in it. On another occasion he told her that he and McCaigue were getting married in June and that he had bought her a £300 engagement ring. He repeated the story about his wife's bigamous marriage and added that the woman was mentally ill and that he had been tricked into the marriage by the Canadian authorities one evening when he was drinking with the other officers of his regiment. Later he told her that he suspected his wife was taking drugs or some other poisons and was constantly sick.

Lehman did not explain how he knew all this, given that Margaret Hayden was allegedly living with her real husband, Stokes; and his cover was almost blown one day when Margaret and their landlady, Mrs O'Callaghan, came into the shop. When they had gone he told Anna Finucane that he had no idea who Mrs O'Callaghan was but that her companion was an 'ex-lady-love' of his and the only person whom he had ever hated.

In March Lehman bought a 150-grain crystal of cyanide, allegedly for testing the sugar content of bottled coffee. He reduced the crystal to powder in the presence of his shop assistants and told them it was acid for testing the stock and that they should not handle it, because it was poisonous. When one of them wondered how it was possible to get his hands on such stuff, he replied, 'There are ways and means!'

By this time Margaret was nine months pregnant but seemed to be in good form, yet on 9 March he called for help from Mrs O'Callaghan, saying that Margaret was very sick. Mrs O'Callaghan hurried upstairs and noted a very strong smell on the landing. She could hear Margaret groaning, and when she went into the room she saw that the woman was unconscious, her face was blue and her forehead shining with perspiration. Lehman was beside himself, dashing to and fro, gulping and groaning, tears pouring down his cheeks.

Margaret had turned purple by the time the ambulancemen arrived. One of them said that he should have called them earlier, but Lehman said he had tried to contact the local doctors without success. By the time the doctors in the hospital saw Margaret, she and her baby were dead. Lehman was informed and burst into tears.

It happened that Margaret's sister was a nurse in the hospital. She came over to the ward and asked Lehman what had happened. 'What did Margaret take?' she asked. 'She was having dizzy spells' was Lehman's reply.

Back in Leinster Road, Mrs O'Callaghan was still disturbed by the bitter smell in the Lehmans' bedroom. She nearly choked when she leaned over the sink on the landing. She had a look around but could see no bottle or any receptacle that could hold the source of the odour. She investigated again the following day and found an empty rum bottle beside the sink in the kitchenette. This surprised her, because she was certain that it had not been there when she had looked around the day before.

When Lehman returned at half past nine that night he was still heaving with sobs and moaning, 'Poor Peg! I knew she had something on her mind!' No-one else had hinted that her death might be other than from natural causes.

He sent a note to Anna Finucane, and when she came around to the house he told her that his wife was dead. For some reason she asked if it had been the result of poison, and he replied, 'I am afraid so.' She wanted to know what sort of poison, and he replied that it might have been an overdose of aspirin.

The next day Finucane returned to help him sort things out and to make phone calls from the nearest telephone kiosk. He asked her to call Nurse McCaigue and say, 'I am speaking for a friend of yours. There has been a death in the family. Could you meet Mr Lehman this evening?' McCaigue turned up at the bar that Lehman had suggested, but he did not keep the appointment. He visited his neighbourhood chemist and, through his sobs, told him that his wife was dead. When the chemist asked if she had been sick for long he replied, 'Since the day before yesterday. Anyway, she was always taking something. She didn't want children.'

A Sergeant Sheppard called to see Lehman that night and told him that the hospital was not satisfied about the cause of death and that it was possible that Margaret Hayden might have taken some poison. 'She got no poison here,' was Lehman's reply. The sergeant searched the rooms and found the rum bottle. Lehman told him that his wife had had a bad cold some days earlier and had taken a glass of rum with cero-calcium tablets.

Some days later, when Margaret was already buried, Lehman and Anna Finucane had a talk. She wanted to know if the police would be asking more questions, and he told her that they probably would but that he would be grateful if she said nothing about his private life and whether he was married or single. This strange request upset her and she told him that she could not oblige him. 'I won't tell any lies to the police,' she protested. 'What about those acids you were working at in the shop?'

'Oh, I got rid of those a long time ago, and anyway you know nothing about them!'

On the following day, when he and Margaret's sister were cleaning out his rooms in Leinster Road, he apparently found a bottle and a crucifix in the pocket of Margaret's coat. It was the bottle into which he had put the flaked cyanide. He gave it to his sister-in-law and told her to give it to the coroner, but then he changed his mind and took it back. He later told his landlady about his find and mentioned that he had also come across a 'terrible' letter from Margaret, which he had burned 'for the sake of the children.'

His next move was to visit McCaigue, who, when he asked if she had heard of Mrs Stokes's death, replied that she had heard of Mrs Lehman's death and wondered where Stokes was all this time. 'If only I could get my hands on him!' was Lehman's response; but McCaigue was not going to let him off lightly. 'Why did you go to the hospital then? You weren't her husband!'

'I did no more than anyone else would have done,' was his reply.

'That's enough,' was her response. 'Our friendship is over.'

The next Anna Finucane heard from him was a letter from County Kildare, where Margaret's family lived.

Dear Anna,

Kevin [Lehman's son] is very ill, therefore my absence. Will be back on Monday.

Please close the shop or do with it whatever you should like or think best. I am terribly sorry.

Will call at your residence when I get back.

Sincerely,

Jim

Not surprisingly, there was no Lehman on Monday, or any other day. Anna Finucane closed the shop and sold off whatever she could to recover some of her £40 investment.

Back in County Kildare, Lehman was spinning yarns to his in-laws: Margaret had not wanted to have the baby because the pregnancy gave her dizzy spells and she had tried to get rid of it by taking pills given to her by one of her friends; the dead baby was black; Inspector Reynolds, the garda in charge of the case, had told him that the bottle he had found had some foreign poison in it. Lehman was interviewed by the gardaí in Ballitore Barracks and made a long statement that took twelve hours to write down. It was mainly concerned with his earlier life.

On 7 March he went to Dublin with his son, leaving debts behind him, as usual. He deposited his son in a convent and went to visit his former landlady. They discussed his wife's death and the newspaper reports. Suddenly he asked Mrs O'Callaghan, 'Wouldn't you think I had done it?' Then he told her he was going to stay with his brother-in-law in County Dublin, walked out the door, and disappeared.

A month later, on Saturday 8 April, a tall, handsome, clean-shaven American airman, James McCaigue, booked into the Oriel Hotel in the Diamond, Monaghan. This was the fifth year of the Second World War, and there were many American soldiers stationed north of the Border. When they had the opportunity they often came south to take advantage of the more widely available butter and beef.

McCaigue told the proprietors of the hotel, and anyone else who wished to listen, that he was based in Belfast but was on sick leave and had come down south for two reasons: to eat good food in order to restore his health, and because his family came from County Monaghan.

McCaigue showed a ring and a woman's watch to the manager, Miss Sherry, and told her they were lucky mascots that had been given to him by a war widow. He booked out the next day to return to Belfast but came back three days later and announced that the army doctor had prescribed an extension of his sick leave. He was in a hurry to go to his room and asked Miss Sherry to sign the hotel register for him.

He had indeed travelled to Belfast, gone to a recruiting office and offered to enlist in the Royal Air Force under the name of James Joseph Feeley, resident at the Oriel Hotel, Monaghan. (There had in fact been a man of that name in the hotel just before McCaigue had booked in.) He said he was London-born, a cook by profession, and had moved to Ireland with his sister, who had purchased a farm near Castleblayney. When asked to produce a passport or identity papers he told the recruiting officer that he had left them behind in Monaghan. He offered to fetch them later but the officer insisted that he could not be enlisted without them. When questioned about this interview, the recruiting officer said that McCaigue seemed to be more intelligent than most recruits but gave the impression that he had recently been on a binge.

Back in Monaghan, McCaigue was technically an alien. Ireland was neutral, so Miss Sherry asked to see his identification. He patted his pockets and looked in his suitcase and discovered that he had left them behind in the barracks. Miss Sherry wondered how he had managed to cross the Border without papers, but he told her that the Customs knew him well and never asked him to show them.

McCaigue always had a word for all the guests in the hotel, and he confided in one woman that he had actually been born a few miles from Monaghan but his parents had emigrated to America when he was nine months old. Their relationship flourished, and he presented her with the ring he had shown to Miss Sherry. This new friendship did not prevent him from striking up an acquaintance with another woman and treating her to lunch in the hotel every day; he even took her several times to the Magnet Cinema in Glaslough Street, not far from the hotel. She too received some gifts from him. He told her tales about his adventures in the Canadian air force. At the time, she accepted them at their face value; it was only later that she wondered how an American pilot could be in the Canadian air force.

It was not only the women in the hotel whom McCaigue charmed. He also became well known in the local bars and in the Westenra Hotel at the other end of the Diamond. Known as 'Captain Lehman', he kept his listeners spellbound with yarns about his adventures as a bomber pilot and a rear gunner in a Flying Fortress over Germany. He told them he would give anything to get back and have another go at 'Jerry' but, on account of his age, he was now grounded. It was a young man's game, he said.

The audience was faithful while McCaigue matched drink for drink. Only once did somebody challenge him. A stranger to the town asked him to show them his identity card. He produced some sort of card with his photograph on it but did not hold it out long enough for anyone to catch the details. It is quite possible that the curious stranger was a policeman.

Otherwise everything went well until McCaigue ran out of money and tried to borrow ten shillings from one of his drinking companions. Once the word went out that he was not buying, his popularity plummeted. One man whom he tried to touch for money replied, 'Haven't you plenty of money in your mouth?' McCaigue had two false teeth lined with gold. They disappeared the following day.

Two days after his abortive visit to Belfast, gardaí went up to his bedroom, arrested him and took him to the local barracks. After a short period in custody he appeared to be sleepy and to have developed hearing problems, but when one of the detectives went behind him and whispered, 'Did you get your cigarettes all right, Lehman?' he reacted immediately and answered in an unslurred tone, 'Yes, sir. I got them, all right.' He then relapsed into his earlier state.

The gardaí had given him a newspaper to read, which bore his photograph on the front page and a notice that they wanted to contact him. When they drew his attention to the photograph and asked him if he recognised the man, he denied all knowledge of him. He was searched, and the two gold teeth were found in his pocket, together with two Dublin tram tickets—a strange find, given that he claimed never to have visited Dublin. He was brought to Dublin and charged with the murder of Margaret Lehman. The gardaí had difficulty in taking a statement from McCaigue, because he had apparently relapsed into a stupor. He did not seem to hear the questions or to understand them.

His trial was a *cause célèbre*, and for the nine days that it lasted the court was filled with a mainly female audience and there were long queues of sensation-seekers as far as the street waiting to get in.

It was agreed that Mrs Lehman had died as a result of the absorption of a fatal dose of cyanide. The defence case was that she had committed suicide. There were long discussions about the relative speed of prussic acid and cyanide, the latter taking much longer to kill because the prussic acid it contained had to be released by the acid in the victim's stomach. Margaret had lived for at least fifty-five minutes after the time that Mrs O'Callaghan had first noticed that she was not well. Counsel and the experts even discussed the assassination of the Russian monk Rasputin, when a heavy dose of poison appeared to have had no effect on him. The doctors for the prosecution confirmed that sudden withdrawal from morphine would result in mental instability and depression in an addict. They also agreed that pregnant women were known to suffer from bouts of instability.

Counsel for the prosecution then began to go through the rambling statement Lehman had made to Inspector Reynolds, but the defence objected to the presence of the jury while legal arguments were being heard, and the jury were sent back to their room. Counsel for Lehman told the court that his client suffered from a bout of amnesia before, during and after the time that the statement was being taken. He had not had the capacity to make the statement voluntarily and it was therefore inadmissible.

Lehman was put into the witness box and questioned about the making of the statement. He claimed he had no memory whatsoever of his actions for a period beginning about eleven days after his wife's death and lasting until the second week of July, when he 'came to' in Mountjoy Prison. He had no recollection of being in Monaghan or of travelling to Belfast or returning to Dublin.

Under cross-examination he told the court that on or about 28 March he had found a letter from his wife in her ration book. In the letter she had said that she was going to take poison. He could remember nothing after reading this letter. Judge Martin Maguire heard evidence from Inspector Reynolds and other gardaí that Lehman had shown no signs whatsoever of confusion or amnesia when making his statement on 2 April in Ballitore Barracks. The judge ruled that the statement was admissible.

Inspector Reynolds gave his evidence and stated that when he had asked Lehman in Monaghan if he objected to being brought to Dublin he had replied that he did not, so long as they didn't bring him back to camp. Evidence of confusion or of cunning? An attempt was then made to halt the case on the grounds that the prosecution had not proved a negative, i.e. that Margaret Lehman had not committed suicide, but Judge Maguire dismissed the point.

When the time came to present the defence case, Lehman told his usual life story and stated that his wife was a morphine addict who had threatened to abort their child if he would not help her to obtain a supply of the drug. He had been unable to lay his hands on any morphine and she began to take aspirins in whiskey. She was constantly vomiting when the pills would not stay down. He had looked for help from an army medical officer, who gave her two injections of morphine.

Obviously, the most dangerous evidence against Lehman had been his experiment with the cyanide crystal. He gave a long explanation of this episode and stated that his inspiration had been an article in an American news weekly that outlined a procedure for testing coffee beans that could be used for bottled coffee. The purpose of the procedure was to establish the correct proportions of sugar and saccharine in bottled coffee, and the test should be carried out with a solution of synthetic uric acid and sodium cyanide. Lehman admitted flaking the cyanide crystal and said he had bought the uric acid in another chemist's shop, the name of which he could not recall. His wife had helped him carry out three or four experiments. He had taken care to warn her that they were dealing with a deadly poison.

At this point he claimed that he had previously sought the advice of some medical students whom he had met in a pub, and it was only after noting what they had to say that he had carried out the experiments. He could not remember the name of the pub and had not learnt the names of the students. Unfortunately the experiments were not successful, which was only to be expected, as it was ground coffee he was boiling in a saucepan before adding the two acids, whereas the point of the operation was to identify the sugar and saccharine in bottled coffee.

When questioned about the events of 19 March, Lehman said that his wife was dizzy on account of a cold from which she had been suffering for some time. At this stage he introduced a new piece of evidence when he stated that in the afternoon he had gone to the flat of a young widow next to the shop and had tea with her and her children until seven o'clock and did not get home until half-past seven. His following deposition contradicted Miss Finucane's earlier evidence that she had asked him if the cause of death had been the result of poison and that he had replied, 'I am afraid so.' He now denied that he had said any such thing; if he had, this would have harmed his case, because at that stage nobody knew what had been the cause of his wife's death. He denied having any discussion of his wife's death with Anna Finucane and denied everything that she had stated about their conversations at this time.

Lehman then treated the court to elaborate explanations about Stokes, who, he now alleged, may have been called Larry Dorset or Dorset L. Stokes. The mixture of fact and fantasy in his written statement had not been convincing, and the defence case was weakened when it was shown that Lehman had changed his story yet again and claimed that the tests had not been carried out by him in the presence of his wife but by a baby-food manufacturer named Dorset!

In court there was a new version of his testimony. He now stated that the man in question was called D'Arcy, not Dorset, and denied that D'Arcy had carried out the tests or had supplied him with the acids. Other oddities in the written statement were claims that his wife did not know that he had bought acids nor did she know where the acids were stored, linked with a denial of knowledge or suspicion of where or how she might have bought or come into possession of poison. He had also denied that he had any knowledge or even suspicion of why his wife should want to do away with herself, as their marriage was such a happy one.

In court, Lehman backtracked on this part of the statement and insisted that it was incorrect. His wife did know where the acids were kept and he had discussed the test in detail with her.

So much for the direct examination; it was now the turn of counsel for the prosecution, George Murnaghan, to cross-examine. His first line of questioning had to do with the viability of the coffee business at the time of the alleged tests. Having elicited Lehman's agreement that the coffee business was on its last legs in March, Murnaghan put it to him that it was too late at that stage to be experimenting with acids. Lehman reflected and then replied that there was still some coffee to be sold and he thought it could be profitable to make his own bottled coffee and sell it. Murnaghan cast doubts on such hopes, given that Lehman had no capital. Lehman said that, if he thought about it at all, he did not see it that way; there were always ways of raising some money.

When Murnaghan suggested that he had never carried out any test on coffee, he did not answer, and when the judge intervened and reminded him, 'It is put to you that there was no reality in reference to your proposed test of the coffee—do you understand that?' Lehman remained silent.

Murnaghan continued to hammer the point home in a manner reminiscent of a Monty Python sketch. 'I put it to you . . . there was no coffee to test . . . Your business had gone . . . it was at the verge of collapse . . . the wolf was at the door.' Lehman's innocent reply was, 'He may have been.'

Following a long and relentless struggle to make Lehman admit the pointlessness of testing acids when there was no possibility of any coffee business getting off the ground, Murnaghan moved on to the hypothetical medical students who could not be identified and to the chemist's shop in O'Connell Street, the whereabouts of which could not be determined and which Lehman could not describe. Having exhausted these topics, Murnaghan switched to Lehman's career and accused him of deserting the American army in 1917 and of having no pension. From there it was a short step to Lehman's many aliases. The cross-examination then returned to the health of Lehman's wife, her alleged addiction, the failure or success of the marriage, and his claims that his wife was already married before she went through a ceremony with him. Lehman's answers to this line of questioning were as vague as they had been in relation to the existence of Stokes. He came badly out of the remainder of his examination, contradicting himself, failing to remember facts that he should have recalled, and making damaging statements.

The cross-examination ended with a discussion of Lehman's moustache, when he had worn it, when he had shaved it off, and where this had happened. Lehman's final words were, 'I can't give the dates on which I shaved my moustache.'

The final act of this drama introduced two doctors for the defence. The first confirmed that cyanide could be used as a reagent for measuring sugar in coffee. The second was a Dr Lee-Parker, a neurologist and psychiatrist, who stated that Lehman was a pathological liar who could not distinguish truth from lies and had probably been disturbed from childhood. This doctor confirmed that the shock of his wife's suicide and the use of morphine, even for medical purposes, could result in 'fugue' or flight from reality and could cause a blackout in which the victim behaved like everyone else but would have no recollection of what he had done. Such blackouts can occur after accidents or could be experienced by an alcoholic. Dr Lee-Parker's final remarks were that it was not unknown for pregnant women to have a nervous breakdown, though it was not common with young, healthy women living in a stable home and happy surroundings. Obviously, this was not the case with Margaret Lehman.

It took the jury two hours to reach its verdict, which was to find Lehman guilty of murder.

Lehman appealed, on the grounds that the evidence of his desertion from the army and his changes of name was prejudicial and therefore inadmissible. The Appeal Court held that his case had indeed been prejudiced and that 'the Court is not able to say that, if the inadmissible questions had been omitted, a reasonable jury after a proper summing up must have convicted the accused on the rest of the evidence.'

The second trial began on 15 January 1945. The preceding publicity had been immense, and a member of the jury would need to have been living on Mars not to be familiar with the case. The judge, Mr Justice Overend, refused to question each juror about his opinion (in those days, to protect the sensibilities of the 'weaker sex', only men could serve on juries) about the case, and counsel for the defence was not permitted to do so either. The only right left to Lehman was to challenge five jurors without showing cause and any other juror in relation to whom he could show cause.

At this trial Miss Finucane's evidence for the prosecution was less damaging than it had been in the first trial. However, new evidence was given about Lehman borrowing a hatpin from her on behalf of his wife, which was connected with an alleged attempt to induce a miscarriage. The defence called no evidence, which not only allowed them to be the last to address the jury but also ensured that Lehman was saved from cross-examination. As a result, the jury did not hear much of the damaging evidence introduced in the first trial.

This stratagem did not help Lehman. He was again found guilty, and when asked if he had anything to say why sentence of death should not be passed on him he said: 'I am satisfied that on my second trial there has been a small degree of fairness. I am innocent, and my conscience is clear.' Mr Justice Overend was visibly disturbed when he pronounced the awesome words about being 'hanged by the neck until dead' and added 'and may the Lord have mercy on your soul.'

Judge Kenneth Deale, who wrote about the Lehman case some years later in his *Memorable Irish Trials*, finished his account with an interesting question: Had Lehman been proved guilty? In other words, had it been proved beyond reasonable doubt that Lehman's wife had not poisoned herself? He tried to answer this question under three headings: means, motive, and opportunity.

1. Had she the means to poison herself? The answer was in the affirmative if she knew that there was cyanide available in the house. This is where a difficulty arose, because Lehman, in his evidence during the second trial, insisted that not only was his wife unaware that he had any acids in his possession but that even if she had she could not have known where he had hidden them. This statement contradicted the import of all his other evidence, which had built a case for her suicide. Judge Deale described Lehman's statement that his wife knew nothing about the availability of poison as 'putting the rope around his neck.'

2. Why should she commit suicide? The facts of the case cried out that she had every cause to escape from her predicament. She had had long enough to learn what her husband was like and how unreliable he was. He had not supported her or the children. She had been left without a penny in England and in Ireland. Twice he had fooled her with promises of a comfortable future on the basis of castles in the air; twice the castles in the air had dissolved. In addition, she cannot have been unaware of his flirtations (if that was all they were) with other women: Nurse McCaigue, Miss Finucane, the young widow—and these are only the ones we know about. Finally, there was yet another pregnancy and the prospect of a further mouth to feed. Depression and suicide were not ridiculous hypotheses.

3. As for opportunity, Judge Deale asked himself whether or not it was possible that she could have taken poison, removed the glass from the bedroom and returned to her bed before the poison began to take effect. She had three or four minutes to do all the above, which would have been quite sufficient. There was another point that counsel for the defence had raised: the strong smell from the sink on the lower landing, as a result of prussic acid being released from the cyanide by the action of hydrochloric acid, something that would be very unlikely in a domestic sink. The contention of the defence was that Margaret Lehman, having swallowed the poison, may have gone down to the landing, vomited in the sink, washed the cup and then returned to bed.

The possibility raised by Judge Deale was that, yes, Lehman was planning to poison his wife, but she had pre-empted him by taking her own life.

Judge Deale also queried Lehman's motive. The murder was pointless. The only evidence put before the second jury concerned his dealings with Nurse McCaigue, but there was nothing to show that she had given him any encouragement: if anything, the opposite was the case. Lehman had a criminal record, of which the jury were, naturally, unaware, but all his crimes involved dishonesty and theft by false pretences; there was never any question of violence. Neither was there any question of an inheritance from his wife. Desertion and flight were not new to him: he had deserted or broken with two other wives. A world war was raging. A new persona, a new alias, and he could have disappeared into any of the armed forces. Moving on had been a way of life for him.

Lehman *alias* Martin *alias* James *alias* Richman *alias* Hiames *alias* Leigh *alias* McCaigue *alias* Feeley was a drifter and what the French call a *mythomane*, whose grasp of reality was obviously minimal. He was certainly a rogue and minor conman, but proved guilty beyond all reasonable doubt? The jury is still out.

More than half a century later, Lehman's ghost would stalk an Irish court when the former Taoiseach Charles Haughey was on trial on two charges of obstructing the McCracken Tribunal. The judge had drawn up a questionnaire that he intended to hand to potential jurors in order to establish whether or not they might be prejudiced against Haughey. Haughey's defence team were in favour of the questionnaire and asked the question: How can an impartial jury be found to retry a person previously convicted of a notorious crime whose conviction may have been accompanied by extensive publicity?

Mr Justice Carney, whose task it was to rule whether or not the questionnaire should be allowed, quoted the old trial of *The People v. Lehman* and pointed out that the Supreme Court had indicated in that case that it was

> well settled that Counsel for an accused is not entitled to question a juror with a view to ascertaining whether a right of challenge should be exercised.

Mr Justice Carney raised the spectre of a notorious gangland boss coming up for trial and the effect that a series of written questions would have on potential jurors. Such an inquisition would not only be offensive to the constitutional imperative that all citizens should be equal before the law but could strike terror into the jury panel when it was hammered home what sort of person it was on whom they were required to reach their verdict.

The questionnaire was withdrawn.

Chapter 10

The man with the golden touch: Paul Singer

P aul Singer, a child of the Dual Monarchy, the Empire and Kingdom of Austria and Hungary, was born in Bratislava on 31 July 1911, five years before the death of Emperor Franz Josef. When the empire collapsed, Czechoslovakia appeared on the map and other parts of the empire were returned to Poland, Transylvania, the new Yugoslavia and Italy.

The Singers, a Jewish family, moved to Austria in 1925 but left for London in 1930, the year the Nazi Party became the second-largest party in the German Reichstag. This was also the year in which some German pundits suggested that Hitler should be made Chancellor because he would be so incompetent that he would be out of office in no time and the German people would wake up to the folly of their flirtation with fascism.

The father's decision may have been influenced by a fall in shares on the Berlin Bourse. In any case it had been a wise move, and the family became sufficiently prosperous to give Paul a good education and send him to university in Lausanne, where he obtained a doctorate in political science.

The recession came, followed by the Second World War. In 1940

Paul Singer made the acquaintance of Irma Wolf, the daughter of a London businessman. After a long courtship they were married in 1946, and he became a British citizen and set up his own business, which did not last very long. His father's Singer finance firm, of which Paul was a director, survived until 1953, when it collapsed, owing £45,000. It was time for Paul to move on again, and he chose Ireland.

In October he came to know a respected Dún Laoghaire auction-eering firm run by Jerome Shanahan and his son, Arthur Desmond Shanahan. Their main business was the weekly sale of antiques from their auction rooms. Singer, a plausible person, convinced the Shanahans that there were better things for them to do and suggested that they join up and go into the stamp business. The Shanahans were impressed by his proposal and on 12 October, with £200 capital, incor-porated a new company, Shanahan Stamp Auctions Ltd. The *modus operandi* was that Singer would seek out stamp collections, bring them back to Ireland and sell them by public auction.

Once the company was in operation, Singer went to London and bought a supply of stamps. The following week they were sold by auction at the Shanahans' premises in Corrig Avenue, Dún Laoghaire, and the company made a profit. The feeling was that there was no way to go but up. Singer continued to travel to London with the money from the weekly sales, and auctions continued to be held. He had a gift for publicity and promotional material and for tempting adver-tisements about how punters could grow rich with no risks. At least thirty thousand investors poured money into the company.

Singer was a master salesman and was soon publishing a magazine, printed on green paper, called *Green I.S.L.E. Philately* (with I.S.L.E. standing for 'Irish Stamp Lovers' Edition'). The first issue, on 22 September 1954, began with a greeting:

Dear Readers, here, there and everywhere,
Here is our Baby, the new magazine about which we have spoken so much. To us, the spiritual parents, it looks beautiful, but what do you think of it, stern Uncles and Aunts?
    But before you pass judgement, let us tell you what we want to make of Green I.S.L.E. Philately. We want to be not only instructive but enjoyable also. We want it to be pleasant not only to the spe-cialist but also to the layman who has a vague interest in philately. We chose articles not only for their philatelic but also for their

entertainment value . . . Tell us what you like, what you don't like, what you want added, what you want omitted. Be outspoken, be rude, but tell us what you really think of Green I.S.L.E. Philately.

We shall take every advice into consideration, and we promise you one thing—issue Number 2 will be better than issue No. 1, and issue No. 3 will be better than issue No. 2, and so on. (No wise-cracks, please, about skipping the next 23 issues and continuing with issue No. 25).

It continued in the same vein. Future issues included articles and recommendations from well-known Dubliners, first and foremost the popular Lord Mayor, Alfie Byrne, whose contribution (if indeed it was written by him) stated:

The reason why I rejoice particularly in your efforts is that here again is a field where Ireland could and should and now certainly will show its independence from the outside world.

Let your magazine show the world the Irish spirit in philately. Let the world know that we, too, have great specialists and that we can make our contribution to this hobby of hobbies, to this Golden Chain of International Peace and Friendship.

At the same time, constant advertisements promising a quick return to investors were being published in the newspapers.

We give you the opportunity to invest small sums from £10 upward . . . we will buy, in your name . . . Stamps which WE KNOW will fetch higher prices in our own Auctions here.

And they worked.

The Irish economy was depressed at the time, and thousands of people jumped at the chance to make a profit. Many were very small investors; some invested their life savings. These were normally cautious people, with money tucked away, whose middle-class con-servatism was dissolved by the promises of a bonanza. In 1958 alone they sent Singer £5,250 to purchase stamps on their behalf; in return they made gains of 20 to 25 per cent on their investments (for a while).

Theoretically, the dividends came from the results of these sales; the reality was that they came from the new investments of those anxious to leap onto the bandwagon. With imperial legerdemain, Singer attributed the inflow of funds to fictitious purchasers. What was also real was the 10 per cent commission that Singer took for himself from each 'sale'. The money to pay these commissions came from the constant flow of investments. Like a child's hoop, the whole thing kept rolling as long as there was the impulsion of spin, greed and credulity to keep it upright.

Singer's person was as impressive—to the gullible or greedy—as the newsletter's claims. He was the epitome of success: bearded, well dressed, cigar-smoking, and stout (almost 20 stone—but those were the days when a degree of obesity was synonymous with success).

A journalist called Séamus Brady, who had been asked by Singer to become his public relations officer, wrote a book about him in 1965, called *Doctor of Millions*. In it he gave the following description of Singer and his life-style:

Singer was now living the life of an Irish lord. He had bought a magnificent mansion on a thirteen-acre site at Foxrock, a fashionable suburb of Dublin, and christened it 'Cairn Hall'. This had formerly been the home of George Formby, the comedian, bought as a haven of retreat for his first wife and himself on his retirement; and he had called it 'Beryldene' after his wife.

The purchase of Cairn Hall was attended by the usual Singer care and caution. He did not buy the house direct. He used a company, H.B. Pipes Ltd, in which he and his wife held all the shares, to buy this Georgian mansion and estate on his behalf. The reason for this device has never been questioned, but it was no doubt a precaution by Singer utilising his knowledge of company law to avoid taxation.

'Cairn Hall' was breathtaking by the time Singer had furnished it to his taste. The furniture was Chippendale, picked up at the best auction rooms in Dublin and London. The curtains were thick velvet. Costly paintings graced the walls. He had a governess for his two children. His Spanish butler, Daro, always wore a spotless white dinner jacket. A chauffeur in livery drove his big limousine. Singer, in colourful dressing gown, always breakfasted continental style on coffee and rolls in the sun patio where he could watch the artificial waterfall cascading over rocks into a pool of goldfish in his huge conservatory. But at 11 a.m. in his office he had his real breakfast: a bowl of soup, with half a dozen raw eggs. Lunch invariably was a five-course affair, the main dish being steak tartare—a pound of raw steak, minced with garlic and herbs, and bound with raw eggs. For dinner at 'Cairn Hall' caviare was always on order. And Singer drank 'black velvet', which is stout laced with champagne.

It is easy to see why Singer was the darling of the press.

He wore an expensive black overcoat and a steel-grey suit but carried a shabby brown pigskin briefcase. He spent much of his time travelling around the world in search of stamps, and every time he returned to Dublin Airport he stage-managed a welcoming group. Rumours spread about women from his Dún Laoghaire staff forming a welcoming party and singing 'For He's a Jolly Good Fellow' when he landed.

The numbers employed by Shanahan Stamp Auctions Ltd continued to increase as the business expanded by leaps and bounds. Few dealers had access to ready cash as he had. He arranged that Shanahans should lodge money for his use in the countries he visited: £100,000 was deposited for his use in the United States and £150,000 in Milan when he was trying to buy a famous collection called the Lombardo-Venezia Collection.

Singer's last trip to buy stamps was to Switzerland, where he acquired a share of a £2 million collection with an option to purchase the remainder. This was the excuse for a party when he returned to Ireland.

The party was held in the Shanahan premises in Dún Laoghaire, which was decorated extravagantly. There were blown-up photographs of the directors on the walls. Edmundo Ross, a famous Latin-American band leader of the period, entertained at least six hundred guests. Claims were made that caviar was flown in from Russia and snails and other delicacies from Paris.

This was only a rehearsal for the fifth birthday party of the company, held on 9 May 1959. Everyone who was anyone was there: the rich and famous of Dublin society, Dáil deputies and a few spruced-up gentry from stately homes around the country. Unfortunately, Singer was not on his best behaviour that night. Allegedly he threw champagne bottles at guests, poured drinks down the front of women's dresses and was generally loutish. This may have been because the staff had discovered that very morning that the firm's impressive premises in

George's Street had been burgled and the Lombardo-Venezia Collection had been stolen. Some say that these stamps were worth about half a million pounds. What is certain is that the collection was not insured for theft but only against fire.

Some £290,000 worth of stamps would be recovered later when, in November, the police arrested a former Shanahan employee in Geneva, a Greek gentleman called Apostolos Tatsopoulos. Newspapers that had helped to build Singer up were now ready to tear him down. In the meantime Shanahans offered a reward of £10,000 for any information leading to the discovery, in good condition, of the stolen stamps.

Ironically, the most recent issue of *Green I.S.L.E. Philately* had published a joke:

Stamp Dealer: Any new orders while I was out?
New Assistant: Only one! Two gentlemen ordered me to put my hands up while they took away the stock.

The rumour machine went into overdrive, investment stopped and, as happens in such situations, panic took over. Nine thousand claims for repayment of something between £1.8 and £2 million (if not more) were made.

Two weeks later the liquidators, Craig Gardner and Company, were called in. Their man on the spot, Gerald O'Brien, established that the assets of Shanahan Stamp Auctions Ltd were about £500,000, of which £55,000 would be needed for the liquidators' fees. The directors were arrested: Paul Singer, his wife, Irma, and the Shanahans, the unfortunate dupes of the colourful conman.

A new saga was about to begin, strung out by the fact that the authorities appear to have made a proper mess of the subsequent proceedings.

The Attorney-General, Aindrias Ó Caoimh, instructed the Gardaí to examine Shanahans' books. The team, led by Chief Superintendent Farrell, discovered that an unseemly amount of money had been lodged abroad, and there were serious discrepancies in receipting payments from these sums for stamp collections. Farrell applied on 28 May to the Dublin Circuit Court for four arrest warrants in respect of Paul Singer, Irma Singer, Jerome Shanahan, and Arthur Desmond Shanahan. They were arrested on 29 May, questioned in Dún

Laoghaire Garda Station and locked up in the Bridewell, where they spent a week before being brought before District Justice Kenneth Reddin.

A preliminary joint charge was read out, accusing the four of conspiring to cheat and defraud Leo Hunt, a Sligo investor, and others. The state prosecutor informed the district justice that there would be other charges, so Reddin fixed bail at £100,000 for Singer, half the sum personal, the rest independent. He was ordered to surrender his passport and to report daily to the Gardaí in Dún Laoghaire. Personal bail of £20,000 each was fixed for the other three accused, together with the same amount in independent sureties. Singer's solicitor, Frank Martin, applied to the High Court for a reduction in the bail demands, and Mr Justice Murnaghan reduced Singer's personal bail to £5,000, with an independent surety of £10,000, and Irma Singer's personal bail to £2,000, with an independent surety of £10,000. In Jerome Shanahan's case the new amounts became £1,000 and £2,000, and for Arthur Desmond Shanahan it would be fixed at a later stage at the same amounts.

The Shanahans had no difficulty in getting guarantors, and Irma Singer was bailed out by her father. She was to hold up proceedings later by insisting that her father's bail money should be invested in a national loan at 5¼ per cent! Paul Singer was to sit in Mountjoy Prison for eighteen months awaiting trial. Ulick O'Connor, who was to act for Arthur Desmond Shanahan, later recalled that Singer, who already weighed 20 stone, ate fourteen fried eggs for breakfast every morning.

Earlier in May the firm of Arthur Cox and Company, solicitors, had announced that the directors of Shanahan's Stamp Auctions Ltd had appointed Gerald W. O'Brien of Craig Gardner and Company, chartered accountants, as liquidator of the company. By the time the bail question had been sorted out, solicitors for investors had placed claims totalling £2 million, and the stamp stocks had been removed to bank vaults.

What followed was a marathon 63-day hearing in the District Court before District Justice Cathal O'Flynn, involving thirty-nine charges concerning £350,000. The charges stated that the four accused

> fraudulently intended to cheat and defraud citizens of the State by inviting them to entrust money for investment in the purchase and sale of stamps at auctions advertised in the public press, by

pretending that these auctions were honestly conducted, whereas, in fact, they knew that the moneys invested were grouped by them into syndicates, and that dividends were paid by the company on money invested, without reference to the prices at which stamps were sold, in that they fraudulently and deceitfully decided that dividends should be paid after auctions were held.

Jerome Shanahan had hearing difficulties, and the judge allowed him to make use of earphones connected to a microphone. Paul Singer, who read a newspaper during the early stages of the trial, was permitted to sit with his defence lawyers for the remaining stages. The sitting for 15 October was adjourned because that was the feast of Yom Kippur, a holy day for the Singers.

Evidence was given that Singer overvalued stamps and described how unsold stamps would be reduced at every auction until they were sold. Two independent assessors from London not only agreed that there was overvaluation but also stated that there had been inaccurate catalogue descriptions. One of them even said that in his opinion Singer was not a philatelic expert.

Members of the Shanahans' staff were called to give evidence of how the business had been conducted. The cashier gave evidence that in at least one year the investments had amounted to £5.25 million. He also revealed that there had been fictitious sales, using the names of people well known in philately circles; they also listed sales to fictitious names. In one instance he demonstrated to the court that the books showed a debt of more than £250,000 to Shanahan's Stamp Auctions Ltd owed by a Mr Zombie. The firm charged commission on transactions that had never taken place, and the amount of profit that was paid to individuals was purely at the whim of Singer himself.

This was all before the investigation looked into the staggering amounts that had been lodged abroad in Singer's name. An insurance broker was called who gave evidence that he had negotiated cover in respect of fire but that when he offered cover against theft, Singer and Arthur Desmond Shanahan had elected to accept burglary risk themselves.

Finally, on 23 January 1960 District Justice O'Flynn discharged Jerome Shanahan and sent Arthur Shanahan and the two Singers on trial on warrants 'to the next sitting of the Circuit Criminal Court.' However, as pointed out by the late Padraic O'Farrell in his captivating book *Tales for the Telling,* that phrase was common enough parlance, but the State did not reckon with the clever Paul Singer, who would use two of its words to his advantage in a manner that would rock the institutions of the State and infuriate its citizens.

Arthur Shanahan and Irma Singer availed of bail, but Paul Singer stayed in prison. He did not, however, waste his time but devoted it to legal study. He was so thorough that he was able to help fellow-prisoners, and it is claimed that he enabled some to gain their release from custody.

After nine weeks he demanded and was given a hearing in the Dublin District Criminal Court. He informed the judge about the delay in sending him for trial and asked for an order releasing him from Mountjoy. The judge refused his request and Singer left the court metaphorically rubbing his hands. The judge had fallen into his trap: Singer had been bargaining on a refusal.

On 11 April the Attorney-General received a letter from Singer to inform him that he (Singer) was still awaiting trial and was accordingly in unlawful custody. The Attorney-General ignored his plea, and on 20 April Singer was pleading before Mr Justice Budd in the High Court, looking for a conditional order under section 6 of the Habeas Corpus Act directing the Governor of Mountjoy Prison and the Attorney-General to release him from custody.

In clear and simple terms, Singer put the facts before Mr Justice Budd. He had been sent for trial in January to the 'next sitting' of the Circuit Criminal Court. He then pointed out that the court had sat on two occasions since the order had been made and he had neither been arraigned nor indicted, nor had the state sought an adjournment on either day. Mr Justice Budd had no choice but to grant a conditional order of *habeas corpus* while keeping Singer in custody for six days, which should give time to the Attorney-General and the governor to show just cause why the order should not be made absolute.

Singer had done a great job on his own; it was now time to call in the heavy cavalry. He engaged Seán MacBride SC and his junior, Noel Hartnett. The next stage began with a short appearance by Paul Singer, Irma Singer and Arthur Shanahan before Judge Conroy in the Circuit Criminal Court. Shanahan was sent for trial but released for the moment on bail, Irma Singer was given an adjournment, and Niall McCarthy, for the Attorney-General, was given an adjournment in Singer's case.

Singer's next appearance was before the High Court, composed of Mr Justice Cahir Davitt, Mr Justice Budd and Mr Justice Haugh. Seán MacBride put forward three contentions. Singer was being held in custody on an order that was spent; his committal order was bad in law and therefore he was being held in custody unlawfully; holding him violated the Constitution and the elements of natural justice.

The application did not succeed. Singer was required to pay £800 costs, and MacBride appealed to the Supreme Court, which on 25 May overruled the High Court and accepted that Singer's interpretation of 'next sitting' was the correct one.

It was as if a fox had been allowed in with the chickens. The police saw their work going down the drain, Singer's barrister was fighting to get a release order, and the Attorney-General's office was looking for a new warrant for Singer's arrest. Everyone was aware that Singer could flee the country. However, no sooner had he walked out the door of Mountjoy than detectives rearrested him. He was driven to the Bridewell and confronted with newly worded charges. The following day Irma Singer, Arthur Desmond Shanahan and his wife, Diana, were arrested; it all happened so quickly that she had to bring her youngest child into court, not having had time to find a baby-sitter.

This third arrest caused a furore among the public and the defence counsel. The famous sharp-tongued senior counsel Ernest Wood rapidly moved to the attack and criticised the Attorney-General as only he could.

So far, I have advised [my junior] to abstain from putting the Attorney General right where he has been guilty of clearly illegal practices. I had hoped that some kind of responsibility would have eventually arisen in the mind of the Attorney General, but it does not appear that this is going to happen. He appears, since Paul Singer exposed him, to have behaved with the irresponsibility of a child.

Unless the Attorney General comes to his senses, and realises the elemental principle of justice that a man cannot stand charged in two courts with the same alleged offence at the one time, I will advise my client to bring proceedings which should not be necessary if the Attorney General realised his responsibility and behaved properly.

I say this in an appeal to the Attorney General to realise that what he is doing in the case of Mr and Mrs Shanahan looks like the act of a forensic teddy-boy who is determined to destroy their family life. He must realise that while this case is pending, and it has been pending for a year now, Desmond Shanahan cannot take up any employment to earn his living while he faces the prospect of appearing day after day in this court, as he did on 63 occasions in the past twelve months. What has happened is a monstrous interference in the rights of the Shanahans and their family. The Attorney General ought to take steps at once to put his house in order—or I shall advise my client to do it for him.

Singer returned to Mountjoy, and the others were granted bail, but the Attorney-General was not to get off lightly. He was also under attack in Dáil Éireann. Some deputies questioned his appointment; some criticised his private practice while holding a public office; others concentrated on his 'costly and clumsy handling' of the Singer case.

On 3 June a special sitting of the Central Criminal Court was held, the outcome of which was that District Justice Walsh held that Singer was being illegally held. History then repeated itself: no sooner had he left the building than he was rearrested. This caused another furore. The Fine Gael opposition had a field day in the Dáil, savaging the Government and its appointees.

Arthur Desmond Shanahan's trial came up on 27 June, and his father gave evidence in his favour. At this stage the veteran of the First World War and former happily modest auctioneer had been reduced to working as a night watchman in England. It was made clear to the jury by the brilliant barrister Ernest Wood that the Shanahans had been the victims of the Singers as much as any investors.

Shanahan was found guilty on 21 July of sixteen out of twenty-one counts and was jailed for fifteen months. Singer's team were still battling, and it would be 17 October 1960 before his and Irma Singer's trials began.

Much of it was about figures. An important witness was a chartered accountant, Noel Gough, who had helped to make an analysis of the accounts of Shanahan's Stamp Auctions Ltd for the Attorney-General and could explain how things were done in the company. He told the jury, as an example, that in one sale, on 29 November 1958, there were 1,266 investors, who had invested a total of £174,397. The value of the stamps allocated to the sale was £42,420, but the amount realised was only £52,319. The total repayment was £215,083. Commission for the company was £21,295, leaving a net payment to the syndicate in the sale of £193,787. The profit paid to investors was only £19,300.

On 11 November the liquidator, Gerald O'Brien, said that the assets of the company were: cash in hand, £2,671, and cash in the National Bank, College Green, £5,930. At a later stage £51,395 would be recovered from a Swiss bank, £30,815 from a bank in Toronto, £1,104 from a bank in New Zealand and £4,942 from a bank in New York. There was £18,479 owing to the company for stamps sold and not paid for. The money in the Swiss and Canadian banks was in the name of Dr Paul Singer or Irma Singer, or both; the money in the New York bank was in the name of Shanahan's Stamp Auctions Ltd.

Singer did not give evidence but he did address the jury for four days. He told them that his name had been blackened and that in his case the 'innocent until proved guilty rule of law' had been reversed. He claimed that he kept the Ten Commandments and paid his staff well. Only the burglary murdered 'the sputnik of philately' that he had made, Shanahan's Stamp Auctions Ltd (a reference to the inauguration of the Space Age by the Soviet Union in October 1957 with the launch of the first artificial satellite, *Sputnik 1*). He claimed that Diana Shanahan was a brilliant woman with a passion for figures. Even when she was having babies she had arranged for an adding machine to be brought to her maternity hospital room. 'She was a queen bee,' he said. Her husband, however, was weak 'and often like putty in the hands of his attractive but very hysterical wife.' He also reminded the jury that the Shanahans had three votes to his two and that his only role was as an agent for the company.

It took the jury an hour and twenty minutes to reach a verdict, and it was that Paul Singer was guilty on nineteen charges of fraud, conspiracy and fraudulent conversion of

£796,514.6s. 2d. To the use and benefit of Shanahan's Stamp Auctions Ltd. Being the amount to which, as alleged, it appeared the company was indebted to investors at the date of liquidation.

The following day the *Irish Independent* reported the scene.

Head erect, his hands clutching the dock rail of the Green Street Courthouse, Dr Paul Singer looked towards the jury in the Central Criminal Court, Dublin, and showed no emotion as he heard their verdict, 'Guilty on all counts, My Lord'. Singer looked straight at Mr Justice Haugh as he heard him tell the jury, 'I fully agree with your verdict, gentlemen, but Singer must wait another week before he knows what sentence will be passed'. The Judge told him, 'I do not intend to propose sentence this evening in the present atmosphere of emotion and excitement. I propose to postpone sentence for one week to give you a chance to think things over. It will be my duty, however, to impose a very heavy sentence'. Mr Justice Haugh said that he would give Singer the week to make up his mind if he would disclose to the liquidator where and when large sums of money were lodged. 'That money is still somewhere . . . Either in credit or in stamps,' he said.

At twenty-five days, this had been the longest criminal trial up to that time in the Republic. In Singer's case alone there had been 1,895 exhibits, which involved 5,000 documents and 10,000 pages.

A week later Mr Justice Haugh asked Singer if he had anything to say. He had, but it was not what the judge wanted to hear.

I have been thinking very carefully about what Your Lordship said last Monday night and I wish to reiterate here and now that all the money entrusted to me for the purchase of stamps was, in fact, so used by me except for 83,000 Canadian dollars which I repatriated to the National Bank, College Green, Dublin. The so-called deficiency arises solely from the difference in evaluations given by Mr Robson Lowe and those which the company offered for the stamps in Dún Laoghaire.

There are no hidden moneys anywhere, and all the money entrusted to me is fully accounted for by stamp purchases and for the investors. I wish to confirm that I am more anxious to help the liquidator to as much money as possible for distribution to the investors and I will always do anything in my power that he may reasonably ask of me. This is my solemn promise.

He reminded the judge that he had spent sixteen months in Mountjoy awaiting trial and in effect had served a 50 per cent longer sentence than Arthur Desmond Shanahan and

much greater mental strain and torture. There is a principle of equality of treatment in Irish Law and I hope Your Lordship will apply this in the interest of fair play, justice and humanity.

In spite of this appeal to Haugh's good nature, Singer was sentenced to fifteen years' penal servitude.

At this point the fan was dirtied. It emerged that the foreman of the jury was a chartered accountant employed by Craig Gardner and Company, the firm in which Gerald O'Brien, the Shanahan liquidator, was a senior partner. He was also an investor in Shanahan's Stamp Auctions Ltd and a claimant against the company in respect of his investment.

Singer was down, but he was not out. On 11 April 1961 he was back at the Court of Criminal Appeal before Mr Justice Walsh, Mr Justice Murnaghan and Mr Justice Ó Dálaigh. Singer told them that no investor had ever lost money, that Arthur Desmond Shanahan had been acquitted of conspiracy and the same should apply to him. He brought to their notice the fact that Haugh was the judge taking the liquidation proceedings in the High Court, and this could give rise to a suspicion that there could be a conflict of interest. He did not put it so politely but bluntly told the judges that Haugh had used his trial 'to further the ends of the liquidation proceedings.'

Singer had done it again. He was given a retrial, and his fourteen-year sentence was cancelled. Delighted with his success, and not afraid to strike while the iron was hot, he reminded the court that his bail figure should be reduced and—hey presto, it was: to a personal security of £3,000 and an independent surety of the same amount. He managed to have the independent security reduced to £1,500.

He had one subsequent defeat and another victory. In the first case he asked Mr Justice Teevan for permission to go abroad for a personal reason, but Teevan refused. In the second matter he asked for the return of the £780,000 that the Gardaí had confiscated more than two years previously, and this application was granted.

The retrial was another long one also. His defence team was Seán MacBride, Gerard Charleton and Paul Callan. After forty-seven days Mr Justice Walsh—no pushover—found that the case against Singer could not be proved either affirmatively or negatively.

The prosecution have to prove it affirmatively—and it is not for the accused to prove his innocence. As the case stands, the prosecution must fail.

He instructed the jury to record a verdict of not guilty, and Paul Singer walked out, a free man.

Wherever he went, it was not to the bankruptcy court, nor was it to a holiday home in the west of Ireland. He simply disappeared from sight; but not from the memories of the opposition, who from time to time used him for baiting the Government.

He still has one defender. Ulick O'Connor is quoted by Padraic O'Farrell as speaking out in Singer's defence.

I think the Attorney General should never have brought the case, because the stamps would have appreciated in value. As it was, investors recouped 50%. Without five years of legal expenses, their losses would have been minimal, if there were any. I believe Shanahan's Stamp Auctions Ltd was a legitimate operation. Paul Singer had acquired part of the Burrus collection. If he had exercised his option to purchase the remainder, he would have controlled the stamp world. Therefore, I believe that Singer's enemies in that same stamp world planned the robbery to destroy him.

Finally, it is worth noting how Singer's time in Ireland also provided fodder for questions in the Dáil. On 29 March 1962 William Norton (Kildare, Labour Party) asked C. J. Haughey (Dublin North-East, Fianna Fáil), Minister for Justice,

whether the recent decision of the courts in the Singer case means the complete acquittal of Mr Singer; if not, whether any further charges are to be preferred against him; and if so, how many charges, and when they will be preferred.

Mr Haughey: Mr Singer has been acquitted on all charges brought against him.

Mr Norton: The legal machine has done this gentleman proudly. It could not happen in a banana republic.

Mr Haughey: I have never been in a banana republic.

Mr Norton: Mr Singer, with all our people's money in his pocket, is in one at the moment and enjoying himself to his heart's content.

If Norton had at the time the power to look into the future he could have added, 'But *you* would not object to having your money in one.'

Two years before, on 10 June 1960, the loophole that Singer's legal studies in prison had exposed had given grounds to the opposition for taunting the Government with the possibility that the Rules of Court had not been respected by the authorities. Sylvester Barrett TD had asked the Minister for Justice if on Thursday 2 June 1960 he had made an order that Paul Singer be brought from Mountjoy Prison to the Central Criminal Court and, if so, if he could state the exact terms of the order and the authority which he had for making it. The Minister, Oscar Traynor, replied that an order was made in the following terms:

> The Minister for Justice hereby orders and directs that Paul Singer, a prisoner at present confined in Mountjoy Prison, be produced at the Central Criminal Court on the 3rd of June, 1960, and from day to day as may be necessary, the Minister for Justice being satisfied that the presence of the said Paul Singer at such place is required in the interest of justice.

Patrick Lindsay TD, a barrister, had then wanted to know if the minister was now satisfied that his order was valid and that the presence of the accused at the Central Criminal Court was in pursuance of a valid order. 'Yes, I am perfectly satisfied,' the minister had said; but this did not get Lindsay off his back. 'In spite of the fact that a *habeas corpus* order was granted there and then in respect of the accused person?'

Before the minister could reply, James Dillon intervened in his best Ciceronian manner.

> Might I ask the Minister, in view of the eminent desirability of the law being vindicated in this matter, justice being done, criminals brought to justice and innocents set free, is it desirable to have recourse to these exotic procedures of which nobody has ever heard before? Is it not much more desirable to proceed according to the ordinary procedures of the law and not create a situation in which the judge presiding in the Criminal Court says: 'What is that man doing in the dock in my court?'
>
> I do not think I am mistranslating what was reported in the public press. Does the Minister not realise that resort to such procedure causes considerable anxiety that the whole system of law is breaking down and that those responsible for criminal acts are not

being made adequately and effectively to answer for their conduct to the appropriate court of law?

Traynor stood his ground.

Orders of this kind are made frequently. There is nothing exceptional in the issue of this particular Order. In fact, this Order was issued in the interests of the prisoner to enable him to appear in court. I cannot understand why this matter should engage the attention of Deputies from the point of view that has just been expressed.

James Dillon, the people's tribune, spoke up again.

Surely the Minister is aware of the general public concern and dismay at the apparent atmosphere of confusion and bewilderment which appears to surround the proceedings in connection with the trial of this man?

It was time for the Taoiseach, Seán Lemass, to enter the fray.

The only fact that has arisen was the unexpected decision of the Supreme Court declaring irregular a practice that had been in operation.

This answer upset Patrick Lindsay. 'That is not so,' he protested. Paddy Smith retorted: 'It is so!' Mr Dillon wanted to move on to more serious matters.

Does the Taoiseach not advert to the fact that, consequent upon that Order, there then arises the extraordinary situation in which the Minister makes an Order directing the production of the accused person in the Central Criminal Court and the presiding judge thereupon appears to inquire: 'What is that man doing here?'

This was getting too close to the bone, and Lemass told him that he did not think that this was a matter they could discuss there; but Dillon, temporary guardian of the sensibilities of the plain people of Ireland, was concerned with the broader picture and insisted:

At least, I suggest to the Taoiseach, these undesirable procedures give rise to considerable public perturbation of mind and create a very undesirable atmosphere of distrust in the efficient prosecution of the law.

Lemass may not have been a lawyer but he had seen how the justice system works, at the very least in the cinema, and answered with an excellent summary of the functions of the men in wigs.

As I understand it, it is the function of counsel defending an accused person to take advantage of any legal technicality open to him to protect his client's interests. It is the duty of the prosecution to see that persons charged with offences are brought properly to book.

Dillon agreed but asked if the Taoiseach thought that the procedure used had been the appropriate way in which to do what the Taoiseach recommended. Mr Lindsay, on the other hand, was perturbed by the Taoiseach's reply.

Is the Taoiseach seriously suggesting, that the finding of the presiding judge in the Central Criminal Court and the granting of an Order of habeas corpus there and then, with an order for costs against the Attorney General, was an irregularity?

The Ceann Comhairle leapt into the breach. 'Surely we cannot discuss this matter here,' he remarked, to which Dillon replied with a question: 'Surely the administration of the law is relevant?' The Ceann Comhairle insisted that court proceedings were not open to discussion in the Dáil, but Dillon was equally insistent on getting it on the record that the minister had mishandled the matter, and told him so.

If, sir, an entirely unprecedented procedure is adopted for bringing a person before the court, a procedure which the presiding judge describes as incomprehensible, it is not improper for us to ask the Minister why he made that kind of Order.

When the Ceann Comhairle replied that he would need to be very fully advised as to whether or not it was an unprecedented order, Lindsay assured him that it was invalid and had been found to be so.

The discussion ended with Lemass kicking for touch and pronouncing that the function of prosecution rested with the Attorney-General.

The second series of queries about Paul Singer took place on 20 March 1962, when James Dillon put five questions to the Taoiseach that certainly gave civil servants a chance to earn their salary. The questions related to the dates on which Paul Singer was first arrested and was first returned for trial to the Dublin Circuit Court by the District Justice, when an indictment against Paul Singer was lodged in the Dublin Circuit Court, and the reason for the delay in lodging the indictment in the Dublin Circuit Court; what directions, if any, had been given to ensure that indictments against persons returned for trial would be lodged without undue delay; and the date on which such directions were given. Their object was to show that the department's action had been one continuous blunder.

Lemass's answer was that Paul Singer had been first arrested on 30 May 1959, was first returned for trial to the Dublin Circuit Court by the district justice on 23 January 1960, and that the indictment against him was lodged on 27 April 1960. The delay of more than three months in lodging the indictment had arisen because of the enormous number of depositions and exhibits that had to be copied, and Lemass was aware of no undue delay in lodging indictments and had been informed that no special directions in this regard had recently been found necessary.

Such frankness was still not enough for Dillon, who asked the Taoiseach to tell him how many counts in the indictment had been quashed by the Court of Criminal Appeal on the grounds that such counts were bad for duplicity. Lemass admitted that there had been four such counts, but Dillon's lust for information was not appeased. He wanted to know whether or not the Taoiseach was aware of the grave public anxiety resulting from the failure of the court to be given an opportunity to adjudicate on these matters because of the technical difficulties to which the Taoiseach had referred earlier.

Lemass's declaration that he doubted whether he could or should say anything that would appear to be a reflection on the courts did not interest Dillon, and accordingly he asked the Taoiseach to consider whether in fact the technical difficulties described by him concerning the judgment of the Court of Criminal Appeal should not be regarded as some reflection on the efficacy of the law officials of the Government in preparing the case for submission to the court.

Lemass back-pedalled and admitted that he assumed that what Dillon said might be so but did not think that the verdict of the court could have been anticipated. Furthermore, he modestly admitted, he was afraid it was all too technical for him to offer an opinion.

As much of the bulldog breed as Winston Churchill, whose debating rhythms were cousin-german to his own, Dillon asked the Taoiseach how many days or parts of days were occupied in connection with the criminal proceedings against Paul Singer (*a*) in the District Court in taking depositions on the first occasion, (*b*) in the *habeas corpus* proceedings instituted by Paul Singer (i) in the High Court and (ii) in the Supreme Court, (*c*) in the District Court in taking depositions on the second occasion, (*d*) in the prohibition proceedings, (*e*) in the first trial in the Central Criminal Court, and (*f*) in the appeal brought by Paul Singer to the Court of Criminal Appeal.

The much-maligned civil servants had not been burning the midnight oil in vain. The prompt answers were: (*a*) 63 days, (*b*) (i) 2 days, (ii) 6 days, (*c*) 26 days, (*d*) 10 days, (*e*) 26 days, and (*f*) 27 days—a total of 160 days.

Dillon then lobbed a hand grenade and asked the Taoiseach whether the foreman of the jury in the first trial of Paul Singer was an investor in Shanahan's Stamp Auctions Ltd, and had a claim against the company in liquidation. The Taoiseach replied that the answers to both parts of the deputy's question were in the affirmative, but Dillon wanted a fuller response.

Did the prosecution, in relation to the jury panel in the first trial of Paul Singer, take any steps to determine who, if any, of the jurymen on the panel they might challenge when a jury was being empanelled to try Paul Singer?

Answer: 'The normal procedure was followed in this case.' Such a defensive movement enabled Dillon to go, like Tiger Roche, for the jugular.

Is it not the Taoiseach's opinion that it was a very strange dereliction of duty on the part of the law officers of the State to allow a jury to be empanelled, when they had a right to object, which contained not only a man who was a servant of the liquidator but a man who had a personal interest in the transactions in respect of which the defendant was being tried?

The syntax may have been twisted, but the sub-agenda was clear. Lemass was now on the defensive and had to insist that the fact that a member of the jury was an employee of a firm of accountants concerned in the liquidation proceedings had become known some days after the trial had begun, and was not regarded as being important by prosecuting counsel, the registrar or the trial judge, nor was it the reason for the subsequent appeal, which was based on the fact that this member of the jury was found to be an investor in the company, a matter that was not known to the prosecuting counsel or to the judge or—if they accepted his affidavit—to the defendant himself.

Nonetheless, Dillon had Lemass against the ropes.

Surely, the fact that the man in question was indirectly a servant of the liquidator and the company in respect of which many of these charges were being tried, was a matter that should have been brought to the attention of the trial judge the moment it became known to the law officers of the State? Is it not a fact that, after this information became available to the law officers within twenty four hours of the proceedings having commenced, they were not brought to the attention of either the judge or the defence?

But Lemass bounced back.

My information is that the trial judge was so informed. The point I am making is that the subsequent successful appeal was based on the grounds that the individual concerned was personally involved as an investor in the company. If the Deputy studies the judgment of the Appeal Court which I had placed in the Library at his request, he will find that the appeal was upheld by the judge on the grounds, first, that the juror should have himself indicated this interest in the case and, secondly, that the trial judge should have warned all the members of the jury panel of the obligation to reveal any such interest.

Dillon, a barrister by training, brushed this weak swipe aside.

Surely, in view of the very peculiar circumstances surrounding this case in which so many people have suffered loss, it was an ordinary precaution for counsel for the State to ascertain if any of the members of the jury were themselves losers or were interested parties in order to take the necessary precautions to ensure that nobody with an interest in the case should be a member of the jury? Even if it had happened after one, two or three days of the trial, it would have been a valid case on which counsel for the State should seek the discharge of the jury and to ask for a trial with a fresh jury which would not be open to any challenge.

The Taoiseach was down but not yet out.

I understand that the responsibility for the preparation of the jury panel rests on the county registrar but I think it fair to point out that it would be a difficult task for him to check each juror, in view of the fact that some 30,000 people in Dublin were said to have been interested as investors in this concern. The fact that the juror in question was interested in that way did not come to light until after the trial was over. That applies not only to counsel on behalf of the State but it was not known to the defendant [he meant the accused], as was stated in his affidavit.

A still dissatisfied Dillon asked the Taoiseach to agree that if the fact was known to counsel for the state at any stage in the trial it should have been brought to the notice of the trial judge and indeed of the defendant also. A now compliant Taoiseach agreed to this assertion with a little twisting of the facts: 'Certainly. The trial judge would have been informed of it.'

Such acquiescence took the fun out of Dillon's game, so he attacked from a different angle and asked whether or not the liquidator of Shanahan's Stamp Auctions Ltd gave evidence at the first trial of Paul Singer and had been called as a witness on behalf of the Attorney-General.

Lemass agreed that the answers to both parts of the question were in the affirmative, which caused Dillon to enquire whether the Attorney-General had been made aware in the early stages of the first trial of Paul Singer in the Central Criminal Court that the foreman of the jury was a member of the staff of the firm of accountants one of whose partners was the liquidator of Shanahan's Stamp Auctions Ltd, and, if not, at what date the Attorney-General was first made aware of this fact.

Lemass was not going to rise to Dillon's bait. He agreed a third time and accepted a disappointed Dillon's first assertion but had to be reminded that the second query had already been submitted to him as question no. 7.

As Dillon had put it that way, Lemass had to admit that his information was that the Attorney-General had been made aware of the fact that the foreman was employed by this firm of accountants a couple of days after the trial had begun, but that it was understood that he had nothing to do with the firm's handling of the affairs of the company. The matter became known through the county registrar, who also, the Taoiseach understood, informed the judge, and it was assumed that any action necessary would have been taken by the court.

Lemass was not going soft after all. He had created an opening for a delighted Dillon to attack once more.

> Would the Taoiseach not agree that, at that stage, something ought to have been done by the Attorney General to inform the court, through counsel for the State, of this fact and that the defendant should certainly have been warned?

Lemass muttered that he had been told that the trial judge had been informed, which gave an opportunity to Gerard Sweetman to jump in and ask if the judge had been informed in open court. The Taoiseach did not think so but felt that in any case this had nothing to do with the appeal, which was not on the grounds that the foreman of the jury was employed by Craig Gardner but that he personally was an investor in the stamp auctioneering company. He suggested that the deputy might study the decision of the judge in the Court of Criminal Appeal, where he would find that no importance had been attached to the character of the juror's employment.

Dillon had read the decision and he could not agree with the Taoiseach's claim. In his view, if necessary a new jury should have been empanelled to try the case; but Lemass continued to stonewall and to insist that his information was that the trial judge was made aware of it, and that, it could be implied, was good enough for him.

Dillon had exhausted that avenue and decided to talk money. He immediately asked if a count in the indictment on the first trial of Paul Singer covered a sum of nearly £800,000 and whether or not this count 'overlapped' other charges and, because of such 'overlapping' and other defects, the Court of Criminal Appeal held that it could not order a retrial on this count involving nearly £800,000. Yet again the answers to both parts of the question were in the affirmative.

A shocked Dillon asked Lemass to agree with him that where a man stands charged with being concerned in the disappearance of £800,000 it is unfortunate that these charges could never be determined clearly by the court on account of technical defects in the indictment and that the matter of fraudulent misrepresentation was never raised, and if so would the Taoiseach also agree with him that these defects reflected gravely on the law officers of the state?

In reply, Lemass insisted that the verdict was set aside by the Court of Criminal Appeal on the grounds that a person interested as an investor in the business was a member of the jury; and when Dillon insisted that it was also for the reasons stated by him, Lemass recommended that he read the decision of the judge in the Court of Criminal Appeal. He did not think it would be right for him to attempt to interpret it.

Dillon continued doggedly in his attempt to prise an admission from the Taoiseach that the law officers of the state had made a total mess of the proceedings, but Lemass would not take the same view. He appealed (no doubt with tears in his eyes) to the majesty and probity of the common law (bequeathed to us by the Saxon invader).

One of the characteristics of our system of law is that a person charged with a criminal offence is deemed innocent until proved guilty, and must be proved guilty in accordance with evidence produced in court and with very complicated procedures and rules designed to protect the interests of the defendant. The fact that the state failed to get a conviction, whether on technical grounds or otherwise, does not necessarily indicate any defects in the State's procedure. Also, I think we should be very careful ourselves not to do an injustice as, no matter what suspicions may be held, the fact is that the individual concerned has not been found guilty.

It would indeed have been very unfair to do an injustice to poor Paul Singer, and James Dillon was not to be outdone in compassion. He declared that he entirely sympathised with the Taoiseach's view of the extreme care necessary in these cases, but, bearing in mind all the Taoiseach had said, he wondered whether he adverted to the fact that a young man, who could be described as little else than the innocent servant of the defendant, had served fifteen months' hard labour for charges arising out of identical incidents?

Lemass, however, saw this as a separate issue and he returned to the judgement of the Court of Criminal Appeal, in which he had, to his surprise, learnt for the first time of the large number of somewhat similar cases in which the verdicts of courts had been set aside because of technical considerations of a similar character.

At this point William Norton of the Labour Party felt that it was time for him to step in and defend the working man. He asked whether or not the Taoiseach was not aware of the fact that a considerable number of honest, credulous Irish citizens had been financially plucked, and that the state's legal machine had done nothing to protect them. Its chief achievement appeared to Norton to be—and he thought others held the same view—to make a legendary character out of the chief plucker of the Irish people.

Lemass's response was to ask the deputy to keep in mind that in this community it is not merely enough to suspect someone: it must also be proved in law. This attitude provoked Gerard Sweetman to speak again and to ask if it was not an obvious fact that charges involving £800,000 were so framed, handled and dealt with that no verdict on the merits of those charges was possible.

The Taoiseach could not accept that it was an obvious fact, but Sweetman recognised an obvious fact when he saw one and asked rhetorically if it was not perfectly clear to everyone in the country, even if it was not to the Taoiseach—or he would not admit it—that what happened was that the courts were not able to give a verdict on the merits of the charges involving £800,000 as to whether they were true or false. Was it not a fact that the matters were so handled by someone that there could not be an indictment?

Lemass was prepared to admit modestly that he could not profess to have any legal knowledge, but it seemed to him that the arguments of the state counsel were the more convincing, a reply that was not good enough for William Norton, who wanted to know what happened the £2 million that the Irish public invested. Neither did it satisfy Thaddeus Lynch, who closed the debate with the sad question, 'What about poor Shanahan?'

———

The third time that Paul Singer's name cropped up in Dáil question time occurred when Noel Lemass put a question to the Minister for Posts and Telegraphs, Michael Hilliard, about the value of postage stamps sponsored by the Conference of European Postal and Telecommunications Administrations and why these stamps should not be processed in the Government's printing office.

When the minister maintained that the matter was complex and that early results could not be expected, Noel Lemass asked the minister to agree that it appeared to be a worthwhile business to get into and that any expense involved in the printing of the stamps in Ireland would be well worth while.

This was the opportunity for which James Dillon had been waiting. He jumped straight in with the remark that Mr Singer had thought so in any case and was now living in the Canary Islands. Seán MacEntee could not resist the lure of a ready joke. 'One canary was singing here today anyway,' he quipped; but it was not a joking matter for Dillon. 'He is living on my and our neighbours' money,' he insisted.

The new Taoiseach and champion hurler, Jack Lynch, spotted an opening. 'Did the deputy put something into it too?' he chortled, but he did not break through Dillon's defence. 'No, but I spent a lot prosecuting them. It cost £250,000 of public money.' Dillon then drove the *sliotar* back into the Government's part of the field, to be countered by a poor defence from Lynch. 'He was two years in jail all the same,' he muttered weakly. 'Two years!' thundered Dillon. 'He ought to have spent the rest of his life in jail!'

Irony of ironies, it was the turn of no less a person than Charles J. Haughey to put his bit in and enunciate the principle that would guide him in his future career: 'I thought Deputy Dillon was a great believer in the principle that a man is innocent until he is found guilty,' said Charles J., looking blissfully into the future. Dillon was not to be swayed by Haughey's sophistry and snapped, 'He was found guilty by a jury, but he wriggled out of it because you did not know how to do your job.'

Like an aggrieved schoolboy, Jack Lynch tried weakly to spread the blame. 'Why did you let him into the country?' Dillon's reply rang, like Cromwell's, across the chamber. 'We could not stop him. There are more rogues than he in the country. In any event, it was you who let him *out* of the country.'

Chapter 11

Tear him for his bad verses: Francis Stuart

Francis Stuart was indubitably a rogue, in the sense of a wolf of the steppes who ran away from the pack and yet from time to time howled to the sky, sniffed their odour and longed to be accepted as one of them and admired. He was not a murderer, a highwayman, a confidence trickster. There was no badness in him, but his history shows that he felt it was a grown-up thing to be an outlaw. He had his militant supporters and critics, but there do not appear to have been many who pitied him. Or perhaps they stayed silent while the reality was that he needed pity and not adulation for qualities that were not his.

There is a strong argument for the view that his questionable behaviour during the Second World War and the controversies that shadowed the end of his life were not his fault but the fault of those who used him for some purpose of their own. There were well-meaning people who felt it was their duty to retrieve him from oblivion, but unfortunately their efforts were hijacked by others with another agenda.

Francis Stuart was both a misfit and a person who needed to be noticed and talked about. As long as he was the subject of discussion, it seemed to be irrelevant whether people praised or criticised him. He portrayed himself as a man who despised worldly things, an ascetic who was above bourgeois rules, and there is no reason to believe that he did not think this to be true.

Stuart was born in Australia in 1902 to Ulster unionist parents. Like many of our rogues, he lost a parent in infancy: in his case his father committed suicide when Francis was only four months old. He was brought to Ireland to live with his grandparents but was educated in English schools, including Rugby.

In 1918 the 16-year-old Stuart met the 25-year-old Iseult MacBride, half-sister of Seán MacBride and daughter of Maude Gonne and a right-wing, anti-semitic French politician, Lucien Millevoye. Some years later he married Iseult. One version of their marriage is that Maud Gonne disapproved, and W. B. Yeats was not over-enthusiastic; another is that it was Yeats and Gonne who arranged the marriage. This latter notion is credible, as it would fit in with the belief that Stuart was an innocent, with a lifelong tendency to obey the promptings of others like a somnambulist.

Stuart took the anti-Treaty side in the Civil War and was imprisoned in Hare Park Internment Camp and the Curragh Camp, both on the Curragh in County Kildare, from August 1922 to November 1923. In the Curragh he was given the job of keeping watch for fellow-prisoners who were digging an escape tunnel, but he fell asleep and so was responsible not only for their discovery and punishment but for the capture of Seán MacEntee and other comrades who were tunnelling into the camp from the outside.

Sixteen years later, and three months after Germany and the USSR had carved up Poland, 37-year-old Stuart landed his first paid job. He was to be a lecturer at Berlin University's English department, sent there by his wife and mother-in-law. He told anyone who was curious that he had come on a mission for the IRA, but was reluctant to say to which IRA group he owed allegiance.

Stuart had some reason to claim the IRA mission. Before his departure Stephen Hayes, chief of staff of the IRA, and Jim O'Donovan, the brain behind the 1939 IRA bombing campaign in Britain (for which Seán Russell, the main proponent of the 'military wing' of the IRA, had sought support in the United States in 1936), commissioned him to request a radio transmitter from German intelligence, the Abwehr, and to ask that a German liaison officer be despatched to Ireland. Stuart claims that he was given half a piece of paper, which he had to produce when he had made contact: when the paper was fitted to its other half, his *bona fides* would be established. He claimed later that he threw away the paper in London because he was not going to indulge in 'playacting like you read about in the old spy books.' How was he expected to prove his *bona fides* in Germany? His attitude was casual. 'Either they believed me when I got to Germany or they didn't. I couldn't care less really.' This remark is significant. There is something touchingly childish about his bluff, like holding back tears when he fell and cut his knee and muttering, 'It doesn't hurt!'

Stuart's own postwar excuse for going to Hitler's Germany was that it was to gain experience as a writer. He wrote later:

When the war looked like breaking out, I didn't want to be caught here [in Ireland]. I mean, for a writer to have been all those years where nothing had ever happened, it was necessary for me to get away.

This hardly explains why he undertook the mission. As it happened, counter-intelligence would not accept that the IRA had sent this lanky, confused Irishman with an English accent until a phone call to a German professor, Abwehr agent and drinking companion of Stuart's in Dublin confirmed that Stuart was who he said he was. Later, Stuart would give Iseult's address to Hermann Görtz, a spy heading off for Ireland. He was already betraying Ireland without being aware of it.

Stuart stayed in contact with German counter-intelligence. Helmut Clissmann, head of the German Academic Exchange Service, who was under surveillance by the Irish authorities, had introduced him to Kurt Haller, who had close contacts with the person who was arranging for Seán Russell to return to Ireland and 'organise'. Russell had impeccable qualifications: he had been out in 1916 and had been one of a unit that accounted for the execution in 1920 of thirteen of the Cairo Gang, the elite team of British intelligence agents and assassins. He was Michael Collins's director of munitions in 1920 and quartermaster-general after the Civil War.

Stuart's masters approached him and suggested that he might sail secretly to Ireland on a Breton fishing boat to prepare the IRA in advance of Russell's arrival. It is not clear what Russell was to do in Ireland, but it was most probably the organising of sabotage operations, or a *coup d'état* against de Valera. In due time Russell set out for Ireland in a German submarine but died from a perforated ulcer before he reached his destination.

With Russell at the time of his death was Frank Ryan, an Irish republican and socialist. After Russell's death the mission was aborted, and Ryan had to return to Germany. Ryan, a charismatic person in his own right, had devoted his life to fighting imperialism, reaction and fascism, had taken part in the Spanish Civil War, was imprisoned in Burgos and condemned to death. His release was eventually arranged by friends but he was not permitted to return to Ireland; instead the German operatives took him to occupied France and then to Germany. He and Stuart moved in the same circles in Berlin and, no doubt out of homesickness, Ryan cultivated Stuart's friendship, but Stuart was to claim later that Ryan had been an adviser to a Colonel Veesenmayer of the ss, a Jew-exterminator, and that he (Stuart) had never liked him. Stuart was to say in 1989 that Ryan had boasted that when Germany had won the war he would be a minister in Ireland, and his comment was:

> I took this as some sort of threat to me to keep in with him. I took that very much amiss. I didn't like this 'When Germany wins the war.'

One can only suppose that Stuart was repeating what he imagined Ryan to have said, given that Ryan had risked his life to fight fascism in Spain.

Stuart also met William Joyce—Lord Haw-Haw—in the broadcasting studios and wrote scripts for him (which Joyce did not use), but he did not socialise with him.

While in Germany, Stuart enjoyed a champagne-soaked Berlin night life with senior Nazi officials but claimed many years later that he said to Frank Ryan in their presence:

> Do you know what? When this war is over, wherever I am, I hope it will be on the losing side, because if it's the winning side it will be intolerable for me. I hope I'll be among the losers and the guilty.

According to Stuart, a founder-member of the Nazi Party asked Ryan whether Stuart was joking, and Ryan answered: 'I don't know what he means, but he's certainly not joking.'

Stuart's first broadcast for the Nazi propaganda machine was woven through with deniable half-truths, beginning with the pronouncement:

I am not trying to make propaganda . . . I only hope that you now have a good idea of what is true and what is false

but ended

> we cannot nor do we desire to escape taking our share in building the new Europe . . . Ireland belongs to Europe and England does not belong to it. Our future must lie with the future of Europe and no other.

The 'New Europe' was the code name for Hitler's New Order, i.e. Nazi dictatorship, the slavery or annihilation of Jews, Slavs, Christians, communists and old-fashioned socialists and the sterilisation or murder of the handicapped, homosexuals and gypsies. Given that it could be argued that Stuart was not terribly smart, it is not impossible that he was not fully aware of the term's meaning.

Stuart linked neutrality to Easter 1916 and said that he hoped and believed that the end of the war would bring back 'our national unity, and that the struggle which began in its latter phase on that Easter morning in Dublin [would] then be, at last, at an end.' In other words, when Germany had won the war it would reward Ireland by ending partition and installing a quisling government. Once again Stuart, rather than being wilfully blind, may not indeed have appreciated what he was suggesting.

In 1942 Stuart claimed that Frank Ryan had suggested to him, and he had fully agreed, that there should be no anti-Russian bias in his weekly talks. (Stuart always seems to have used the words Russia and Russian rather than Soviet Union, USSR or Soviet.) It is understandable that Ryan, a member of the Republican Congress wing of the IRA, should take this view, in spite of his experience of the Soviet Union's treatment of its allies in Spain, but Stuart's blindness to the reality of the USSR's invasion of Poland and the Baltic states reveals an unfortunate incapacity to recognise reality.

Stuart, by his own testimony, considered that the USSR's stance in this war was 'honourable' because it had been attacked by Germany. Here again one can only dig for a benign explanation. It is quite possible that when he was deciding what was honourable behaviour he never considered the Molotov-Ribbentrop pact, or the genocide by starvation of the Ukrainian and Southern Ruthenian farmers, or the mass deportations of whole populations to central Asia, or the show trials of the highest-ranking commissars and army officers. Living, as he seems to have done all his life, in his own self-obsessed cocoon, it is quite possible that he remained unaware of the massacre of Polish soldiers in the Katyn Forest and the subsequent campaign of lies that the Allies dared not dispute, or the behaviour of the Soviet army, waiting in Praga on the other bank of the Vistula during the tragic Warsaw Rising in 1944 when the bestial slaughter of young and old, Christians and Jews, who identified each other by their Polishness, not their religion, was being carried out by Stuart's German paymasters.

Hardened as we have become, Stuart's inability to grasp, or his unfortunate blindness to, the inhuman atrocities committed by the Nazis in August and September 1944 is, to put it at its mildest, bizarre. Once again it should be stressed that Stuart, engulfed in his own private world, may, in all innocence, never have considered that such dreadful things could happen.

It is sad to have to say so, but it cannot be denied that Stuart's radio talks endorsed the evil of the Thousand-Year Reich, which would cause the deaths of 55 million people, which was determined to obtain 'lebensraum' by annihilating all 'subhuman' Slavs, and had begun in 1939 by shooting the priest, the schoolteacher, the doctor and the chemist in every Polish village that was invaded, which was already operating extermination, prison, transit, concentration and collection camps for Jews and gentiles (all of them deadly, whatever their classification). Once again one can argue that he may have known nothing about these horrors when in Berlin, but it is strange that he did not learn about them after the war, though he was by then sufficiently alert to sue the *Irish Times,* which was forced in 1999 to print the lie that he had 'never expressed anti-Semitism in his writings.' Unfortunately he lost the high moral ground when he happily pocketed the money he had squeezed from the newspaper; but perhaps he passed it on to a home for hares or old cats.

Even an impartial commentator like the novelist Colm Tóibín has admitted that passages of Stuart's work are clearly anti-semitic, adding that he found that *Black List, Section H* 'arose from something darkly and deeply rooted in his psyche—the need to betray and be seen to betray.' Tóibín also considered that this need 'arose from something else too—a passionate belief that every organised structure, and that includes liberal democracy, is rotten.' This may be so, but it can also be argued that Stuart's behaviour and blunders were the result of his innate passivity. After all, he was a writer in the 1920s and 30s, a period marked by a casual anti-semitism in popular novels that is shocking in the twenty-first century.

Given that the controversy that arose in Stuart's old age concerned his elevation to the rank of *saoi* (wise man) by Aosdána, the state-sponsored academy of writers and artists, it is excusable to wonder why he accepted his badge of office, a gold-plated torc to wear around his neck. Here again this strange acceptance can be explained by his passive attitude to life: driven to action by extreme situations, such as saving his life, it does seem that at other times he drifted in a dreamlike state with the flow of life. 'Make me a *saoi*? Okay, so make me a *saoi*.'

On the negative side it is also indisputable that Stuart's talks provided ammunition for those who claimed that Germany was assisting the IRA in its attempts to overthrow the Irish government. It is significant that when Stuart urged his listeners to 'give special preferences to those men who have shown themselves sincerely concerned for the welfare of the whole people of Ireland,' the Fianna Fáil government (which was under threat from extremist republicans such as Ailtirí na hAiséirghe and Córas na Poblachta) was impelled to lodge a complaint at the German embassy, because it and others in the know had no trouble in interpreting his references.

This was not the only time that Stuart went too far (again possibly without realising what he was doing). When he interfered in the forthcoming general election of 1943 by warning voters to vote against Fine Gael as a party that was threatening the desire of the majority for a free and united country, the broadcast provoked de Valera and his Government to protest yet again to the Foreign Office in Berlin.

Francis Stuart has been making broadcasts to this country discussing the forthcoming elections and advising people to vote against Fine Gael. Such broadcasts are an unwarrantable interference in our internal affairs and are apt to prove most embarrassing and harmful to the government. Please act immediately to ensure that nothing of the kind will be broadcast in future.

His talks continued to upset the Department of External Affairs to such an extent that Frederick Boland, assistant secretary of the department, protested to the German ambassador in Ireland that the holding up of McAteer [an IRA activist] was likely to be resented by many people [in Ireland] and to furnish a concrete example for use by those who charged Germany with aiding and abetting the IRA against the Government.

An Irish army monitor questioned Stuart's continuing claims not to be a propagandist in the light of his hardening stance, which was becoming 'steadily and openly pro-German'. He made his point when the Red Army had encircled the German Sixth Army at Stalingrad, less than a month away from General von Paulus's surrender. Stuart said:

What the men, officers and generals of the German Sixth Army are doing at Stalingrad is altogether beyond the ordinary standards of bravery.

And he added a few weeks later:

Last Wednesday the German people received news of the end at Stalingrad. If I were a German, I would be proud to belong to a nation which could produce such men. As it is, I am glad to be among them.

This is not at all how he would feel when the war ended and he was in flight and (in spite of his stated desire to be among the losers and the guilty) intent on saving his hide by not falling into the hands of the Americans or the British. Nowhere did he say how proud he would have been to belong to the thousands who died for their country in Warsaw.

So what did Stuart talk about? In 1976 he gave an interview about the broadcasts, in which he claimed: 'These broadcasts didn't usually deal with politics; they dealt very often with literature, both English and Irish, and even with other literature.' Unfortunately, the old man's memory was faulty in this instance: his broadcasts hardly ever mentioned literature. It is noteworthy that whenever he did talk about Yeats, Synge or Pearse he used the justification that 'a nation's soul is revealed in its soldiers and poets' to link them to Liam Lynch and Cathal Brugha, two hate-filled zealots; and when he had made his brief obeisance to literature he would return rapidly to such topics as Stalingrad and the failure of the German army to capture the city.

'The Irish would understand what the German people felt,' he assured his audience. 'This has moved Germany more than any other event of the war, for while such victories as the fall of Paris might be attributed to the perfection of the German war machine, this is a triumph of flesh and blood.'

One wonders if the same sense of triumph was felt by the unfortunate German conscripts who were facing years in the frozen wastes of Siberia, most of them never to return.

The facts do not support the claim that Stuart's broadcasts were merely anodyne strolls through the Celtic Twilight. On 5 August 1942 he confessed to being sick and disgusted with the Old Order under which he and his listeners had been existing and which had been created by the great financial powers in whose shadows they lived. He comforted the IRA by assuring them that the past had belonged to the politicians and the financiers but that the future would be theirs. 'Politicians and financiers' was, of course, Nazi shorthand for Jewish bankers and businessmen. Here again Stuart may genuinely have failed to realise what he was saying and how it would be interpreted. He also told his listeners that he wanted to bring something of Germany and German ideas to the people of Ireland. In 1942 that meant only one thing: Nazism, the realisation of *Mein Kampf's* promises and the elimination of all Jews, homosexuals and mentally retarded or handicapped people.

What were Stuart's private thoughts during the years that he was speaking on behalf of the Third Reich? His diary reveals that, with his permanent innocent, adolescent solipsism, he was not worrying at all about the cataclysm that had torn Europe apart; his only concerns were the opinions that critics in the English press expressed about his work, and the renewal of his Irish passport. Is it an example of his naïveté or of his passive arrogance that he was annoyed because the Irish government had refused to renew his passport and that he took time to record his suspicions that Britain had been responsible for the delay? Stuart was forty by now—nine years older than Michael Collins when he was killed—and it should be an attempt to understand him rather than to criticise him to say that there is a childish element in this tendency to find someone to blame.

Whether or not a case can be made for the assertion that Stuart had not, before 15 May 1943, stepped over an invisible line between the defence of neutrality and open encouragement of the German armed forces, he did jump over the line in one sense when he encouraged soldiers from Northern Ireland to desert and join the German army. He assured them that desertion

> has been proved to be not a very difficult thing to do in the latest form of warfare where there are no very determined lines and where there is rapid movement . . . Wait patiently until you are actually at the front and then . . . go over to the Germans or Italians . . . And I can promise you that you will be received as friends and well treated as soon as you've explained who you are . . . [This] is better than that you should get killed in fighting for the continuance of the enslavement of [your] families and friends under the government of Sir Basil Brooke.

Here again it is quite credible that he did not understand how seriously such a suggestion could be taken by the British army. That he (or his tutors) were still hoping for, or promising, a German victory is evidenced by the following reassurance:

> And I say that you will be treated with every consideration, both during the war and as long after it as you would have to remain away from your home.

As David O'Donoghue points out in *Hitler's Irish Voices*, the result would in fact have been death or a prisoner-of-war camp. Stuart's contention was also ill informed. The only European front at the time was against the Soviet Union, and no British troops were involved in that conflict. Such a call to soldiers to desert would be regarded by the British authorities as treason deserving of the death penalty.

After the war Stuart admitted that this was the case and childishly boasted that his capture by the French 'was not accidental' and that he deliberately moved to the regions of Germany that were 'obviously going to be where the French were fighting'—another strange admission from the man who wanted to be among 'the losers and the guilty'. He also admitted that it was not only luck that ensured that he did not fall into the hands of the French maquis or Italian partisans, a situation in which a shaved head would be the least of his worries and a bullet or a rope would have been the more likely outcome. His desire for abnegation had not included execution; and it was his determination not to share the martyrdom of the admirable soldiers at Stalingrad that saved his life.

It is hardly surprising that years later, with his unfortunate naïveté or the forgivable forgetfulness of old age, he was to say, when asked if he could have been put to death as a collaborator:

> It could have been possible but it would have been so unlikely really, for a neutral writer with quite a readership, who had made certain broadcasts. There was no question of treason. As a neutral you can express opinions even on a combatant's radio service. I don't say there weren't travesties of justice . . . That would have been one.

One cannot help admiring that 'quite a readership'; and it is quite possible that he considered the Nürnberg verdicts to have been such travesties of justice. Francis Stuart was a rogue, and rogues are different. It's not their fault.

Stuart would not have featured in this book if he had not been a writer, and it may be argued in his favour that, in the words of Colm Tóibín, the impulse to write novels comes from 'the dramatic revelation of matters that are hidden and dark and difficult.' This is an interesting theory, though it is easy to name many excellent novels that are gloriously free of all matter that is hidden or dark or difficult; but that is not the point. Fiction is one thing, real life another. A novel may be a white horse, but to broadcast on Zimbabwe's radio station is to gallop with the Four Horsemen of the Apocalypse, and to pettifog with the splinter of treason is to ignore an awful beam stamped *Support of a belligerent reduces neutrality to shreds.* Malcolm Lowry, the author of *Under the Volcano,* was an alcoholic rogue who revealed matter that was hidden, dark and difficult, but the only destruction in which he indulged was self-destruction.

What is sad, even frightening, is the possibility that when Stuart wrote 'Needless to say, during the whole business, I didn't take it—the support of an evil regime—into account,' he was telling the truth. In one sense that was one of the big lies that Goebbels recommended. In another, it illustrates Stuart's frightening innocence.

A slip of the tongue could at times betray his inner thinking. When warned of the danger of giving comfort to the Soviet Union, his comment was: 'Luckily, I have some fairly well-placed protectors,' i.e. there are grown-ups who will look after me. Protectors were something that this holy misfit would always manage to acquire in Germany and Ireland, before and after the war. One wonders who his German protectors were.

When asked on television in 1997 if he was sorry for what he had done, Stuart replied that he was not sorry, and when asked about regrets added, 'Non, non, je ne regrette rien, rien du tout [No, no, I regret nothing, nothing at all].' A sceptic might have asked him, 'Did you learn anything by your experience?' to which the honest and genuinely innocent answer would have been, 'Non, non. I learnt nothing.'

————

This brings us to the controversy that had arisen a year earlier when a man who publicly despised all honours and acclaim embraced the ultimate contradiction in a life chock-a-block with contradictions. This happened when he accepted elevation to the office of *saoi* of Aosdána and permitted the President of Ireland to put a golden collar around his neck. One cannot help thinking of the dog-collar that read,

I am His Majesty's dog at Kew.
Pray tell me, sir, whose dog are you?

Stuart's elevation to the rank of *saoi* deserves recording because of the controversy that surrounded it. Máire Cruise O'Brien's description, in her memoirs *The Same Age as the State*, of her treatment by Haughey's artistic apparatchiks is fascinating and not a little frightening.

In her brief connection with Aosdána, Máire Cruise O'Brien (née Máire Mhac an tSaoi) was subject to two shocks. The first was when, as a poet writing in Irish, she was voted in as a member and discovered that no-one in the Aosdána secretariat 'was willing, or perhaps competent to conduct business in Irish—in spite of the Celtic Revival terminology in which the organisation clothed its proceedings.' Her second shock occurred when she realised that Francis Stuart had been elected to the highest rank of this ersatz neo-Celtic body. So great a mistake did she consider this to be that she was compelled to propose a motion, on 26 November 1996, that Aosdána 'should define its abhorrence of the Fascist and racist views expressed throughout his life by Francis Stuart and never repudiated, and should deprive him of his office of Saoi.' At an extremely rowdy meeting she was shouted down, and her motion was defeated. Three days later she wrote in the *Sunday Independent*:

> I could wear Mr Stuart as a fellow-member and a pensioner of Aosdána, though with difficulty. I find I cannot live with him as a laureate. Of the arguments put to me before the meeting, the most important philosophically was the contention that aesthetic judgement should be independent of moral values. \

Then—bravely in the face of the implacable Stuart cultists—she told her readers that the emperor wore no clothes.

> I do not suffer from this dilemma because I do not think that Mr Stuart is a good writer. He is a fashionable writer, a notorious writer, even, in a historical context, a useful writer. He is not a good one, he does not write well. His weird, artistic voyeurism is psychologically interesting, but his style—once he departs from straightforward narration (which he does at the drop of a hat)—is depressingly Edwardian, dated and baroque, like James Stephens on a bad day, or Oscar Wilde without the wit. In the extract from his work in the *Field Day Anthology of Irish Writing*, the horrible prose blankets the immediacy of the horrors described. Mr Stuart's is the kind of prose that lends itself to the Myles na gCopaleen school of literary analysis: what colour is the moon if it is 'the colour of grey-blue decaying flesh'? Answer: grey-blue.

She pointed out that Stuart's self-proclaimed 'affection for Jews' was based on the fact that he saw them as pimps, smugglers, even quasi-collaborators, similar to an old-time Southern colonel's liking for blacks. He liked their defects—a common and not very subtle form of racism. She could well have referred to the condescending affection of the writers Somerville and Ross for their stage-Irish peasantry, in contrast to their open mockery of the emerging (and threatening) middle classes.

In a subsequent letter Máire Cruise O'Brien made a telling point.

> What we are doing is not merely forgiving Mr Stuart's past, we are exalting it ... It is ironic that we have accorded Mr Stuart that very

seal of establishment approval which he himself has always maintained was the kiss of death for the artist. He must be laughing like a drain.

The wrongheadedness of elevating Stuart was not confined to the inadequacy of the recipient as a writer of no merit: Máire Cruise O'Brien's motion was justified as a measure to nullify Aosdána's endorsement of what he, irrespective of his motives or understanding, represented—all apologists of evil.

Of course Francis Stuart, to do him justice, was a leaf that flew or fell as the wind blew. It must be stressed yet again that the fact that he qualifies as a rogue does not make him wicked. His non-conformist behaviour often seems to have developed from his inability to make his own choices. His marriage to Iseult Gonne, his journey to Germany and his other activities seem to have been done in a dreamlike state, an inner laziness or 'anything-for-peace' attitude. Later he would come to realise what he had done and try to justify it after the fact. While he can hardly be blamed for this dysfunctional behaviour, there is a valid reason for criticising the turgid novels, which appear to have been ground out in a continuous stream of self-justification and *nostalgie de la boue*. From an artistic point of view, Stuart's elevation to the rank of *saoi* diminished the coinage. Máire Cruise O'Brien's reasonable proposal supported this view: 'Give the man the money, but don't slap him on the back and tell him what a great fellow he is.'

With hindsight it is obvious that the debates about Stuart's *œuvre* focused on the wrong questions. It should not have been on the contradictions between art and morality but rather the imbalance when a writer uses cardboard figures to hawk his personal obsessions. This is not literature: it is 20 per cent propaganda and 80 per cent justification. Graham Greene's main fault was to trawl his readers through his characters' dreams. If an artist is sufficiently gifted they can get away with it. Unfortunately, Stuart did not fit into that category. Without being aware of it, he was the victim of spiritual arrogance, a self-canonised holy sinner. While sensibly showing no aversion to fame and rewards, he claimed, in his sub-Dostoevskian moods, to be justified by failure. He proclaimed that he espoused the poor and the downtrodden; but there is no evidence of his lifting a finger to help any of them. He drank to excess, cheated on his wife and his partners—but there are many who would claim that such peccadilloes only made him a better writer. At the same time one should always be suspicious of people, like Adolf Hitler, who prefer their pets to their fellow human beings.

It is interesting that there was no mention in the Aosdána bear-fight of Stuart's novel *Memorial*, an account of a paedophile novelist and his rape of an emotionally disturbed and suicidal but willing girl in her early teens. This fantasy girl, who is obsessed with small animals, is conveniently killed when she and the narrator go up to Northern Ireland from the midlands or the Aran Islands to take part, in some undefined way, in a battle with the British forces. All the other characters are wooden mouthpieces for Stuart's obsessions. The book may or may not, like all Stuart's novels, have an autobiographical element. It is loaded with semi-literate quotations from the Scriptures; and the following gems (which would be idiotic if they were not sinister) are typical:

'Do you know, Liz, there are children and adolescents in this holy land of ours for whom rape would be a lesser evil than constant exposure to the fact of small, helpless creatures, which their natural instinct is to cherish, being cruelly hunted and tortured while they have to learn to suppress their pity as a weakness?'

and

A severe hangover is a minor crucifixion. You're up on your cross in view of the respectable, wage-earning citizenry.

In other words, an attack of the dry gawks is a sacrifice that will save the world. For some unknown reason, Stuart's Lolita figure is Swiss, perhaps to make the situation more kinky.

Why should one criticise this failure on moral and literary grounds and praise Lolita? Because Nabokov was an impeccable wordsmith, and his Lolita is believable. His splendid prose, masterly word-play and detached humour take the sting out of his work. Unlike Stuart's wet dream, there is nothing prurient in it, though there is an atmosphere of intense sensuality. The plot is intriguing, and Humbert Humbert's fantasy world comes tumbling down when he meets the suburban housewife that the adult Lolita has become. Nabokov's characters are simultaneously harmless and shrewdly painted portraits that give their comic-book liveliness the necessary substance to engage the reader.

Memorial, on the other hand, is embarrassing sub-porn, a letter to a girl who is safely dead (no chance of her becoming a housewife). It combines pseudo-intellectual examinations of Scriptures and fantasies about Mary Magdalene as a dancer in a strip-tease joint—in short, an adolescent wet dream written by a seventy-year-old fantasist.

By way of contrast, another non-establishment writer and master rogue, Céline (Louis-Ferdinand Destouches), wrote about real people, avoided artificial, contrived plots and shunned patrons and approbation. There was no question of him being taken into the bosom of the Académie Française. He was refused the Prix Goncourt. Celine lived his unhappy life to the full without seeking the 'kindness of strangers'. In the French cavalry during the First World War not only did he undergo the horrors described in *Voyage au Bout de la Nuit* but was wounded in battle and earned a decoration for his actions. In spite of a very elementary education he studied to obtain a medical degree and worked for the new League of Nations before taking up a permanent position as a doctor, catering to the genuinely poor and downtrodden in Paris. He broke many literary conventions of the time and was not afraid of slang and vulgar speech. His subsequent books were innovative, chaotic and anti-heroic visions of human suffering. An anti-semitic, full of contradictions, he was simultaneously openly anti-Nazi. Though he was anything but a happy man, his works were the epitome of black comedy, where misfortunate and often terrible things are described humorously. Hyper-real and polemical, his main strength lay in his ability to discredit almost everything and yet not lose a sense of enraged humanity.

In relation to Céline, one can agree with Hilaire Belloc's self-obituary that 'his sins were scarlet, but his books were read'—and still are. Will this be the case with Francis Stuart twenty years from now?

Céline's books were about others; Stuart's were always about himself. (This is not necessarily a fault: so were Malcolm Lowry's.) In considering Céline's entitlement to roguehood, his private reactions and his works are equally important. For example, Stuart's reaction to jokes or jeers about Hitler was to wonder what Hitler really was and to identify with the Austrian monster.

Anyone who is the butt of these small city-made mentalities seemed to me to be probably someone of consequence. I began to find out something about Hitler and the new Germany and then,

of course, I was completely fired by enthusiasm, for here was someone who was freeing life from the money standards that dominated
it almost everywhere I had ever been, not excluding my own
country; here was someone who had the vision and courage to
deny financiers, politicians and bankers [i.e. Jews] the right to rule.
Nor did the word dictator frighten me—I saw that as it was. Our
lives were dominated by a group of financial dictators and it
seemed to me at least preferable to be ruled by one man whose sin-
cerity for the welfare of his people could not be doubted than by a
gang whose only concern was the market price of various com-
modities in the world markets.

When it was no longer profitable to support the dead Führer,
Stuart's campaign of denial began. This does not necessarily mean
that he was clever enough to switch horses when it suited him: it
may well be that he got things in perspective. On the other hand, it
does seem that his first instinct was to whitewash his role in the Nazi
propaganda machine.

In April 1946 he turned to Basil Liddell Hart, the well known writer
on military topics, who had praised one of his pre-war novels.
Unfortunately for those who would try to be understanding, he began
with what English schoolchildren (and possibly Tony Blair) call
'porkies' (short for the rhyming slang 'pork pies'—lies):

> Your help would be especially valuable. As you know . . . I was
> deeply opposed to Nazism and state tyranny, and my experience
> during the war only deepened this opposition. It is not the hard-
> ship of detention here, but also the hold-up in that work which I
> believe I could do now, that is hard to bear with patience.

When, in October 1946, he was rearrested by the French, Madeleine
(Gertrude?) Meissner, his companion and guardian angel, also wrote
to Liddell Hart.

> Please, please dear sir help him! Francis Stuart has such a fine and
> rare soul, the influence of which humanity has great need.

Sympathetic though one might be to Stuart, one cannot help feeling
that this is going a little too far. It is easy to love the masses; it is

harder to be kind to individuals. That said, we must recognise that it is of the nature of rogues to have undeserved luck. There is no doubt that Stuart's second wife, Madeleine (Gertrude) Meissner, was a saint who got work for him in Germany and, as a cleaning woman, supported him in London.

In Stuart's defence one could say that his desire to be an outlaw, to be loathed by well-meaning liberal people, was not a disguise. He longed for the dock, to be accused in front of everybody and despised in public, while obsessed all the time with his own righteousness. It may be that he was fighting against guilt arising from his father's suicide. He longed for public disapproval as much as he longed for (and won) the love and support of a small group of friends. He also, in his own contradictory way, longed for fame as a novelist and man of letters.

A very fair and balanced view of Stuart may be found in an honest review by Colm Tóibín of *The Wartime Broadcasts of Francis Stuart*, edited by Brendan Barrington—fair, because Tóibín begins with a statement of his admiration for Stuart as a writer and his support of Stuart's elevation to the rank of *saoi*. He also admits that *Black List Section H's* favour was hard to win and that

> the book was not well written . . . the contempt in it certainly implied a contempt for liberal and democratic values as well as for many people . . . and there was something oddly forced about H's outlaw status.

There are critics who state that the book, contrary to the views of many, is not autobiography, and their arguments are convincing. There are some who believe that Stuart 'went to Berlin to be cut off from conventional demands on his feelings and to find himself in isolation,' a view that does not chime with David O'Donoghue's remark, in *Hitler's Irish Voices*, that 'Stuart was settling well into his new life,' or with the St Patrick's Day party held in the Hotel Kaiserhof, not far from Hitler's Chancellery, where Stuart entertained diplomats, writers, a national newspaper editor, the head of the German Red Cross and a representative of the Irish legation and his secretary. Stuart was not bearing witness to atrocities when he was making a threesome for golf with the Irish representatives in Berlin, nor was he in isolation when he visited night clubs and drank champagne with 'rare and highly influential' members of the Nazi Party.

Brendan Barrington also expresses some doubt about the emperor's clothes.

> Stuart's allegiances to the anti-Treaty side in the Irish Civil War and to the Third Reich in the Second World War have usually been explained as arising from non-political forces in his psyche: a sense of adventure, a compulsion to betray, a mystical desire to suffer. These forces were undoubtedly present but they existed alongside a political consciousness that was far more highly developed, and also rather more discriminating and conventional, than has generally been recognised. The wartime broadcasts . . . are concerned primarily with politics, and could not have been written by someone as politically naive, or gormless, or blindly revolutionary as Stuart has usually been depicted as being.

Barrington also examines Stuart's claim in 1996 that he had 'spoken and written several million words in my life. No one could ever point to a sentence of mine that was or is anti-Semitic,' and counters this claim with a pamphlet that Stuart wrote for the IRA in 1924, when he was twenty-two:

> Austria, in 1921, had been ruined by the war, and was far, far poorer than Ireland is today, for besides having no money she was overburdened with innumerable debts. At that time Vienna was full of Jews, who controlled the banks and the factories and even a large part of the Government; the Austrians themselves seemed about to be driven out of their own city.

Ireland should overcome the British influence, Stuart suggested, as Austria had overcome the Jewish influence.

Casual and less than casual anti-semitism survives in all types of writing by Stuart from the 1930s forward. He even made anti-semitic comments in letters to his wife from Germany in 1939 (these are quoted in Geoffrey Elborn's biography, published in 1990).

What is unfortunate—though not surprising, in the light of the enormous personal affection that the elderly Stuart inspired—is that so many writers and scholars have been enthusiastic participants in this re-imagining, creating a myth of Stuart that is far more palatable to contemporary sensibilities than the literary and political persona of the man who wrote and delivered the talks printed in Barrington's collection.

Barrington's balanced case, having considered all the evidence, is that the holy fool, the awkward, apolitical and damaged figure of H in *Black List, Section H* is an invention, a fictional disguise for a more political and nastier self. Barrington found Stuart's efforts at patriotism to be ridiculous and quotes Stuart's assertion that

> if a committee of six average Irishmen, let us say a farmer or two, a National University student, a Civic Guard and an IRA man, were formed into a committee with sovereign powers to settle all the present problems of the world, they would make a far better job of it than Churchill and Roosevelt and company.

A strong argument could be made that this nasty image is the result of a lack of development rather than a conscious wickedness.

Finally, to put the whole question of Stuart and his broadcasts in context, it is worth while remembering that on 2 August 1942, the day after Stuart noted in his diary that he had written the first of his weekly talks, two Carmelite nuns, Edith Stein (described as 'a witness to God's presence in a world where God is absent') and her sister, Rosa, were arrested by the Gestapo in the chapel of the Echt Convent in the Netherlands. The sisters, born into a Jewish family, had, like Francis Stuart, converted to Catholicism. On 7 August, with 985 other Jews, they were deported to Auschwitz. A few days before her deportation Edith had dismissed the possibility of a rescue. 'Do not do it!' she told those who wanted her to escape. 'Why should I be spared? Is it not right that I should gain no advantage from my Baptism? If I cannot share the lot of my brothers and sisters, my life, in a certain sense, is destroyed.'

Her last words in Echt were addressed to Rosa: 'Come, we are going for our people.' Four days after Francis Stuart's first broadcast, Edith Stein, her sister and the other Jewish victims were gassed to death.

Chapter 12

The tribunal rogues: Charles Haughey, Des Traynor, Patrick Gallagher, Ray Burke, Liam Lawlor

W hile tribunals of inquiry are accepted in Irish life today as an integral variation on bread and circuses, they are not a new phenomenon but have been in operation since at least 1925, when they began with an investigation of retail prices. In the following year they dealt with the matter of ports and harbours, and in 1928 a tribunal inquired into the shooting of a Timothy Coughlan.

From 1929 food seems to have been the abiding interest, and tribunals were appointed to decide whether or not the mixing of maize meal and maize products with home-grown cereals would be in the national interest and in 1934 on how to treat the marketing of butter, pig production, and the grading of fruit and vegetables.

Two tribunals were held in relation to disasters: a fire in Pearse Street in 1936 and another at St Joseph's Orphanage, Cavan, in 1943. The 1940s saw tribunals that would be more familiar to the 21st-century public: an inquiry in 1943 into dealings in Great Southern

Railway shares, allegations in 1946 concerning a parliamentary secretary, Dr Con Ward, and the disposal of Locke's Distillery in 1947.

Ten years later there was an inquiry into cross-channel freight rates;
and it would be another ten years before the death of a man in Garda
custody would be the subject of a tribunal. This was followed two years
later by an examination of a television programme on illegal money-
lending and, six years after that, by one on allegations made by two Dáil
deputies against the Minister for Local Government.

The money really started rolling in for the men in wigs with the
Whiddy Island disaster in 1979, the fire at the Stardust Club, Artane,
Dublin, in 1981, and the 'Kerry Babies' case in 1984. Since then there
have been:

(1) the Tribunal of Inquiry into the Beef-Processing Industry, 1994,
which investigated alleged irregularities in the way the beef industry
was being operated,

(2) the Tribunal of Inquiry into the Blood Transfusion Service
Board, 1997, which investigated the infection of large numbers of
people in the 1970s and 80s by contaminated blood products,

(3) the Tribunal of Inquiry into Payments to Politicians (Dunne's
Stores), 1997, otherwise the McCracken Tribunal, which investigated
payments to politicians, particularly Charles J. Haughey and Michael
Lowry,

(4) the Mahon Tribunal (formerly the Flood Tribunal), to investigate payments to politicians in the context of planning decisions,

(5) the Moriarty Tribunal, which inquired into payments to politicians, including Charles J. Haughey,

(6) the Lindsay Tribunal, to inquire into the infection with HIV and
hepatitis C of persons with haemophilia, and

(7) the Laffoy Commission, to examine claims of child abuse in
industrial schools.

Whether or not it is part of the definition of the word, it is
definitely a characteristic of rogues that their activities cause harm,
pain or suffering to others. When one is describing rogues and their
activities, the temptation is to concentrate on the immediate damage
they cause, but the consequential damage should not be ignored. In
the case of the tribunal rogues, serious harm and suffering was certainly identified with regard to the child victims of industrial schools,
those who were infected by contaminated blood and those who were
infected with HIV and hepatitis C.

But when summing up the consequences of roguery, consideration should be given to indirect effects, such as the cost to the taxpayer, which has been considerable. On this topic a fascinating paper, entitled 'Tribunals of inquiry: Want not, waste not?', was presented to the annual conference of the Dublin Economics Workshop in Kenmare in 1999 by Frank Barry of the Department of Economics, National University of Ireland, Dublin, and John O'Dowd of the Faculty of Law in the same institution. This paper is essentially an examination of the question of costs in tribunals. One of the topics examined is the manner in which lawyers' fees are calculated and paid, which might cause the words 'legal rogues' to trip off the tongue of the man or woman in the street.

Barry and O'Dowd are uneasy about the possibility of a monopoly being exercised but soften their approach by recognising that a certain 'monopoly power is a by-product of the way we (or, more accurately, the lawyers) have set up our legal system.'

The government's view of tribunals is equally instructive.

> Tribunals of Inquiry are established by resolution of the Houses of the Oireachtas to inquire into matters of urgent public importance. *It is not a function of Tribunals to administer justice, their work is solely inquisitorial.* [My emphasis.] Tribunals are obliged to report their findings to the Oireachtas. They have the power to enforce the attendance and examination of witnesses and the production of documents relevant to the work in hand. Tribunals can consist of one or more people, a lay person, or non-lawyer may be the Sole member of a Tribunal. Tribunals can sit with or without Assessors (experts in the subject concerning the Tribunal). Assessors are not Tribunal members. Sittings are usually public but can, at the Tribunal's discretion, be held privately.

So much for the official line; but Barry and O'Dowd point out that, although they (and, no doubt, most other people) would prefer tribunals to limit their scope to the inquisitorial, i.e. to establishing a narrative of the events that have caused public concern and nothing more, tribunals

> almost invariably degenerate into the adversarial, in other words, into duels between the prosecution and the defence which are not

intended to unearth the truth, the whole truth and nothing but the truth but to establish a particular case, on the one hand and to demolish it, on the other, like any contentious litigation in the Common Law system.

Barry and O'Dowd remark ruefully that such a gladiatorial contest 'again appears to be fundamental to the way in which the Irish legal system works,' and they quote from a comment on the record of the Employment Appeals Tribunal.

While the procedures of the Tribunal were intended to be informal, speedy and inexpensive, the increasing involvement of the legal profession . . . has tended to make the hearings more formal, pro-longed and costly, with an over-emphasis on legal procedures and technicalities.

The McCracken Tribunal was an early victim of this approach. It began by summoning witnesses to give sworn evidence in private sessions, before the public phase, but was prohibited from proceeding in this manner as a result of a challenge by Liam Lawlor. The great advantage of the aborted 'McCracken method' would have been that there would be no danger of an abuse of the subject's 'constitutional right to a good name,' and, accordingly, there would have been less excuse for lawyers to stonewall and run up costs.

Professor Gwynn Morgan of the National University of Ireland, Cork, pointed out in the *Irish Times* on 18 December 1999 that tribunals are merely fact-finding bodies, not rights or liability-determining bodies. They should not, therefore, allow the same rights to their subjects as they would be granted in the adversarial climate of a court of law, and con-sequently the absence of the need to protect such rights with the same ferocity would, as a result, significantly reduce the costs of the procedure.

Barry and O'Dowd went on to compare the Beef Tribunal and the famous O. J. Simpson murder trial. They demonstrated that the legal costs awarded to Larry Goodman in the beef tribunal amounted in the end to £6 million (although the original bill had been £9 million), whereas the fees paid to Simpson's spectacular dream-team of leading American attorneys was the equivalent of £1.6 million; but in poor little Ireland 'the State felt itself required to pay the legal expenses of both sides.'

In addition, Barry and O'Dowd draw attention to the fact that

[Judge] Hamilton, in the Beef Tribunal, judged that, though the Goodman group appeared to be guilty of some wrongdoing, they were not guilty of many of the charges laid against them and so he awarded costs to everyone (i.e. against the taxpayer), though it remains unclear as to the wrongdoing of which we (the taxpayers) had been found guilty.

Writing about the tribunal in the *Irish Times* in 1997, Professor Morgan argued that such an order was legally questionable, as it treated the tribunal as if it were a criminal trial. How interesting that, not too long afterwards, Liam Hamilton was awarded the post of Chief Justice!

In May 2005 the Law Reform Commission published a *Report on Public Inquiries, Including Tribunals of Inquiry*. It recommended procedural changes concerning the selection of an appropriate type of inquiry, drafting appropriate terms of reference, the rights of individuals and organisations to be heard and represented, and the awarding of legal costs.

On 1 September 2005 the Minister for Justice, Equality and Law Reform, Michael McDowell, announced a draft bill to consolidate and modernise the law regarding tribunals of inquiry. The main features were that the process for setting and amending terms of reference should be clarified, and a tribunal would be required to produce, within three months, a statement of estimated costs and the duration of the tribunal. This statement would subsequently be amended if there were any significant development requiring change. The Government, for stated reasons and following a resolution of both houses of the Oireachtas, would have the power to dissolve a tribunal; new provisions were to be set out governing the taking of evidence, including the costly practice of orally 'reading in' evidence already available in written form and not disputed; the situation with regard to granting legal representation before a tribunal would be clarified; the responsible minister would be given the power to request from the tribunal an interim report on the general progress of an inquiry, or of a particular aspect of an inquiry; tribunals' reports would be admissible in civil cases and the facts in a report or the opinions expressed would constitute *prima facie* evidence, unless the contrary was shown; and the situation with regard to the awarding of costs would be clarified Co operation with the tribunal would remain the principal determinant for an award of costs. No provision would be made for continuing 'stage' payments to third parties; and regulations to be made by the Minister for Justice, with the consent of the Minister for Finance, would set out the maximum amounts of legal costs recoverable.

Unfortunately, the bill does not seem to have found its way onto the statute book. It may be at its second reading.

CHARLES J. HAUGHEY

With one bound our hero was free. The miraculous escape was from the Circuit Criminal Court on 26 June 2000, where the former 'Boss' Haughey had been the leading player in *The People (at the suit of the Director of Public Prosecutions) v. Charles Haughey,* charged with obstruction of the McCracken Tribunal. One of the instruments of his release was a headline in the *Irish Independent* of 27 May 2000: 'Jail Haughey, says Harney, telling of bids to silence her.'

The Tánaiste had been, to put it mildly, indiscreet. She was reported to have stated that the accused should be convicted, that her assessment of disclosures that big business had provided him with £8½ million over seventeen years was that he should spend time in prison, that his age should not protect him and, finally, that an enormous number of 'shocking revelations' had passed over her desk in the Department of Enterprise, Trade and Employment as a result of thirteen separate inquiries that she had instituted.

Mr Justice Haugh noted the prosecution's insistence that the publicity was not such as would give rise to a real or substantial risk that Haughey would not receive a fair trial, as he was not being charged with corruption but that he had knowingly misled the McCracken Tribunal—an entirely different matter. However, he agreed with the defence that there was a real and substantial risk that Haughey would not receive a fair trial at that time, which did not mean that the matter could not be brought up again. His order, accordingly, was that all further proceedings be stayed without the leave of the court. Yet another lucky escape for Charles J. Haughey.

Many successful people, particularly men, claim that they made their own luck. Other seeming winners, determined to shape their own destiny, end up by attracting bad luck. Charles Haughey, in spite of years of apparent success, could be said to belong to the second group.

Charles Haughey was born in Castlebar, County Mayo, on 16 September 1925. His father was a soldier in the new Free State army. From the Christian Brothers, Charles went to University College, Dublin, and King's Inns and qualified as an accountant and a barrister. He would certainly have flourished in the latter profession.

At the age of twenty-six he married Maureen Lemass, the daughter of the Tánaiste, Seán Lemass—a wise move. Six years later he was elected a member of Dáil Éireann and two years after that was given the post of parliamentary secretary to the Minister for Justice. From 1961 to 1964 he was Minister for Justice—rapid promotion. He transferred to Agriculture for two years and moved on to Finance in 1966. His stay in that department lasted for four years and might have been longer if he had not been demoted because of allegations that he had been involved in the illegal importing of arms for use in Northern Ireland. The first instance of bad luck.

Following six years of chicken dinners with the rural Fianna Fáil cumainn, he returned to the fold and was appointed Minister for Health and Social Welfare in 1977, from which pinnacle he and his supporters began a campaign of destabilisation of the Taoiseach, Jack Lynch—behaviour that was quite alien to the Fianna Fáil ethos. As it happened, Lynch by then was not keen to continue in power. Two years later, in the contest for Taoiseach, Haughey defeated his old friend and neighbour George Colley and on 11 December 1979 took office, an elevation that intensified internal divisions in Fianna Fáil that would last as long as he was in the Dáil.

Once again his period in office was only two years. The following general election was blighted by more bad luck. Fianna Fáil lost two traditional seats to H Block candidates and was deprived of its overall majority, but Haughey's personal luck turned when the new Fine Gael-Labour government fell apart after seven months or so. On this occasion he copperfastened his lucky streak by brokering a deal not only with an independent, Tony Gregory, but also with Sinn Féin the Workers' Party. He was back in power without an overall majority but managed to cling on for nine months. The tide had begun to turn and the ground had been laid for a degree of confusion within the monolithic Fianna Fáil party that had not been known since its foundation.

After the collapse of Haughey's Government in December 1982, scandals arose about the tapping of journalists' phones, and the party slid into disarray with heaves and rumours of heaves, culminating in the expulsion from the party, on an open vote, of Des O'Malley on the grounds of 'conduct unbecoming'. It would be five years before Fianna Fáil got back into power, and when it did succeed it was without an overall majority. This was a truly historic moment, as Fianna Fáil would never again be able to form a Government on its own, even though a refusal to go into coalition was one of Fianna Fáil's 'core values' and Haughey himself had earlier declared that 'coalition Governments go against every fibre of my being.'

Haughey deserves some credit for laying the foundations for the Celtic Tiger, but in fairness it must be said that it could not have happened if Alan Dukes, leader of Fine Gael, had not announced his 'Tallaght strategy', an undertaking by his party to support the Government in its efforts to work towards prosperity. The enormity of this concession, putting country before party, contrasted with Haughey's automatic impulses in opposition to resist every proposal of the ruling party. In succession he fought against the vital Anglo-Irish Agreement, a much-needed divorce referendum and Fine Gael's earlier timid attempts to stimulate economic growth.

In April 1989, gambling on achieving the now elusive majority, Haughey called a snap election and lost four seats. He did not even get a majority in the vote for Taoiseach. Irony of ironies, the bitter fruit was a coalition cobbled together with the Progressive Democrats, a party headed by former Fianna Fáil deputies: Des ('conduct unbecoming') O'Malley, Mary Harney, Bobby Molloy and Pearse Wyse. The tide was beginning to turn, and in 1990 Haughey's candidate for President, Brian Lenihan, was defeated by Mary Robinson.

'Events, dear boy, events,' was Harold Macmillan's explanation of the gremlins that upset political applecarts. Events cancelled Haughey's hope of taking his rightful place ahead of Daniel O'Connell or Charles Stewart Parnell. The aura of the Arms Trial lingered, making him an untouchable in the eyes of the unionist community and a suspect to the British government. His silence in relation to the actions of the IRA in the nine years before he became leader of Fianna Fáil and Taoiseach had been interpreted as support, but when he got power his actions alienated republican supporters without gaining new friends.

Haughey had two personae: the critic, knocker and objector in opposition and the copycat of formerly despised policies when in government. He had an initial success with Margaret Thatcher in 1980 and elevated relations to, in his own words, a 'new plane'. Neutral observers give him credit for helping to lay the foundations of the Anglo-Irish Agreement that would eventually be adopted. Unfortunately, enough was never enough, and what he convinced himself he could achieve was always beyond the limits of feasibility. This inability to reach unattainable goals generated childish tantrums and erratic behaviour that, more often that not, were destructive.

Before the Arms Trial had been forgotten and he had been taken back into the inner fold of Fianna Fáil, Haughey had pushed a policy that called on the British government to encourage the unity of Ireland by agreement and to declare its intention to make an ordered withdrawal from Northern Ireland. However, once he became Taoiseach he changed course: not only did he announce that his aims were to secure Irish unity by peaceful means and to maximise border security but he also condemned the Provisional IRA and its campaign of violence.

Luck was on his side: British army casualties in the North were mounting, as were security costs. The United States was increasing political pressure, and Margaret Thatcher was persuaded to enter into dialogue. The two leaders met and at first got on well together. He agreed to develop 'new and closer political co-operation between the two governments.' Unfortunately, they were at cross-purposes. Thatcher wanted an internal Northern settlement, but the SDLP, given false hopes by the Irish Government, would not agree: they wanted a broader political initiative.

Seán Donlon, the Irish ambassador in Washington, was unpopular with Sinn Féin and militant Irish-Americans, so Haughey tried to remove him. Though he did not succeed, this abortive move was interpreted as a blatant sop to the Provos.

'Events' took centre stage when Haughey was orchestrating the Dublin Castle summit of December 1980. They began in the Maze Prison in Northern Ireland. Thatcher insisted on 'criminalising' Provisional IRA prisoners and removing the rights due to political prisoners. Hunger strikes began, ten prisoners died and Haughey lost the next general election. Before these tragic events took place, Thatcher and Haughey agreed in Dublin Castle to devote their next meeting to 'special consideration of the totality of relationships within these islands.' The Minister for Foreign Affairs, Brian Lenihan, then put his foot in it by stating that all political options were now open, which was not how Thatcher saw things. Any suggestion, she implied,

that the government of Northern Ireland and its constitutional status
could be altered would be 'damaging and counter-productive'.
Haughey's response was, on the one hand, to put her at ease with
references to the consent of the majority in Northern Ireland while
continuing to hammer home the notion of Northern Ireland as a
'failed political entity'.

In the Republic, the economy was crumbling. In 1981 inflation and
unemployment were both rising, and Haughey called a general election.
Once again 'events' were waiting in the wings. Two hunger-strikers were
elected to Dáil Éireann. Fianna Fáil lost its majority, Haughey lost
power and the republicans despised him. However, he took comfort
in his knowledge of why these disasters had come about: it was all
Thatcher's fault!

'Back in opposition' equalled 'back to hard-line rhetoric.' Fianna
Fáil became the 'Republican Party' once again; it could not lose votes
to Sinn Féin. In the process, Haughey excoriated Garret FitzGerald for
suggesting that there was a need to dismantle sectarian laws in the
Republic and accused him of abandoning an aspiration to unity.
Haughey was once again facing up to the reality that his leadership of
Fianna Fáil had never been secure—the second appearance of the new
phenomenon in a political party that had always looked on itself as a
'family'. The first appearance had been when he attempted to sabotage
Jack Lynch. There were moves against him now, but they were timid
and unsuccessful.

When Thatcher went to war with Argentina over the Falklands,
Haughey saw an opportunity to vent his spleen against her and
exploited Ireland's membership of the UN Security Council to spit in
Britannia's eye. He broke ranks with the then EEC countries by
discontinuing sanctions, an action that led to the tapping of the
telephones of the journalists Geraldine Kennedy and Bruce Arnold
and of Bruce Arnold's wife, Mavis. Anglo-Irish relations sank to a new
low. Later, his extreme demands for the New Ireland Forum would
split Fianna Fáil and prepare the way for the Progressive Democrats.
It was about this time that Geraldine Kennedy was the victim of a
'threat campaign' carried out by Fianna Fáil bully-boys and that
Government members were required to pledge their loyalty to
Haughey as their leader.

In his usual way of approving when in power and denigrating
when on the opposition bench, knocking anything that he could not

claim as his own, Haughey refused to accept the terms of the Anglo-Irish Agreement of 1985, which Fine Gael and the Labour Party had brought about with the support of the Social Democratic and Labour Party (SDLP). He threatened to repudiate it when he was back in power and sent Brian Lenihan to the United States to campaign against it. Unfortunately for him, Mary Harney and Des O'Malley voted with the coalition Government. By now Haughey had run out of choices, and in the end it would be Albert Reynolds who would change Fianna Fáil policy and adopt 'political consent as a necessary part of any Northern settlement.'

While all this was going on, Haughey was mysteriously becoming wealthier and wealthier and his life-style was increasingly the subject of rumour and conjecture. Though he clearly loved to flaunt his wealth, he always insisted that his financial affairs were out of bounds for journalists. Almost twenty years later the Moriarty Tribunal would be given estimates from the Revenue Commissioners that Haughey's expenditure from 1977 to 1997 was possibly £9.9 million and certainly not less than £6 million—quite large sums for a man whose only income was apparently his salary as TD and, from time to time, Taoiseach. The Revenue Commissioners negotiated with Haughey's agents and settled for a figure of £6.9 million, which they agreed could be viewed as representative of the total gifts he had received in that period.

Ben Dunne had given him £1.3 million, which enabled him to entertain his expensive mistress in the best restaurants in Ireland and abroad, to buy designer clothes and spend thousands on Charvet shirts, custom-made for him in Paris—all this at a time when many people were paying up to 65 per cent income tax.

In spite of this prosperity his luck ran out once again, and 'events' reared their ugly heads in 1992 when a former Fianna Fáil TD and Minister for Justice, Seán Doherty, appeared on the late-night television chat show 'Nighthawks'. In an apparently off-the-cuff interview he discussed phone-tapping at length with the presenter, Shay Healy. At a subsequent press conference he stated that Haughey had known that the phones of Geraldine Kennedy and Bruce and Mavis Arnold were being tapped in 1982 and added that he had personally handed over transcripts of the tapes to his leader.

How much money Haughey received from benefactors will probably never be known. The Moriarty Tribunal was told that the Revenue

Commissioners had accepted a payment of £3.94 million (€5 million) in 2003 by way of settlement of an estimated tax bill of £5.5 million (€6.98 million). At the time it was the largest settlement ever made by a taxpayer. Haughey told the Revenue Commissioners that he had received no gifts of money since 1997 and was living on borrowings from a building society. In 2003 he sold his home, Abbeville, to private developers for a reported €35 million.

It is estimated that C. J. Haughey spent more than €12½ million during his time as a politician. He certainly made reluctant tax settlements of more than €6 million, which may have been the result of 'sweetheart deals'. He was lucky, as the Moriarty Tribunal could have arrived at a liability for €14 million. Over twenty years the Taoiseach had never declared a single payment made to him. His potential liability for capital acquisitions tax was €13.9 million, but, given that he might not have long to live, the Revenue Commissioners accepted that any relevant payments were gifts. They knew he would fight them all the way and considered that this inadequate settlement was better than drowning in a legal quagmire.

When Haughey died, on 13 June 2006, media comment often fell into the San Andreas fault between his achievements and his private life, when in fact the two moved together and affected each other. The more serious writers concentrated on his political failures and triumphs as leader of his party. References to his character were made, but somehow a reason was always found to consider criticism inappropriate at any given time. Some commentators described him as a 'lovable rogue'—an epithet that, with its connotations of a cuddly misfit, was never appropriate in Haughey's case. He was capable of charm when things were going his way but vicious when he was opposed.

The fact that some of Haughey's obituaries contained references to Frank Sinatra and the song 'My Way' linked the former Taoiseach, consciously or unconsciously, with the infantile amorality of the selfish child who, consumed by his own egoism, is indifferent to the feelings or needs of others. Like many of our rogues, his character betrayed a flagrant insecurity that had to be bolstered by the trappings of what he saw as the aristocratic life, membership of the Horse Show set and an anachronistic aping of the Anglo-Irish ascendancy.

Patrick Gallagher, one of his benefactors, confirmed this when he said:

Haughey was financed in order to create the environment which the Anglo-Irish enjoyed and that we as a people could never aspire to . . . Someone had to live in the big house.

At the end of the day, Haughey's story is one of tragedy. The last nine years of his life were consumed by the unravelling of the tapestry that he had woven and, fight and lie as he might, it became the sorry farce of the Wizard of Oz exposed as a carnival barker, the Medici of Donnycarney, revealed as a little man willing to make expansive gestures with other people's money.

Tiger Roche was an unfortunate rogue. Fighting Fitzgerald was a psychopath. Redmond O'Hanlon had the excuse that outlawry was the only way to deal with an oppressive regime. Bishop Hervey was a spoiled child who treated the world as his toy. Myler Magrath was a survivor. What they all had in common was that they were larger-than-life figures, doing what many of us might do in our fantasies but would not have the courage or audacity to carry out. Charles Haughey's hero was Napoleon Bonaparte, which tells us something about him.

It will take time before he can be categorised. When Haughey died, in 2006, the coverage was, as might be expected, mixed. The economist and broadcaster David McWilliams wrote that Haughey

dominated Irish political and financial life during the least successful economic period this State experienced . . . At home, his approach was pure populism—no matter how down and dirty it had to be. Abroad, it was all pomp and propriety—nationalism at home and European solidarity abroad.

A typical story about Haughey recalls an occasion when he was holding talks with Tomás Mac Giolla, president of Sinn Féin the Workers' Party. Haughey kept referring to Mac Giolla as 'Mr President,' while his own entourage kept saying 'Yes, Boss' and 'Right, Boss.' During a break Haughey put them straight, and when the talks resumed they fell over themselves to refer to him as 'President' (i.e. of Fianna Fáil).

Peter Murtagh of the *Irish Times* and joint author (with Joe Joyce) of *The Boss* took the view that Haughey, to keep himself in power, created a climate of fear and intimidation, demanding and getting from the majority obsequious loyalty. In October 1982 he insisted that every member of the Government sign a written declaration of loyalty to him personally. This was when Des O'Malley's days within the party began to be numbered. Murtagh also claimed that Haughey believed that he should be leader of Fianna Fáil for his lifetime, or until he hand-picked his grateful successor. He represented Ireland, and to oppose him was treason. He used the Garda Síochána for personal political ends, particularly in relation to phone-tapping, which ended with the resignation of two senior officers.

Murtagh's description of Haughey's Ireland was not the Ireland of Saints and Scholars or of Gaelic chieftains but a country in the grip of 'cronyism, backhanders, golden circles, political strokes and [the] absence of principle in public affairs.'

Tales about folk heroes or villains are an oral way of passing on the story of a generation or a country. Shane Coleman, political correspondent of the *Sunday Tribune,* writing shortly after Haughey's state funeral, put his finger on this point. 'His flaws and strengths said more about Ireland in the second half of the 20th century than we might wish to acknowledge.'

The journalist Richard Delevan saw Haughey's contribution in a different light from that promoted by his supporters.

With the exception of some of the stewardship of Haughey's father-in-law, Seán Lemass, Ireland had been shooting itself in the foot economically since the foundation of the state. Charley Haughey happened to be left holding the gun when the country finally couldn't afford any more bullets.

Delevan's summing up does not see Haughey as a glamorous rogue to be emulated.

We do ourselves no favours if we let observers believe Haughey to be the first of a new current breed, rather than the last of an old one—and one whose ways of doing business should be buried with him.

This brings us to the sordid matter of the misappropriation of funds collected to pay for a liver transplant in the United States for Haughey's friend and colleague Brian Lenihan. In the conclusions of his 700-page report, Mr Justice Michael Moriarty said that it gave him no satisfaction to find that Haughey 'deliberately sought to raise funds in addition to what he knew or must have known was required to meet the cost of Mr Lenihan's treatment, and that he ultimately applied part of those funds for his own use.' Moriarty was satisfied that Haughey was fully aware of his pivotal role in all these matters and that his attempts to attribute responsibility to others in relation to the Lenihan funds were 'reprehensible'. It was clear that there was 'no proper or effective system put in place to record funds collected for the benefit of Mr Lenihan.' The 'haphazard system' of collecting and recording funds 'facilitated the misappropriation of funds by Mr Haughey as did the determination that such funds should be lodged to the Leader's Allowance account.'

Haughey had begun a campaign to raise funds for Lenihan in late May 1989, when he knew that the Voluntary Health Insurance (vhi) Board would make an *ex gratia* payment of £50,000 towards the cost of Lenihan's treatment. Haughey also knew that the additional expenses to be met could amount to £100,000. He nonetheless fixed £150,000 to £200,000 as the figure to be raised. Moriarty found it to be evident that Haughey had personally misappropriated a donation of £20,000 made by Dr Edmund Farrell for Lenihan's benefit, and that he took a series of steps to conceal his actions, including channelling the proceeds of the cheque through the bank account of Celtic Helicopters Ltd. He had also personally misappropriated £25,000 contributed to the Lenihan fund by Mark Kavanagh on behalf of Custom House Docks Development Company Ltd when he remitted that cheque to the Fianna Fáil party as a donation to party funds while retaining a further £75,000 provided for that purpose by Kavanagh. The chairman also found that Haughey's evidence to the tribunal in relation to the Lenihan funds and the use of those funds for his personal benefit was 'less than candid'.

An amusing aspect of the Haughey regime was revealed by Mary Raftery, a producer with rte's current affairs programme 'Today Tonight', who was assigned to cover Fianna Fáil's 1986 ard-fheis. When she went into Haughey's office he shook her hand and, without speaking, clicked his fingers. A cavalcade of lackeys came in bearing suits, ties and shirts. 'Take her in there and get her to pick out what I should wear for the speech,' he ordered them. Raftery's inner reaction was that this was a strange way to treat rte, a neutral national broadcaster. It was not part of her job description to make the leader of any political party shine before the public. Her impression was that Haughey and his party felt that, as with everything else in the country, they owned RTE. She did not pick out any suit, tie or shirt!

This was not, however, the first such incident. It was the practice at ard-fheiseanna and other political meetings to set the cameras at eye level, as a neutral and fair way to capture speakers. A camera filming from below gives the speaker an aura of power and importance. The Fianna Fáil organiser had no time for eye-level shots. An enormous photograph of Haughey had been set up behind the podium, and the camera was to take its picture from a low angle. A silent battle followed. Raftery would give orders to her crew that the camera podium should be raised to eye level; whenever she turned to take care of some other matter it would mysteriously drop.

Later the same year RTE's advertising revenue was capped to make room for competitors. This was read in the organisation as a silent threat that any stepping out of line with the godfather's party meant further restrictions of resources. Two years later, when documentary evidence was acquired showing that Patrick Gallagher had bankrolled Haughey with funds from his bank, the 'Today Tonight' team contacted Haughey for his views of this matter. An immediate threat of legal action followed. The programme was not made, not only because of the cost of a legal action but also because of the 'climate of fear for the future of the public broadcaster which Haughey had so directly engineered.'

Charles Haughey will be remembered and talked about when other non-rogue politicians are forgotten; it is safe to forecast that stories will circulate for many years to come. In this sense he has certainly left a heritage to posterity. Not only will the anecdotes circulate but they will be bipolar. The gaps between them can be summed up by two letters to the *Irish Times* after Charles Haughey's death.

The last great leader of the Irish people has fallen, and we are the less for it. Sinne Fianna Fáil, atá faoi gheall ag Éirinn.

It is customary not to speak ill of the dead. In the case of Charles Haughey there is no need. The unvarnished truth is sufficient to tarnish his reputation for ever.

The prize for the most laid-back view of the Boss's career must go to Bertie Ahern: 'Okay, maybe there were a few blips along the way, but that's life.' In the other corner of the ring, Michael Clifford, a journalist writing in the *Sunday Tribune*, pulled no punches.

> He lied and lied again, and even when the lies weren't working, he kept lying . . . A man widely acknowledged to possess a first-class brain didn't know that his bagman, Des Traynor, was running a criminal empire in the Cayman Islands and skimming money to keep him in the style to which he was accustomed. When the country was on its knees, Haughey was living it up, bought by a cabal of the elite. Meanwhile, his bagman was chief executive of a parallel state, and Charlie was their man in the fools' paradise.

Charles J. Haughey was given a state funeral, attended by the President, members of the Council of State, the Taoiseach and Government, leaders of opposition parties, TDS, MEPS, members of the judiciary, aides-de-camp, senior army officers and representatives of the Garda Síochána. He had made all the arrangements himself and left his family €30 million, as well as the island of Inishvickillane.

A significant part of Haughey's legacy will be the collection of aphorisms uttered by him or about him as part of Irish folklore.

An Irish solution to an Irish problem.
>> (The Family Planning Bill, 1979, to make contraceptives available but only to married couples on a doctor's prescription)

Grotesque, unbelievable, bizarre and unprecedented.
>> (GUBU—Haughey's opinion of the finding of a murderer, Malcolm MacArthur, in the Attorney-General's apartment)

You're dealing with an adult, and no banker will talk to me in this manner. If you take drastic action I could be a very troublesome adversary.
>> (When AIB demanded that Haughey return his chequebooks he 'became quite vicious' and told them that 'I have to live')

Go dance on someone else's grave.
>> (Haughey's advice to his detractors)

'Here's something for yourself.'

'Thanks, big fella.'

(Dialogue between Haughey and Ben Dunne as the latter slipped
him a large sum of money)

Coalition Governments go against every fibre of my being. I and
the Fianna Fáil party just have to accept reality.

(On going into coalition with the PDS in 1989)

I can instance a load of fuckers whose throats I'd cut and push over
a cliff.

(On political enemies within Fianna Fáil)

I have an unshakable belief in the family as the basic unit of society.

(A philanderer's opposition to the divorce referendum, 1986)

A failed entity.

(The Northern Ireland 'statelet')

What I have to do, I do with great sadness and great sorrow.

(Before sacking Brian Lenihan, on the demand of the PDS, in 1990)

Right, lads, you know what I want. What do yous want?

(Haughey's proof of pragmatism, a grasp of reality and a sense of
humour when negotiating a deal with Tony Gregory TD in order
to stay in power)

I'll give you what you want, but remember, for Jaysus' sake, that I
can't nationalise the fucking banks.

(Reminder to Gregory and friends that, though he would give them
anything they wanted, it had to be within the limits of the possible)

Well, lads, as Al Capone said, it was nice doing business with you!

(Acknowledgement of final agreement with Gregory and his allies)

I don't think he was cut out for the hurly-burly of politics. He
would be unable to look you in the eye and tell a lie. In politics you
have to be able to lie and cheat. I don't think he would have made
the contribution he made if he was elected to the Dáil.

(Haughey's view of Martin Mansergh's future as a politician)

When it comes to memoirs, my attitude is 'never justify, never explain.'
(*Omertà*—the law of silence)

Uno duce, una voce! In other words, we are having no more nibbling at my leader's bum.
(P. J. Mara to journalists at a time of dissension in Fianna Fáil
over the report of the New Ireland Forum)

It always makes me happy and proud when being driven home to
Kinsealy to know that I was responsible for the new houses and
homes that had replaced the slums.
(An admission by Haughey, who had forgotten that he had
ordered the houses to be built as a political stroke to stay in
power and keep his creditors at bay)

Jump out the fucking window.
(Haughey's advice to a flustered TD whom he had just bawled out
and who stuttered that he couldn't find the door)

I wish to say categorically that I was not aware of the tapping of
these telephones.
(Haughey's variation of Bill Clinton's 'I did not have sexual
relations with that woman')

How do I stop all this sewage coming out of the newspapers? Is
there any God up there?
(Haughey's reaction when his resignation seemed to be imminent
following the tapping of the phones of Geraldine Kennedy and
Bruce and Mavis Arnold)

Are its policies and its leader in future to be decided for it by the
media, by alien influences, by political opponents or, worst of all,
by business interests pursuing their own ends?
(Haughey's query when it seemed that he would be removed by a
party vote)

Hitler should have finished the job.
(One of many similar phone calls made, in the week of the fiftieth
anniversary of Hitler's election as Chancellor, to Ben Briscoe TD
following his proposal that Haughey should resign)

Take me to my people.
(Haughey's order to his chauffeur, having survived a party vote
against him)

I have done the state some service—they know it. No more of that.
(Haughey's quotation from *Othello* in his resignation speech)

I pray you in your letters,
When you shall these unlucky deeds relate,
Speak of me as I am; nothing extenuate.
(The continuation of the previous quotation and the justification
of this chapter)

Nothing about me was ever run-of-the-mill.
(Admission at the Moriarty Tribunal)

He made the rules—for everyone else!
(Medb Ruane, art critic, columnist and broadcaster)

He was very kind and charitable when what he gave was not out of
his pocket.

(Anon)

When challenged, he did not forbear to call in aid the most ignorant and unthinking elements in the country to browbeat and
intimidate his opponents.
(Comment in the *Irish Independent* after his death)

DES TRAYNOR

We have said that a majority of rogues suffer from anti-social personality disorder, that is, they are sociopaths, with little regard for the
feelings and welfare of others. They are emotionally immature, are
self-centred and do not know the meaning of guilt. They lack moral
sense and chronically indulge in anti-social behaviour. We have also
noted that they can be impulsive, can fail to plan, can be aggressive,
irritable, irresponsible, and display a reckless disregard for their own
safety and the safety of others. These are the spendthrifts, the raparees
and highwaymen, the compulsive duellists and the murderers. As they
are the majority, it follows that there must be a minority who,

although it too does not know the meaning of guilt, is immune to impulsiveness, knows how to plan and covers its tracks. Des Traynor was an excellent example of the latter.

Des Traynor was not a colourful or penny-dreadful rogue but was instead a low-profile mastermind in Irish financial circles for many years. He began his career as an articled clerk in Haughey, Boland and Company, chartered accountants—Charles Haughey's firm—and worked there until 1969. He remained a lifelong friend of Haughey and was often referred to as 'Haughey's bagman'. When he left Haughey Boland he became one of the founding directors of the private bank of Guinness and Mahon (GMCT) and later chairman. He remained with the bank until 1986. In his later years he was one of the leading figures in the business community and became chairman of Cement Roadstone Holdings PLC in 1987, a position he held until his death in 1994.

Nothing to complain of there or to ring any warning bells. However, if we dig a little deeper we find that Traynor became the mastermind behind a widespread system of tax evasion and fraud that benefited a golden circle of businessmen and politicians, thanks to a 'see no evil, hear no evil' attitude on the part of the Central Bank and the Revenue Commissioners. He masterminded a network of organisations—among them Guinness and Mahon (Ireland) Ltd, Ansbacher (Cayman) Ltd, Cement-Roadstone Holdings PLC, and all their attached ramifications—that had one joint purpose: the facilitation of bogus offshore accounts, that is, accounts where cash was nominally in banks outside the jurisdiction but where an equivalent amount had been deposited in a bank in Ireland. This arrangement enabled John Doe to withdraw from his Irish bank real money that would not be liable to tax because, technically, it was not there at all. It was all in the sleight of hand. Now you saw it, now you didn't.

This Ansbacher deposit tax evasion scheme lasted for more than two-and-a-half decades, from 1970 until it was exposed by the McCracken Tribunal in 1997.

Bogus offshore accounts, it should be noted, are not the same as bogus non-resident accounts, which often involved money that had possibly changed hands in the form of cash but had never, in any case, been declared. The function of bogus non-resident accounts was to enable their holders to avoid paying the deposit interest retention tax (DIRT), which it was the duty of banks to deduct from deposit accounts. The holding of bogus non-resident accounts was another form of so-called 'victimless' crime. While the DIRT scam was operating, the amount of money stolen from the state may have amounted to £10 billion.

The fraud that Traynor devised worked as follows. A client would give money to Traynor, who would invest it in Ansbacher (Cayman) Ltd, a company based in the Cayman Islands in the Caribbean, where it earned interest. Simultaneously a 'mirror' account would be opened in Guinness and Mahon (Ireland) Ltd, a subsidiary of a bank of the same name in London. Owners of a Guinness and Mahon account had access to their money but paid no tax, because, technically, their deposits were offshore and therefore not liable to tax. Lodgements and withdrawals were, however, scrupulously documented. There were also discretionary trusts and 'back-to-back' loans secured by offshore deposits.

Obviously, the money loaned was not liable to tax, because, with the use of mirrors, the authorities were tricked into believing that it would be repaid. In short, Traynor in effect ran a private bank for twenty years from his office in Dublin, evading tax and laundering money. The charm of the scam was that technically the money was owned by Ansbacher Cayman, so his clients were not guilty of any offences.

Guinness and Mahon (Ireland) Ltd offered 'relationship banking', which told the investor that it 'aimed to relieve the administrative burden with managing your own finances, while providing peace of mind through our professional and discreet approach.' From 1976 to 1986 Traynor was the deputy chairman of Guinness and Mahon, and during that decade 35 per cent of the bank's liabilities were made up of Ansbacher deposits, which amounted to at least £50 million but which, when everything is put together, may have been more than £100 million.

Though Traynor was convinced that his offshore scheme was successfully hidden from prying official eyes, there must have been some doubt in his mind, because at one point he sent a warning to one of his colleagues stressing the importance of secrecy. The advice was entitled 'Towards Minimising the Footsteps'. The list of corporate bodies (Irish and non-Irish) covered by the document shows how intricate Traynor's scheme was: Guinness and Mahon (Ireland) Ltd; Guinness, Mahon and Company Ltd, London; Investee Bank (UK) Ltd; Henry Ansbacher Holding PLC; First National Bank of Southern Africa; CRH PLC; Bank of Ireland Private Banking Ltd; IIB; Clients of Ansbacher (Cayman) Ltd; Hamilton Ross Company Ltd; the Auditors of Guinness and Mahon (Ireland) Ltd, the Central Bank of Ireland and Exchange Control.

Everything went well until Ben Dunne of Dunne's Stores was involved in a much-publicised escapade in Florida in February 1992 involving cocaine and a young woman from the 'Escorts in a Flash' agency, and unpleasant facts began to emerge that caused the Minister for Industry and Commerce to apply to the High Court to have one or more competent inspectors appointed to look into the affairs of Ansbacher (Cayman) Ltd and to report back to it. The grounds for the application were that there were circumstances suggesting that Ansbacher's affairs were being, or had been, conducted with intent to defraud its creditors or the persons connected with its formation or management. In this case the main creditor would be the state or Irish taxpayers, or both. The High Court granted the application and told the inspectors to look behind the corporate veils of the multifarious companies that Traynor had controlled or influenced. The High Court inspectors got to work, and their report was published on 6 July 2002, by which time Des Traynor was dead.

What did they find, and how did Traynor's roguery manifest itself? He did not need to hold up travellers on the highway, or to abduct marriageable young women of means. Instead, in the words of Paul Appleby, director of corporate enforcement, his company Ansbacher (Cayman) Ltd secretly operated in Ireland for more than twenty years and conducted business that seems to have contravened prevailing banking, tax, company and other legislation. Appleby stated that when the activities of Ansbacher (Cayman) Ltd came to light in 1997 the nation was shocked that such activity had occurred and had remained hidden from official authorities for so long. He claimed that, in a sense, the revelations infected Ireland's collective psyche in subsequent years, creating suspicions that it was possible to evade legal or other obligations without effective sanctions, thereby undermining respect for the rule of law and damaging public confidence in the country's institutions.

Unfortunately, as the inspectors pointed out, there would be some difficulty in bringing prosecutions arising from the matters investigated by them.

It is fair to suggest that Des Traynor and all his friends who infected Ireland's collective psyche created a climate in which businessmen were encouraged to believe that it was possible to evade legal or other obligations without effective sanction, and that their illegal behaviour undermined respect for the rule of law and damaged public confidence in the country's institutions.

With regard to Ansbacher (Cayman) Ltd, the inspectors found that Traynor had devised a so-called 'memorandum account' system operated by Guinness and Mahon and GMCT in a deliberately complex and secretive manner that concealed the names of the clients while allowing them to lodge and withdraw funds to and from accounts held nominally for GMCT. Loans were obtained from Guinness and Mahon for GMCT clients on the security of their GMCT deposit, but the existence of this deposit was deliberately omitted from the loan agreement documents. In other words, the general regulatory system of Guinness and Mahon was hidden from the Central Bank and Revenue auditors.

Under Traynor's stewardship, Ansbacher established places of business in Ireland, first at the premises of Guinness and Mahon and later at the premises of Cement Roadstone Holdings. It knowingly breached those sections of the Companies Act (1963) that set out the obligations binding companies incorporated outside the state when they establish a place of business within the Republic. This means that it carried on banking business in Ireland without holding a licence, which is a serious criminal offence.

The inspectors also found that GMCT, in conjunction with Guinness and Mahon, operated a sham trust structure and that there was evidence that their discretionary trust scheme facilitated widespread tax evasion. The inspectors were satisfied that Traynor had conducted the affairs of Ansbacher in order to defraud deliberately the Revenue Commissioners. In doing so, it also defrauded the Irish taxpayer.

It was not the job of the inspectors to declare verdicts of guilt; that was for the courts. All they could do was to propose that Ansbacher, as a result of Traynor's scheme, could be guilty of a number of criminal offences: the common-law offence of conspiracy to defraud and the offence of knowingly aiding, abetting, assisting, inciting or inducing another person to make or deliver knowingly or wilfully incorrect returns, statements or accounts in connection with their tax liabilities. It could also have breached at least three Irish acts, as well as the Cayman Islands Banks and Trust Companies Law (1989).

The inspectors then reflected further on Des Traynor's responsibility and cautiously concluded that there was evidence tending to suggest that he had facilitated the operation of sham trusts on behalf of

Ansbacher's clients and the carrying on of a banking business by Ansbacher and Hamilton Ross in Ireland without a licence.

That was not all. Traynor deliberately enabled Ansbacher and Hamilton Ross to operate in Ireland in such a way that they could defraud the Revenue Commissioners and avoid their liability to corporation tax. He facilitated the improper use of subordinates in Ansbacher and Hamilton Ross's unlawful business activities. He also arranged for money to be paid to various clients without any deduction of tax.

Cautiously, the inspectors suggested that all the above could amount to criminal offences, before moving on to a gentleman named John Furze, a Cayman Islands banker who operated the Cayman end of the Ansbacher deposit illegal operation while Des Traynor was running the show in Ireland, and concluding that he had conspired with Des Traynor to conduct Ansbacher's affairs with intent to defraud the Revenue Commissioners. They also concluded that Furze had consented to or approved several of Traynor's dubious activities that could have been criminal offences under the Cayman Islands Banks and Trust Companies Law (1989).

The inspectors concluded that from 1971 to 1991 Guinness and Mahon, i.e. Des Traynor, conspired with Ansbacher to defraud the Revenue Commissioners and might have committed the offences of conspiracy to defraud and of being involved in the making or delivering of incorrect tax returns. They also found that Guinness and Mahon aided and abetted Ansbacher in the crime of carrying on a banking business in Ireland without a licence.

The inspectors stated that there was evidence that Guinness, Mahon and Company Ltd in London could have committed the offences of conspiracy to defraud and breaches of tax legislation.

The Central Bank did not escape criticism, but it suffered a rather gentler rap on the knuckles. The inspectors concluded, while accepting that Guinness and Mahon and Des Traynor had fed misleading information to it, that the failure of the bank to test, appraise and gather information that was available to it resulted in the true nature of Ansbacher's activities going undetected for longer than ought to have been the case. In plain English, Des Traynor and his minions, under the noses of the authorities, had broken the law for twenty years and robbed the exchequer of millions. If such chronic indulgence in anti-social behaviour does not betray a lack of moral sense, what does? If this is not roguery, what is?

The inspectors' report did not, however, disturb Des Traynor, as he had died eight years before it was published.

PATRICK GALLAGHER

Patrick Gallagher was a young man spinning in the maelstrom that was Ireland in the 1970s, a decade when money was there for the making but also for the sharing with those who were considered to have power. In 2006 a columnist described Gallagher as using Dublin between 1973 and 1981 'as his personal playground' and identified him as 'one of those children who liked smashing their toys.' Some twenty years earlier, in *In Dublin,* she had written: 'Patrick Gallagher plays Monopoly with the streets of Dublin; and St Stephen's Green is where he likes to land.' This was the period when, as can be seen in rebroadcast television programmes, villages became soulless suburbs.

Gallagher was the son of a particular type of Irish self-made man. Having emigrated to England in the hard times and laboured on building sites, such men did not flush their wages down the toilets of Cricklewood pubs but put them by until they could branch out on their own and build their own construction empires. They are dotted around Britain today, keeping a low profile, living quiet lives, educating their children in public schools and avoiding all publicity. They are known, however, among their own and are generous in their support of expatriate Irish charities and societies.

Gallagher's father, Matt Gallagher, from Tobercurry, County Sligo, was more colourful than most of his peers, one of the first of a generation that was eager to step into the shoes and the Big Houses of the Anglo-Irish in the style of their hero, Charles J. Haughey. Matt Gallagher's dictum was 'Fianna Fáil was good for builders and builders were good for Fianna Fáil, and there was nothing wrong with that.' Unfortunately, not everybody agreed with this slogan.

Young Patrick, who grew up in a big house near Mulhuddart, County Dublin, was educated at St Gerard's in Bray and Clongowes Wood College, having already become a company director at the age of twelve. We do not know how often young Patrick took leave from St Gerard's or Clongowes to attend board meetings before he joined the business at the age of seventeen, but it is an important fact that he was only twenty-two when he inherited the awesome responsibility of seventy construction companies.

The young master began by turning his back on construction and moving into the wider world of property development. Six years later he was to show his ability with the purchase of a mock-Georgian office block in St Stephen's Green, appropriately named Seán Lemass House, for £5.4 million and its resale five days later to the Irish Permanent Building Society for £7.65 million. Unfortunately, coups like this would become less profitable a few years later with the introduction of a special capital gains tax on development deals. Nevertheless Gallagher went from strength to strength, and within nine years of taking control of the Gallagher companies he owned the Slazenger site in St Stephen's Green and the former Alexandra College site in Earlsfort Terrace, the Phoenix Park Racecourse, Donaghmede Shopping Centre, a three-house block in Lower Mount Street, Castle Howard in the Vale of Avoca and Dolanstown Stud. In addition he owned development land in Boyle, County Roscommon, more development land in County Limerick and prime sites in the greater Dublin area. It is worth noting again that at this time the tenants of many of the office blocks in the city were state or state-sponsored bodies. An inside track to Government Buildings was beneficial, if not mandatory.

From Ballymacarney Stud Farm in County Meath, Gallagher moved to Straffan House, on 550 acres of County Kildare countryside bisected by the River Liffey. The original Straffan House had been built in the 1830s by Hugh Barton of the famous wine family, based on the model of Château Louveciennes west of Paris. The Barton family had continued to live there until 1949. One of the four subsequent owners was a mysterious Iranian general. In 1989, Gallagher sold the property to the Jefferson Smurfit Group, and it is now the K Club and Hotel.

Like Paul Singer, Patrick Gallagher was driven about Dublin in a Rolls-Royce, and it is claimed that he once told a meeting of a bank board that 'the three most exciting things in life are sex for the second time (you never get it right the first time), the first winner at Royal Ascot and a flight on Concorde.'

Unfortunately, the very traits that make freebooters successful are also those that bring about their downfall; the attempt to swallow a bit of the action can unfortunately become the wolfing down of a very indigestible mouthful. In due course the Gallagher empire, in accordance with this law, began to resemble Shanahan's Stamps—with one vital difference. Whereas Singer gambled on the greed of speculators,

Gallagher sold properties on which he had only paid a deposit
Greedy banks supplied him with the cash for these operations.

It was about this time that Gallagher purchased the 4½-acre
Slazenger site and then tried to sell it on to Irish Life for £15.75 million. The deal was stillborn, and other possible purchasers melted
away like snow on a sunny day. His timing had been wrong. Ireland
was now in recession, and interest rates were soaring. The business
community was cautious and there was no demand for office space.
Not even the prime site in Earlsfort Terrace could come to Gallagher's
rescue. His problems were compounded by the purchase from his
uncles of one side of Earlsfort Terrace for £9½ million. They had
bought it for £1½ million and let it deteriorate. The *Irish Times* had
celebrated their coup with the headline '8 million harvest for weed
growers.' Unfortunately for the uncles, the £9½ million had not been
handed over; all they got their hands on was a deposit of £450,000.

The Gallagher companies were now £25 million in debt, and no
help was forthcoming from any source. Gallagher tried to buy the
H. Williams supermarkets as a source of ready cash, but the banks
would not play. It is said that at this point he owed £100,000 a week in
interest payments. The cumulative value of his companies was falling
and in a short time had dropped from £60 million to £26 million, and
Gallagher's debts now amounted to £30 million. A receiver was
appointed, and about this time Gallagher went to live in South Africa.

As might be expected, Charles Haughey features in the Gallagher
saga. The Gallagher Group was associated with a bank, Merchant
Banking Ltd, of which a number of members of the Gallagher family,
together with persons associated with other companies in the
Gallagher Group, were directors. The bank, which collapsed in 1982,
subsequently went into liquidation and would be on the agenda of the
Moriarty Tribunal in 1999. The tribunal was investigating a number of
specific payments to Haughey about which it had been unable to
obtain any information except of the most limited kind but where the
circumstances of the payments suggested that they required further
examination.

Documents made available to the tribunal gave it reason to suppose that Charles Haughey had been the recipient in 1976 of two loans
from Merchant Banking Ltd of £6,000 and £2,500. Gallagher could
not be questioned about these loans, as he had gone to South Africa
for urgent medical attention. The tribunal had been interested in these

loans because they were repaid only on the liquidation of the bank in 1982, no demands had been made for repayment, no repayment schedule was agreed in respect of principal or interest, and no security, except for a promissory note, was sought by the bank in relation to these loans, which would at the time have been quite significant sums. The 'loans' had never been loans.

When Merchant Banking Ltd collapsed it owed £4.5 million to depositors, and six hundred people lost their life savings. Gallagher, however, was not ready to throw in the towel and moved to England, which was in the middle of a property boom. Unfortunately, once things start to go wrong they go very wrong. A Belfast subsidiary of Merchant Banking Ltd, Merbro Finance, was under investigation at the time, even though its depositors were protected, and it emerged that Gallagher had spent £120,000 of the depositors' savings on two paintings that were not listed in the bank's assets. He was arrested in London in 1988, tried in Belfast and pleaded guilty to theft of the £120,000 and to three charges of providing false information. A charge of conspiracy to defraud the Bank of England and to defraud depositors was also pressed. Gallagher was sentenced to imprisonment in October 1999 for lying to the Bank of England in order to obtain a licence to conduct a deposit-taking business and so finance his own high-risk adventures.

When the bank went into liquidation in the Republic, the liquidator's report was sent to the Director of Public Prosecutions in 1984 and forwarded to the Garda Fraud Squad. The report noted that seventy-nine possible criminal offences might have been committed in the Republic; but Gallagher was never charged with any wrongdoing. No evidence had been offered in the Belfast court because of the guilty pleas. This may have been the reason, or excuse, for the amazing failure to prosecute in the Republic.

Nothing happened for five years. Then, in 1989, 'Today Tonight' planned a programme about the Gallagher collapse, making use of the liquidator's report; but the DPP asked them not to broadcast for fear that any future proceedings could be prejudiced. RTE waited for three months but finally ran out of patience and transmitted the programme, which revealed evidence of false records, false returns to the Central Bank, falsified books, an asset fraudulently obtained and fraudulent statements. Seventy-nine per cent of the bank's assets had been siphoned into Gallagher Group companies, and depositors' money had been loaned to Gallagher companies. Instead of perform-ance bonds, county councils were given deposit receipts as security to ensure that housing estates would be completed. These deposit receipts were, literally, not worth the paper they were printed on.

In spite of these revelations the DPP decided in September 1991 not to proceed against Gallagher. Five years later the liquidator reached a High Court settlement with him, but the amount of the settlement was never disclosed. A large number of depositors lost their money.

A depositor who did not lose money was Charles Haughey. The Gallagher links with Haughey went as far back as Taca, the Fianna Fáil fund-raisers. 'You scratch my back and I'll scratch yours' was the slo-gan. The Gallagher Group had close connections with Des Traynor, who was invited onto their board. It was not long before the group's affairs were being run from the Cayman Islands.

Eventually, Gallagher was released on bail and tried to raise £1.2 million to compensate the creditors. He was given £165,000 by Ben Dunne, for whose benefit he had made £750,000 available when the latter was kidnapped by the IRA.

Two days after Haughey became Taoiseach, Patrick Gallagher, who had been helping him with his political expenses to the tune of £3,000 a year, was asked to assist in clearing the new Taoiseach's £1 million debt to Allied Irish Bank. He handed over £300,000, which, to straighten the Gallagher books, was described as a 'tangible' quid pro quo, giving him the right to purchase land from Haughey. This was all very fine, except that the small print allowed Haughey to stop the sale before it went too far, with the result that the sale never took place and the £300,000 handed over as a deposit could not be recouped.

The Revenue Commissioners knew nothing of this until the 1980s but by then were unable to prove wrong-doing. Counsel in the Moriarty Tribunal described the whole deal as 'a sham used as a vehi-cle for Mr Gallagher to get money to Mr Haughey.' Haughey replied that such a suggestion was totally false, but never returned the money.

Gallagher did eventually come back from South Africa but died in 2006.

RAY BURKE

In olden times, when pirates sailed the Spanish Main between Port-au-Prince and Cartagena, they buried their doubloons and gold beakers in deserted islands, which possibly included the Caymans.

Present-day pirates have other means of hiding their loot.

Ray Burke, former Government minister, is an example of what can be done to hide one's takings. Investigators from the Criminal Assets Bureau, in the course of a search of his home, discovered a folder of information that showed that over a period of nine years, from 1982 to 1991, his earnings were over £97,000, whereas he had declared income from deposit accounts at just over £5,000.

The Flood Planning Tribunal found that in 2002 Burke had received corrupt payments of almost €250,000, and that the acquisition of his home in north Co. Dublin was also corrupt. In October 1997, in spite of Bertie Ahern's denunciation of the opposition's 'persistent hounding of an honourable man,' he had been forced to resign from his office because of a scandal over a payment to him of £30,000 from building interests. Where did it all go?

Ray Burke began his political career as a Fianna Fáil member of Dublin City Council and then took his father's seat as a Fianna Fáil TD for Dublin North. From 1967 to 1978 and from 1985 to 1987 he was also a member for the Swords area of Dublin County Council, which later became Fingal County Council. Between 1987 and 1989 he held three ministerial posts: Energy and Industry, Justice, and Foreign Affairs. Known as 'Rambo' for his gung-ho political style, he had been a political ally of Bertie Ahern, who famously declared on one occasion that he would climb every tree in north Dublin to find the evidence that would clear Burke's name.

Burke was a director of a firm of auctioneers and estate agents in Swords and became a director and secretary of Ray Burke and Associates Life and Pensions Ltd in 1984 but resigned two years later.

His fall from grace began on 3 July 1995 when a notice appeared in two daily newspapers offering a £10,000 reward to anyone providing information leading to the conviction of persons involved in corruption in connection with the planning process. This notice was placed on behalf of unnamed clients by a firm of solicitors in Newry.

This was followed by a series of newspaper articles that accused Burke of receiving payments from property developers in Dublin in return for securing planning permission for housing. In June and July two developers were named: Bovale Developments and Joseph Murphy Structural Engineers Ltd (JMSE), a Santry firm. Burke denied everything, and the *Sunday Business Post* published another article, headed 'The other side of the coin,' that introduced James Gogarty, an elderly employee of JMSE who said that Burke had been given two envelopes, which totalled in bulk the size of a nine by four inch brick, each containing £40,000, and that one of them came from JMSE.

Burke claimed he was the target of a vicious campaign of rumour and innuendo but agreed that he had been visited by Michael Bailey of Bovale and James Gogarty of JMSE. His version was that he had accepted, in good faith, a sum of £30,000 from the latter. He threatened to sue the perpetrators of any further libels.

He resigned as Minister for Foreign Affairs and as a member of Dáil Éireann, and the Flood Tribunal was established on 4 November to inquire into his affairs.

Tom Brennan and Joseph McGowan were builders and property developers from County Mayo who controlled various companies. Brennan had a building company called Oakpark Developments Ltd, the core business of which was the development of high-density housing estates in the Swords area. It did not build individual houses, with one notable exception: Ray Burke's home, 'Briargate'. Burke's auctioneering and estate agency, P. J. Burke (Sales) Ltd, acted as sales agent for the houses built by Brennan and McGowan's connected companies.

Burke admitted to the Flood Tribunal in July 1999 that a company registered in Jersey, Caviar Ltd, held a bank account in Jersey into which £35,000 had been lodged in April 1984 and £60,000 in October 1984, the proceeds of political fund-raising carried out by Brennan and McGowan in Britain. The tribunal made contact with a firm of advocates in Jersey, Bedell and Cristin, and obtained documents called the 'Caviar file', which referred to a company called Canio Ltd. The tribunal was pleased to learn that there was a compulsory disclosure procedure in Jersey, which it could make use of if information was not forthcoming voluntarily.

The first matter was 'Briargate'. The tribunal held that Burke had not bought the house in a normal commercial transaction. Documents from the Revenue Commissioners showed no evidence that Burke had paid any money to Oakpark Developments Ltd, nor was there any declaration of the costs of construction. The tribunal found that the motive for providing such a benefit was an improper motive connected with Burke's position as an elected representative on Dublin County Council.

The tribunal also found that the current account of P. J. Burke (Sales) Ltd at Bank of Ireland, Whitehall, had received a payment of

£1,000 per month from Kilmanagh Estates Ltd, a Brennan and McGowan company, which was not the way that estate agents' fees are normally paid, which is as a commission related to the value of the properties sold, and therefore were most probably retainers for Burke himself.

It then moved on to payments made outside the jurisdiction and to offshore bank accounts that Burke had opened and operated when he was at all times a resident of the Republic. Such activities were prohibited by exchange control legislation, something that the Minister for Justice should have known, but Burke, without any reasonably comprehensible explanation, had opened accounts in Belfast, Manchester, Douglas (Isle of Man), London and St Helier (Jersey). He had 'no reasonably comprehensible explanation' for opening an account with Foster Finance (NI) Ltd in Belfast. He had failed to inform the tribunal about the Bank of Ireland account in Manchester or that £14,584.49 had been transferred from it to his Dublin account in 1977.

An opening lodgement of £50,000 had been made in AIB Bank (Isle of Man) Ltd, though the account-holder was named as Patrick D. Burke, with an address in Hampshire, which was that of Burke's sister-in-law. AIB (Isle of Man) had been instructed to communicate with him at that address, and the correspondence was redirected to him in Swords. A payment into the account had been made by a company called Kalabraki, which was wholly owned by Tom Brennan. There were four withdrawals from this account, none of which coincided with the date of elections in which Burke was a candidate, which would be expected if the payments had been donations towards contesting elections. Another account had been opened in the name of P. D. Burke with the same address in Hampshire as that of the Isle of Man account. Burke claimed he had operated an account at that branch for years, but this claim was not substantiated.

Another account was found in Hill Samuel and Company, Jersey. It had been opened by a St Helier firm of advocates, Bedell and Cristin, in the name of Caviar Ltd, a company registered in Jersey. Nine days later an account had been opened at Hill Samuel and Company (Jersey) Ltd in the name of Canio. Burke had instructed Bedell and Cristin to place all correspondence, including bank statements, in a sealed envelope and to send it to Mr A. Burke at the office address of Burke's Dublin solicitor. The three shareholders of Caviar Ltd were

members of Bedell and Cristin, who had all executed a declaration of
trust in respect of the shares they held. In this document they
declared, in private, that they held the issued shares as nominees of
and trustees for Mr and Mrs P. D. Burke of Church Lane, near Alton,
Hampshire. Bedell and Cristin had also set up, in a similar fashion,
companies individually or jointly owned by Brennan and McGowan
or by Brennan, McGowan and John Finnegan (a well-known Dublin
auctioneer and estate agent). Caviar Ltd had been set up for the sole
purpose of receiving funds for and on behalf of Ray Burke.

The tribunal did not accept that the accounts in the Isle of Man
and Jersey were opened solely for the purpose of maintaining the
confidentiality of Burke's affairs or for the proceeds of political fund-
raising conducted abroad. Legitimate political donations received by
a politician were not taxable in the hands of the recipient. There was
no use of the money for political purposes: rather, the operation of
the Caviar account was consistent with the money being maintained
on long-term interest-bearing deposits.

Burke had explained that his dealings in Jersey were to ensure that
his wife would have access to the Caviar account (in the words of
the tribunal) 'in the event of his being hit by the mythical bus.' The
tribunal considered this explanation to be untrue, because the
account was to be operated on the sole signature of P. D. Burke and
there was no instruction to allow for access by Mrs Burke. The excuse
also demonstrated that the fund was not for any political purpose but
was rather a private arrangement. The tribunal concluded that

> Burke opened offshore accounts to conceal the fact that he was the
> recipient of the funds contained in these accounts because the cir-
> cumstances in which he came to be paid these sums would not
> withstand public scrutiny.

There was no need to board a Spanish galleon: it all came to him.

The tribunal then held that Burke's failure to disclose the existence
of the Isle of Man account was a deliberate attempt to conceal the
existence of a £50,000 deposit. The payment of £60,000 to Caviar Ltd
had come from Canio Ltd and was obtained from funds borrowed from
Lombard and Ulster Banking Ireland, which were secured on the interests of Canio Ltd in lands at Sandyford, County Dublin. Once again
Burke had lied. The tribunal established that the beneficial owners of

Canio Ltd were companies owned beneficially by Brennan, McGowan and Finnegan. The last-named owned it through a company, Foxtown Investments Ltd, that, interestingly, had been established for Finnegan by another rogue, Des Traynor, and was wholly owned by College Trustees Ltd, which was—surprise, surprise—a subsidiary of Guinness Mahon Channel Islands Ltd, in turn owned by Guinness and Mahon (Ireland) Ltd.

Having examined these multifarious dealings, the tribunal found that the corporate structures involved were a labyrinth that stretched from Jersey and Guernsey to Tortola in the Caribbean, and the only common features were the involvement of Messrs Brennan and McGowan and land transactions that resulted in large sums of money being distributed between Messrs Brennan, McGowan and Finnegan in Jersey.

The tribunal declared that it was satisfied in all circumstances that these payments to offshore accounts were corrupt.

Another matter that concerned the tribunal was Burke's relationship with a company called Century Communications Ltd, the brainchild of Oliver Barry, a promoter of musical events and manager of artistes for some twenty-five years, who had been a member of the RTE Authority for approximately three years. The other backers had close links with Charles J. Haughey.

In January 1989 Century had been awarded the first independent national sound broadcasting contract in the country. The tribunal found that a lodgement of £39,500 had been made to one of Burke's bank accounts on 31 May 1989, of which £35,000 was a donation from Oliver Barry. The power to award contracts rested with the Independent Radio and Television Commission, an independent statutory authority. Nonetheless, some months earlier Burke had issued a directive that made a significant reduction in the level of transmission fees payable by Century to RTE.

The following year Burke promoted legislation that, among other things, restricted RTE's income from advertising in order to benefit independent broadcasters. The tribunal investigated this action and many other proposals by Burke in favour of Century, which was in serious financial difficulty at the time. He even put forward a Broadcasting and Wireless Telegraphy Bill that would give him the sole power to select licensees and grant licences.

The promoters of Century were determined to set up a national radio service, with the help of Gay Byrne, who advised them that a local station would be less expensive and could be profitable. In due course Byrne's confidence in the project declined and he dropped out, even though he had been offered £1 million for what he understood would be a three-year contract.

The new act provided for a Television Commission that would award a number of sound broadcasting contracts, including one for an independent national sound broadcasting service. The IRTC granted the franchise to Century under a seven-year renewable sound broadcasting contract. RTE understood that it would receive a reasonable commercial return for giving Century access to its sites and installing separate facilities at a reasonable rent. Everything was to be done on a commercial basis, without any subsidy, direct or indirect, to Century.

A reasonable charge for a fourteen-station national FM network covering the twenty-six counties would have been in the region of £800,000. Nonetheless Burke issued a directive ordering RTE to provide access to its fourteen FM sites and two AM sites (Dublin and Cork) at an annual charge of only £35,000, together with easy terms in relation to maintenance charges for Century's equipment, and several other easy terms.

These figures were radically different from what had been agreed between RTE and the minister: £35,000 instead of £252,000 per annum for access, £30,000 for maintenance instead of £355,000, with £1,000 for each subsequent visit to be charged at actual cost plus 25 per cent.

The tribunal found that Burke's directive was a total reversal of the previous position. It was contrary to the advice of his department and was not supported by any independent evaluation. Burke came up with excuses that the tribunal did not accept, on the grounds that there was no evidence that would allow him to conclude that the charges he fixed were fair and reasonable. It then found that Burke had not acted in the public interest but to serve the private interests of the promoters of Century Radio (and, no doubt, his own).

It all came to an end for Burke on 24 January 2005, when he began a six-month prison sentence for tax offences. He had pleaded guilty to a charge of knowingly or wilfully furnishing incorrect information during the Government's tax amnesty of 1993.

LIAM LAWLOR

Liam Lawlor was another buccaneer who had treasure to bury. He saw the inside of Mountjoy Prison, not once but three times, because he obstructed the work of the Flood Tribunal. He did not go gently into the dark night of the 'Joy but, like any self-respecting rogue, twisted, turned and dragged his feet.

Mr Justice Flood, when inquiring into the activities of Ray Burke and his associates, had set out clearly what was required of witnesses under examination by the tribunal.

> Any person, duly summoned to do so, who gives evidence to the Tribunal which is material to its inquiry, which that person wilfully knows to be false or does not believe to be true or who by act or omission obstructs or hinders a Tribunal in the performance of its functions, commits a criminal offence.

This pronouncement prepares us for the examination of another characteristic of a rogue: the determination to avoid, by all means, punishment for their wrongdoing and a willingness to use any stratagem, including lavish expenditure of their own or other people's money, to do so. This was certainly the case with Liam Lawlor.

Born in Dublin in 1945, Lawlor was educated at Synge Street Christian Brothers' School and Bolton Street College of Technology. He ran a refrigeration company before he was elected to Dáil Éireann in 1977.

Lawlor, whose constituency was West Dublin, made a habit of losing his Dáil seat, but he always recovered it. He became chairman of the Oireachtas Joint Committee on Commercial State-Sponsored Bodies, even though he was a director of a Larry Goodman food company and earning £6,000 per annum from this. He lost a Dublin County Council seat in 1991 either because he had spoken out against Charles Haughey or because of a public backlash against the epidemic of section 4 rezoning motions. These were motions that allowed county councils to overturn the decisions of planners; when Fianna Fáil ruled the roost in Dublin County Council for six years, from 1985 to 1991, they passed 185 such motions. Many of these had been proposed by Lawlor, against the heartfelt protest of the planning officers. They were welcomed, if not instigated, by property developers who had bought agricultural land at knockdown prices and who made a killing when this agricultural land was rezoned for housing or shopping centres.

When the tribunal's climate got too hot for Fianna Fáil, Lawlor resigned from the party but continued to support it in the Dáil.

In 1989 he got into trouble in a controversy about a conflict of interest between his role as chairman of the Oireachtas Joint Committee on Commercial State-Sponsored Bodies, his post as a non-executive director of Goodman's Food Industries Ltd, and his access to a consultants' report on the Irish Sugar plant in Thurles that Food Industries Ltd was planning to buy. In the light of these and later developments it is ironic that Lawlor was at one time vice-chairman of the Dáil Ethics Committee.

It has been said that Lawlor was called 'Lord Lucan', because of his huge Mercedes car and his large house in Lucan, which was valued at between €2 and 3 million but was to be faced with seizure in 2004. He trailed rumours of blackmail, bribery and corruption. He provided ample fodder for the rumour machine and ended up before a tribunal of inquiry. In his case the tribunal was inquiring into certain planning matters and payments in the West Dublin constituency.

'Lord Lucan' may not have been enough for him. A letter, dated 1990, has come to light addressed to a Mr Mardan in the Iraqi embassy in London. It relates to visas that he had obtained for Iraqi officials following representations made at a reception to celebrate the twenty-second anniversary of the 17th of July Revolution in Iraq. Throughout the letter Lawlor is referred to as 'His Excellency', which excellency invited a Mr al-Algavi to visit the 'Irish Parliament Buildings'.

Why was Lawlor in Mountjoy? Because on 8 June 2000 Mr Justice Flood ordered that he make discovery on oath of, and produce to the Flood Tribunal, all documents and records in his possession or power relating to accounts held in financial institutions either within or outside the state. He was also required to reveal any interest held by him in any company and the relevant documents and records in his possession or power. He was ordered to supply information concerning the tax amnesty and the moneys in respect of which such amnesty was granted to him, including records in relation to the source of any relevant moneys and the accounts in which they were held.

Mr Justice Flood had applied to the High Court for orders compelling Lawlor to comply with these orders and to attend before the tribunal to give evidence in relation to these documents. Instead of complying without delay, Lawlor had contested the order in the High Court and, when that court held against him, had appealed to the Supreme Court—not only an expensive exercise but also a waste of time, because the Supreme Court supported the decision of the High Court. Lawlor had, however, succeeded in spinning things out.

The High Court had acknowledged that the tribunal had unearthed wrongdoings, in relation to which Lawlor had been less than frank, involving land deals in Ireland, a Jersey company, Longwater Investments Ltd, and a bank account in the Liechtenstein Landesbank in Vaduz, as well as 109 other bank accounts in various countries. The trial judge said that, given that Lawlor's non-compliance had been of a serious character, several weeks' imprisonment would be appropriate, but he was mindful that what might be regarded as a draconian power ought not to be exercised 'too prodigally' or in a manner that was inconsistent with the requirements of the Constitution. In those circumstances he decided that Lawlor should serve a further week's imprisonment.

Lawlor spent more money and hired further lawyers to go to the Supreme Court, where he and the state spent a great deal of time (and no doubt frightening sums of money) in deciding whether or not he should go to prison for a week or so. The Supreme Court stated that there could not be the slightest doubt about the significance of Lawlor's failure to make discovery of (i.e. to produce) the relevant documents, as required by the Rules of Court, and that, to put it at its mildest, his averment on oath that he was not involved in the purchase or ownership of, nor had he any interest in, certain lands that had been the subject of dispute, either before or after their acquisition, was less than candid. In other words, Lawlor had consciously been guilty of a serious failure to comply with his discovery obligations.

Seen in the context of the uncontested finding of the trial judge on 15 January 2001 that Lawlor had already been in contempt of the High Court orders 'in a deliberate and most serious manner,' meriting a sentence of imprisonment of three months, his further failure to comply with his discovery obligation was rendered even more serious.

The judge then referred to the Liechtenstein Landesbank accounts and found that Mr Justice Flood had been legitimately concerned to obtain all the documents evidencing the source and ultimate destination of the substantial sums lodged to those accounts. The tribunal and the High Court therefore were fully entitled to infer from the evidence available to them that Lawlor had possession of a significant quantity of documents in relation to the Landesbank accounts, and if he did not have them then there were people, such as the officers of the

Landesbank, who could be required to produce them. A most likely person, in particular, was a Dr Kieber, the official of the bank with whom Lawlor had dealings. The documents were in existence and it was Lawlor's duty to do everything he could, as quickly as possible, to get those documents from Dr Kieber and any other person in whose possession they might be.

Lawlor had not taken any such steps by the time the period fixed for completion of the discovery had expired. Mr Justice Flood had given him permission in January 2001 to contact Dr Kieber but he had confined himself to writing one letter to Dr Kieber in April and had done nothing more.

The Supreme Court judge then dealt with Lawlor's failure to comply with the rules governing the supply of information to the court or the tribunal and stated that, while the rules in relation to the discovery of documents should not be interpreted in too narrow a way, which could be counter-productive, this was not the case with Lawlor. The judge emphasised that Lawlor would have been fully aware of his obligations in this regard, as this had been specifically referred to in an earlier application to the High Court the previous January. He was, accordingly, satisfied that Lawlor had failed to comply with the relevant orders of the tribunal and of the High Court and that, as none of the instances of non-compliance could properly be characterised as technical or minor in their nature, this was a serious matter. Therefore, it could not be considered as excessive or disproportionate to impose a further week's sentence of imprisonment and a fine of £5,000—or indeed a significantly increased penalty. The result was that the judge dismissed Lawlor's appeal.

On the other hand, because of these court hearings Lawlor left two legacies for future rogues: one that they might not appreciate and one that would help them to spin things out and strengthen the tendency to turn 'inquisitorial' inquiries into 'adversarial' battles.

The first legacy was the emphasis that the Supreme Court placed on a section of its Rules of Court that confirmed that rogues could not wriggle out of their responsibilities. The second legacy is described in the paper 'Tribunals of inquiry: Want not, waste not?' by Barry and O'Dowd, which describes the difference between private inquisitorial procedures, where witnesses cannot claim that their constitutional 'right to a good name' is threatened, and adversarial procedures, involving the legal profession, which tend to make the hearings more formal, prolonged and costly, with an over-emphasis on legal procedures and technicalities.

What was Liam Lawlor's gift to future tribunal rogues? When the Flood Tribunal attempted to adopt a more inquisitorial system of private sessions (without the presence of the public), in which lawyers for the tribunal, as part of their preliminary investigations, would question Lawlor without the presence of the tribunal chairman and where Lawlor's 'right to his good name' would not be an issue, his lawyers rushed to the High Court, where Mr Justice Nicholas Kearns found that the tribunal chairman did not have the jurisdiction to make such an order. Mr Justice Kearns said that the power sought to be exercised by a tribunal is not merely procedural but a matter of considerable substance and therefore requires a specific mandate or statute. If the tribunal or the houses of the Oireachtas felt that the present powers of tribunals were inadequate, he said, legislation could be introduced to widen and extend the powers.

The result is that Lawlor's fellow-rogues, when appearing before a tribunal, can if they so choose continue to spin things out indefinitely. So far there does not appear to have been any effort to introduce the required legislation.

Lawlor's life ended suddenly through no fault of his own. On a business trip to Moscow in 2005 he was being driven into the mad stampede that is the daily journey into the city. The car crashed and he was killed instantly. He was sixty years of age.

Select bibliography

— Barrington, Brendan (editor), *The Wartime Broadcasts of Francis Stuart, 1942–1944*, Dublin: Lilliput Press, 2000.

— Barrington, Sir Jonah, *Personal Sketches and Recollections of His Own Times* (revised edition), Glasgow: Cameron, Ferguson and Company, [1876].

— Barry, Frank, and O'Dowd, John, 'Tribunals of inquiry: Want not, waste not?', paper presented to the annual conference of the Dublin Economics Workshop, Kenmare, 15 October 1999.

— Béaslaí, Piaras, *Michael Collins and the Making of a New Ireland*, Dublin: Phoenix Publishing Company, 1926.

— Boyle, Andrew, *The Riddle of Erskine Childers*, London: Hutchinson, 1977.

— Brady, Séamus, *Doctor of Millions: The Rise and Fall of Stamp King Dr. Paul Singer*, Tralee: Anvil Books, 1965.

— Childers, Erskine, *The Framework of Home Rule*, London: Edward Arnold, 1911.

— Cosgrove, John, *A Genuine History of the Lives and Actions of the Most Notorious Irish Highwaymen, Tories and Rapparees . . .* (twelfth edition), Dublin: W. Jones, [n.d.].

— Costello, Francis J., *The Irish Revolution and its Aftermath, 1916–1923: Years of Revolt*, Dublin: Irish Academic Press, 2003.

— Cruise O'Brien, Máire, *The Same Age as the State: The Autobiography of Máire Cruise O'Brien*, Dublin: O'Brien Press, 2003.

— Deale, Kenneth E. L., *Memorable Irish Trials*, London: Constable, 1960.

— de Búrca, Pádraig, and Boyle, John F., *Free State or Republic?: Pen Pictures of the Historic Treaty Session of Dáil Éireann*, Dublin: Talbot Press, 1922.

— DeLorean, John Z., and Schwartz, Ted, *DeLorean*, Grand Rapids (Mich.): Zondervan, 1985.

— Joyce, Joe, and Murtagh, Peter, *The Boss: Charles J. Haughey in Government*, Dublin: Poolbeg Press, 1983.

— Kerrigan, Gene, and Brennan, Pat, *This Great Little Nation: The A–Z of Irish Scandals and Controversies*, Dublin: Gill & Macmillan, 1999.

— McCarthy, Colm, 'Corruption in public office in Ireland: Policy design as a countermeasure,' *Quarterly Economic Commentary*, autumn 2003, p. 59–73.

— Maxwell, W. H., *Wild Sports of the West: With Legendary Tales, and Local Sketches*, London: Richard Bentley, 1832.

— Mulcahy, Risteard, *Richard Mulcahy (1886–1971): A Family Memoir*, Dublin: Aurelian Press, 1999.

— O'Donoghue, David, *Hitler's Irish Voices: The Story of German Radio's Wartime Irish Service*, Belfast: Beyond the Pale, 1998.

— O'Farrell, Padraic, *Tales for the Telling: True Life Stories of Irish Scandals*, Cork: Collins Press, 1996.

— O'Halpin, Eunan, *Defending Ireland: The Irish State and Its Enemies since 1922,* Oxford: Oxford University Press, 1999.

— Pakenham, Frank, *Peace by Ordeal: An Account, from First-Hand Sources, of the Negotiation and Signature of the Anglo-Irish Treaty, 1921,* London: Jonathan Cape, 1935.

— Reed, Christopher, Obituary of John DeLorean, *Guardian* (London), 21 March 2005.

— Somerville-Large, Peter, *Irish Eccentrics: A Selection,* London: Hamish Hamilton, 1975.

— Tóibín, Colm, 'Issues of truth and invention' (review of *The Wartime Broadcasts of Francis Stuart, 1942–1944,* edited by Brendan Barrington), *London Review of Books,* vol. 23, no. 1 (4 January 2002), p. 6–11.

— Walsh, John Edward, *Sketches of Ireland Sixty Years Ago,* Dublin: J. McGlashan, 1847.

TRIBUNAL REPORTS

— *Report of the Inspectors Appointed to Enquire into the Affairs of Ansbacher (Cayman) Limited* . . . Dublin: Stationery Office, 2002.

— *Report of the Tribunal of Inquiry into Payments to Politicians and Related Matters* [Moriarty Tribunal]: *Part 1,* Dublin: Stationery Office, 2006.

— *The Third Interim Report of the Tribunal of Inquiry into Certain Planning Matters and Payments* [Flood Tribunal, now the Mahon Tribunal], Dublin: Stationery Office, 2002.